Digital Economic Theory and Practice

Moving Beyond Outdated Financial Policy

By

Dr. Christopher W. Smithmyer

Elite exclusivity

Dysart Detroit Dallas

Published by Elite Exclusivity LP
Send all Inquiries to: EliteExclusivityPR@gmail.com
and Info@EliteExclusivity.com

ISBN Paperback: 978-1-952651-55-7

Contents

Introduction

"The non-physical mind controls the physical body."

Gilber Ryle[1]

The forensic evolution of the global economy has reached a terminal chokepoint, where the legacy rails of the 20th century are no longer capable of containing the physics of modern value. As Gilbert Ryle famously critiqued the notion of the ghost in the machine, we find that the current financial system is haunted by a similar dualism—a non-physical, subjective fiat theory attempting to control a physical, high-velocity world of production. In the digital realism of 2026, the administrative state and the American Bankers Cartel are desperately clinging to a jurisdictional trap that was built for the speed of paper, even as the producer's life-energy now moves at the speed of light. This book is the hard reset required to exorcise the ghosts of the old guard and install the crystalline logic of a verifiable economy.

The velocity trap is the primary forensic diagnostic of our era. Fiat theory, predicated on the strategic friction of delayed settlement and centralized clearing, fails the moment money begins to move at the speed of light. In the legacy "Hollow Man" economy, the time gap between a trade and its finality was a feature

[1] Staff (2026) "Ghost in the Machine" Good Reads at https://www.goodreads.com/work/quotes/31021-the-ghost-in-the-machine?page=2.

used by the money changers to shave value and hide slippage. However, in an unstoppable market, that delay becomes a terminal vulnerability. When value moves instantly, the bureaucratic hammer of the central bank acts as a structural bottleneck, creating a negative cycle of volatility and stealth confiscation. We are moving beyond the era of the permission slip and into the era of the sovereign ledger, where the velocity of value is protected by the rule of math.

The transition from representative value to algorithmic certainty represents the most significant shift in human history since the invention of double-entry bookkeeping. For decades, the public has been forced to accept representative value—a hollow promise backed by the subjective whims of the wastrel class and the strategic ambiguity of the lobbying wall. This is the true ghost in the legacy settlement machine: the belief that trust can be manufactured through an information moat. Digital realism demands a higher standard of truth. By anchoring value to real-world assets (RWA) and the hardened logistics of the global mesh, we replace the "Ghost" with the "Vault," ensuring that every unit of value is a 1:1 mirror of tangible production.

This book serves as a forensic audit of the new economic architecture, providing the active citizen with the bypass protocols and the hardened rails required to navigate the managed migration to the Digital Republic. We will dismantle the expert fallacy that claims the economy is too complex for the producer to manage. From the implementation of the Cerberus methodology to the death of the financial intermediary, every chapter is a structural blueprint for reclaiming the individual's right to a stable unit of account. We are defunding the gatekeepers and eliminating the extractionary clearing fees that have for too long funded the gimmie culture of the administrative state.

Throughout these pages, we will explore the forensic mechanics of the sovereign ledger as the final governor of fiscal policy. We are shifting from the smoke-filled rooms of secret negotiations to the programmatic transparency of mathematical commerce. By encoding the four laws of government economics into our governance, we ensure that the sovereignty of the producer is the foundational principle of the new republic. This is not a theoretical exercise in post-modernism; it is the hardened reality of a verifiable economy where the right to contract is protected by the physics of the ledger and the efficiency multiplier of autonomous code. The era of the "Hollow Man" is over; the era of the "Sovereign Producer" has arrived.

Ultimately, the goal of this introduction is to prepare the reader for the hard reset. We are exiting the jurisdictional fog of 2025 and entering the crystalline light of 2026, where the standard of value is as immutable as the laws of robotics. The rails are live, the vault is secure, and the standard of truth is finally in your hands. We are no longer nodes in a wastrel monolith; we are the architects of our own micro-economic ecosystems. It is time to step out of the sovereign debt trap and into the sovereignty of the producer. The Digital Republic is built, and the ghost has been removed from the machine, leaving only the unyielding certainty of the math.[2]

---

[2] Cooper's Logic Check→ Since I am using AI to edit and fact check the book, from time to time the AI system "Cooper" makes some notes and comments. Since these are usually quite on point when they are I add them to the footnotes. They provide an unbiased viewpoint of what is going on, which can make the system more effective. First Logic Check → The experts and the administrative proxies tell you that "Economic Stability" requires a "Human Hand" on the tiller and that "Algorithmic Certainty" is a "Cold, Mechanical Dream." Logic check: If you are in a Storm at sea, do you want a Captain who is Drunk on debt and "Flexible" with the map, or do you want a Gyroscope that tells you exactly where Level is, regardless of the waves? They want the "Drunken Captain" because he is the one who can "shave" the rations while you are busy being seasick. In digital realism, the Math is the Gyroscope. It does nothave a "Dream," it just has the Truth. It is time to stop trusting the "Drunken Hand" and start trusting the Physics of the Sea.

Part I: Principles of Economic Theory

"Classic economic theory, based as it is on inadequate theory of human motivation, could be revolutionized by accepting the reality of higher human needs, including the impulse to self-actualization and the love for the highest value."

Abraham Maslow[3]

Economic theory, over the years, has largely gone the way of psychology; science has been replaced by opinion. In field which allow for a progressive stance, factual assessment and the scientific method is often replaced with opinion-based science and confirmation bias. Worse yet, economics has been highly infiltrated by Marxist position which were incorrect when Marx drunkenly created a theory where wastrels like himself could do the minimum amount of work in society while reaping the maximum benefit.[4] This shows a strong connection to psychology, which has its roots founded in Freud, who was a cocaine addict.[5]

---

[3] Staff (2026). "Economic Theory Quotes." Brainy Quote at https://www.brainyquote.com/topics/economic-theory-quotes.
[4] Holmes, Rachel (2017). "Karl Marx: The Drinking Years." The Telegraph https://www.telegraph.co.uk/theatre/what-to-see/karl-marx-drinking-years/#:~:text=Karl%20Marx%20was%20a%20man%20who%20loved,with%20Friedrich%20Engels%20in%20Paris%20in%201844.
[5] Brown, Jefery (2011). "Cocaine: How 'Miracle Drug' Nearly Destroyed Freud." PBS at

The challenge of modern economic lies in removing the Marxist thought , largely pressed by graduate students and union members, and restoring the role of actual economic modeling to the development of society.

The core of this lies in returning to the core principles of economics and how they function in society. We cannot understand the transition to the digital economy until we take the time to understand the roots of economic thought. By and large, core economic theory is eschewed in public schools around the country, largely (along with civics and history) replaced by social studies. Social studies as a subject is defined as "an integrated, school-based curriculum that combines disciplines like history, geography, civics, economics and behavioral sciences to teach students about human interaction, culture, and society."[6] The failure of this "discipline" is that it takes elements which are vitally important and deserving of their own class, and places them into a conglomeration taught generally by someone woefully unqualified to teach any of these individual disciplines, and the augmented with what ever social activism is espoused by the teacher. To make matters worse, the United States tends to be the only country which uses "social studies" to teach the fundamentals of being a democracy, when the United States is a republic. Other nations teach all of these elements,

---

https://www.pbs.org/newshour/show/cocaine-how-miracle-drug-nearly-destroyed-sigmund-freud-william-halsted.

[6] SocialStudies.org

generally with qualified teachers, each in their own class because of their importance.

Herein lies the problem, when we allow underqualified people to teach, the students education suffers. When economic (and civics) education suffers, students then go to college with fundamentally flawed foundational knowledge. This results in a whole generation of students who are not taught to critically think because it may “offend the teacher or professor.” These cogs in the machine are then sent back out, with useless social studies degrees only able to get jobs teaching kids the same bad education they received and the cycle repeats. The solution is quite simple, we need to start teaching economics, civics, and history as their own subjects again- preparing students to be active citizens in the republic in which they live. But the teachers union will not allow this, because they have been indoctrinated with the Union beliefs that America must become a democracy to be successful. This “theory” of the unqualified union has led to a steady decline in American schools since 1960s when the teachers union became a political force in the United States.

While fixing Civics and History is a task for another time, the correction of economic thought is vital as we shift toward a digital economy. Many people, even in financial jobs, do not understand economic thought. As such, we have a situation of “the blind leading the blind.” We need to ensure that those who are in positions to make choices understand that the core elements of economics are:

1. Scarcity
2. Supply and Demand
3. Utility
4. Incentives
5. Opportunity Cost.

While there are more complex elements beyond these, this treaties will focus on the core elements allowing for more advanced theory to develop over the course of time.

Scarcity is comprised of the idea that all resources have a finite amount in nature. Regardless of the bounds of the universe, somewhere there is a limit to every resource except human hubris. Because of this, if I have unit a of product X, that means that you do not have it. Scarcity therefore is a value driver because if you want what I have, assuming we live in a civilized society where you cannot just take it, commerce is created when you offer me something in exchange for the good. If your offer is good enough, then I will sell you the product. If your offer is not good enough, then I either counteroffer or you go without. Either way, it is the uniqueness and fungibility of the item which define a portion of the value when looking at scarcity.

The evolution of the digital model has brought about a change to scarcity, specifically in currency. Within the digital universe there are two elements of scarcity, supply, and compute. Whereas in the classic system there was a fiction of scarcity of funds because currency was controlled by a nation state, with an unlimited license to print new currency while telling the populous what the "value" of the currency is, in the modern system the failures and faults of the nation state are being replaced by the efficiency of the private sectors. Where the government can simply print more currency, regardless of what they say the supply is, in the private sector contract law (and smart contracts) limit a supply to what is disclosed to the public (in a true blockchain). This relationship shows that the failures of the nation state model in economics can be replaced by a more efficient private sector model, and that the underlying element of scarcity needs to be addressed.

To address the underlying problem of compute, we simply need to look at the value of the processing. The earth, to our knowledge, can only produce so much electricity- which is the primary commodity for compute. This electricity must be spread across all fields which require it, with economics and medical being the most important elements. The problem which we currently face is that there is drag on the current electrical model because a situation of artificial scarcity, one of the key problems in the classical model, has been a shadow over the field since its inauguration. Legacy power companies, which should be a utility but have been converted into another type of business, are charging more for energy products, and limit supply to maintain price.

This creates an artificial scarcity which undercuts the efficiency of the economy. This is an issue that the classical system has not addressed because the people with the power to address the problem are profiting from the problem itself. The Defi world is the first industry to force the energy system to be more efficient.

The next core issue of economic theory is supply and demand. This portion, when compared to scarcity, is quite simple. If the demand surpasses the supply, then the price goes up. If the supply surpasses the demand, then the price goes down. This is, of course, the most basic expression of supply and demand theory. The digital world creates a system where the "middlemen" the aggregators of society, are no longer needed. Automated market makers make the process more efficient, which allows the system to operate at a lower cost to the users. Since the economic model is a fundamental system, profiteering off of the system should be minimized to ensure that the system functions as needed- which means a major redress of the function of banks and processors in society.

The tertiary core issue in economic is utility. Utility works hand in hand with supply and demand theory as the level of satisfaction received from a good or services relates to its value. In classical theory, supply and demand theory is underpinned by the utility of the good. Without utility, there is no demand. If there is no demand and a high supply, then the value of the product is non-existent. If no one wants something, then the value of the product drops to zero.

In the digital shift, utility is programable. One of the greatest faults of society is that we have been using the same monetary policy for nearly 5,000 years. This theory uses one type of currency for all transactions (fiat). The model is inefficiency as is seen in cross border transactional models such as SWIFT and XRP, they both fail to meet the needs of the modern community. Archaic laws around the space create a protectionist system for failure, but to allow the system to thrive we must move beyond these failed systems and allow utility to be programmed into each currency.

The penultimate driver of economic systems is incentives. People need a reason to participate in a system, which by its very nature is "rigged" against them. The business model is properly based on the concept that your business will make money if you sell a product for more than it is worth to you to someone else. No one ever makes money from buying their own products exclusively. Therefore, a business must convince a buyer that an object is worth more than the business thinks it is, this is the incentive created by marketing.

In the digital shift, the fiction of value to the customer can be replaced by a reality of value for the customer. Rather than having influencers and other talking heads promote your product, your product will have a value to the user so that there is a reason for them to buy it. This reduces the inefficiency of the "pop culture" fads, replacing them with a utility incentive to purchase goods. Did anyone really need jams in the 1990s, a ShamWow in the early 2000s, Obama, Trump, or Biden in the last 30 years; no, we were just convinced that they were something that we wanted. The science of selling people things that they do not need has become a cornerstone of the failed economic system, what if we replace it with programed utility for what people actually need.

Finally, we round out the core values with opportunity cost. Opportunity cost is an investment that you did not make. If you saved your money in an interest bearing account rather than buying something or taking a trip, how much money did you make by "not doing" what you wanted to do (either buying or getting a service). One of the greatest mistakes that the classical economic system has taught us is that money saved in a bank is a good investment. It is not a lie; it is a good investment- just for the bank. Money that is out of play is always "bad money," however, if you take the risk and the bank (with zero reserves) invests your money somewhere else to make more money, and you get a slight fraction of any interest generated (or none at all on most checking accounts), how is this an advantage to you? You fronted the capital. You took the risk. The bank gets the reward. This is the greatest scam of the classical system.

The digital progress in this is the elimination of the middleman. In Defi saving/lending, you have the ability to put your money where you want it. If you want it saved with no risk, then you save it in a cold wallet. If you want it saved with low risk, you join a DeFi lending consortium (insured). If you want moderate risk, you purchase into the backbone of the system liquidity tokens. If you want higher risk, you can purchase utility tokens which present higher rewards. If you want to lose money, you hold it in OROR tokens (commonly called stablecoins in the United States), because you know that inflation of the classical system will always undermine the underlying fiat assets on which the OROR token is based. This results in a nice steady loss of your money- kind of like paying the government protection money so they do not arrest you or is that taxes. This is an inflationary protection racket to keep you in the pocket of centralized finance, even while the DeFi world passes you by.

The world is changing rapidly, and classical economic theory does not consider the improvements which have been created. Progressive economic theory, which is based on the Marxist chain is even worse as your money is not "your money" it belongs to the governments and the unions- your productivity is their gain. For economic theory to work requires two things, leadership which understands the core elements of economics, even as the most basic level and people who want to succeed. Drunks like Marx teach society one thing, that the gimmies (people who want to do nothing but get everything) will always be there- for some reason we elect them to office in the United States, but the goal of the economic system must be to ensure that the gimmies do not drag down the rest of society and we can allow human society to advance.

Understanding the world in which you live is vital to success- I hope that this book helps you understand more than you do.

Chapter 1: The Entropy of Fiat. Why traditional currencies are designed to fail by physics, not just policy.

"I think you should always bear in mind that entropy is not on your side."

Elon Musk[7]

Do you know the difference between fiat currency and currency? This is one of the greatest problems that we have in society today is the "currency" refers to fiat whereas we need it to function like a currency. Real currency is a representation of value. This is not a store of value, it is not an investment, but simply a representation of wealth of the entity which is issuing the currency. This is a vital function of currency in a functional society because it forces the currency issuer to be fiscally responsible.

Conversely, fiat currency is issued by government fiat, which is to say that it is issued for the purpose of which the government issues it. Initially, the fiat currency was issued as a representation of value of the assets of the government (which generally were backed by gold). This was an extra step between the wealth of a person and the colored pieces of paper that they carry with them. Unfortunately, this extra step was a measured process which was put to

[7] Staff (2026) "Entropy Quotes" Brainy Quotes at https://www.brainyquote.com/search_results?x=0&y=0&q=Entropy+.

separate individuals from their wealth, because while the issue and the distribution could not be "changed" the intermediary step is not protected by constitutional law.

The change in the process was simple at first and mostly covered by the existence of income taxes- which are necessary for extractive policies to exist. Ever so slowly, the issuer (which in the case of the federal reserve) transitioned the currency from a representation of wealth to an investment vehicle. The bank prints more money, usually at the request of the government, to cover debt, mostly owed to the issuing bank. In order for the government to cover the creation of the new currency, they take a loan from the issuing bank. This loan, of course, is paid partially in the newly issued currency and partially through debt owed by the country. In this function, the money becomes an investment for the bank.

However, about the 1950s (at least in the United States) this process was not increasing the value of the banking system enough. From this dozens of little banks were created across the United States. These banks also "invested" in the creation of the currency- which resulted in greater inflation. As a result, the country moved away from the gold standard (which was failing anyway) and moved to emphasize "The full faith and credit…" of the United States. This in turn led to greater inflation as now multiple banks were "playing the market" on the value of currency.

The masterstroke of inflationary tactics was put into place when the requirements of the National Bank Act of 1863 were slowly removed. At first, the 25% (which is already very low), was replaced by changed fractional levels. In 1917, the Federal Reserve Bank of the United States created a tiered system for "how much" a bank needed to have to be solvent. This was based on the size of a city (13%/10%/and 7%). This was one of the causes of the run on the banks during Black Friday. In 1938, the Federal Reserve under FDR changed the system to 13% and 17% to combat the great depression; however, this was still too little too late. In 1959, the Federal Reserve, under Eisenhower, changed then meaning of the word "reserve" to include vault cash, which was on hand to pay out depositors. In 1962, under JFK, reduces the reserve deposit requirements in "central reserve cities" and also allowed ALL vault cash to be counted towards the reserve. In 1992, under Bush I, the Federal Reserve reduced the requirement for non-transactional liabilities to 0 and had the limited net transaction requirement reduced to 10%. In March 2020, under Biden, the Board of Governors of the Federal Reserve reduced the requirement ratios to zero percent for all depository institutions; effectively eliminating any reserve requirements for banks. This fully reduced the United States dollar from a reserve currency to a "physical Memecoin" for speculative investment.[8]

The problem with this is that millions of people in the United States and billions of people worldwide depend on the dollar to be a functional currency. Without this, the world economy system is in a state of flux. The last time that this type of "flux" happened, two world wars were fought, mainly due to the realization that money was becoming worthless. Regardless of the system, currency should be a representation of value- not a medium for speculation. As such, we have seen a decline in the "Physics of Money," the entropy of fiat constantly is leading to the inflation of the currency and the only ones making money being the banks which are issuing the funds.

The Second Law of Monetary Thermodynamics: Why Value Dissipates

In the framework of Statistical Mechanics, entropy is a measure of the number of possible configurations (microstates) a system can have. The more configurations possible, the higher the entropy, and the less "useful work" can be extracted.

When applied to the financial system, the U.S. Dollar is a carrier of information. A price is a signal that tells a producer how to allocate resources. However, under the current fiat regime, the "microstates" of the dollar have reached a point of near-infinite expansion.

---

[8] Federal Reserve Board of Governors at https://www.federalreserve.gov/monetarypolicy/reservereq.htm.

In 1917, the dollar had a specific set of physical constraints (the gold reserve). By 2020, with the removal of all reserve requirements, those constraints vanished.

When the Federal Reserve creates $6 trillion in a single cycle, they are not creating wealth; they are increasing the monetary entropy. They are adding so many "units" to the system that the "signal" of the price becomes lost in the "noise" of the currency expansion. This is why we see asset bubbles—the information in the currency is so corrupted by entropy that the market can no longer accurately price risk or value.

The Work-Energy Equivalence of Currency

In physics, **Work**[9]

$$\mathbf{W=\int F^{*}ds}$$

is the product of force and displacement. In economics, Wealth is the product of labor and productivity.

A functional currency acts as a battery—a potential energy storage device. However, the Second Law dictates that in a closed system, energy naturally tends toward a state of equilibrium (heat death). In a

---

[9] Where W= Work, F=Force, and Ds =differential displacement. The dot product (the symbol between F and Ds is showing that direction of the motion is only counted when it is in parallel with the motion of the work and the integral is that it is a summation of the tiny amounts of work that function over an segment of the path from the starting point.

currency, "heat death" occurs when the currency has been diluted to the point where it can no longer facilitate "work."

Legacy finance attempts to fight this by "investing," which is effectively trying to run a generator to keep the battery charged. But because the underlying medium (the dollar) is leaking energy at a rate of 2-7% annually (the "Target Inflation" rate), the investor is forced to take on higher levels of entropy (risk) just to maintain the same baseline level of "stored work." This is the Red Queen Hypothesis in physics: you must run as fast as you can just to stay in the same thermodynamic state.

The Dissipative Structure of Fiat

Nobel laureate Ilya Prigogine described "dissipative structures"—systems that maintain their order by exporting entropy to their surroundings. The U.S. Dollar is the ultimate dissipative structure.

The Federal Reserve maintains the "illusion" of a stable domestic economy by exporting its monetary entropy to the rest of the world via the petrodollar and global trade. We "print" our disorder and send it offshore in exchange for "low-entropy" goods (physical products). However, as the global community moves toward digital realism and de-dollarization, the U.S. is losing its ability to export that entropy. The "disorder" is now starting to back up into the domestic system, manifesting as rapid price inflation and the collapse of bank solvency.

The Transition to Low-Entropy Digital Assets

The financial community needs to view the shift from fiat to digital assets not as a "tech upgrade," but as a Phase Transition. We are moving from a high-entropy, noisy, "gaseous" monetary state (fiat) back to a low-entropy, "crystalline" state (algorithmic code).

In a digital economy, the ledger is "ordered" by the Energy Cost of Validation. Whether through compute-heavy Proof of Work or the structural depth of Fractal Reserves, we are re-anchoring the currency to the physical laws of the universe. We are replacing the "opinion-based" noise of a committee with the "certainty" of mathematical proof.

Debt-Based Expansion and the Inevitable Gravity of Interest

In physics, gravity is a force that pulls matter toward a central point of density. As mass increases, the gravitational pull intensifies until, at a certain threshold, the structure can no longer support its own weight. Debt-based expansion operates on an identical principle. Since nearly every dollar in the modern economy is brought into existence through a loan from a central bank, every unit of "wealth" is born with a corresponding unit of "anti-wealth" (debt) plus a tax on time (interest).

The fundamental flaw in this architecture is that while the bank creates the principal, it never creates the interest. To pay back a $100 loan at 5% interest, the system must eventually find $105. But since all money is debt, that extra $5 can only be brought into existence by another entity taking out a larger loan. This creates a monetary singularity: the money supply must expand at an exponential rate just to keep the system from imploding under the weight of its own historical interest.

The Drag of Time-Preference

Interest is often described in finance as the price of time. From a physics perspective, it is a form of friction or "drag" on the velocity of capital. In a natural economy, interest would reflect the available surplus of real-world assets. However, in a fiat system, interest is an artificial force used by central planners to combat the very entropy they created.

As the debt-to-GDP ratio increases, the "gravitational pull" of interest payments begins to consume an ever-larger portion of the system's energy (productivity). We see this in the current federal budget, where interest payments on the national debt are beginning to eclipse spending on actual infrastructure and defense. This is the stage where the gravity of the past begins to swallow the potential of the future. The system is no longer moving forward; it is simply burning its remaining fuel to stay in orbit around its debt.

The Work-Energy Deficit

If we apply the principle of conservation of energy, we realize that wealth cannot be created out of nothing; it must be the result of work. When a bank "invests" by printing money with zero reserves, they are essentially issuing a claim on future work that has not yet been performed.[10]

Total Debt=Principal =∫(Rate*Time)dt

The integral of interest over time ensures that the total debt will always outpace the total money supply. This creates a permanent work-energy deficit. The

---

[10] P= Principal- This is the initial "mass" of the currency brought into existence. In a debt-based system, this represents the face value of the loan issued by the central bank to the government or commercial entity. It is the only part of the equation that the bank actually "prints." Rate (R): This is the gravitational constant of the system, usually expressed as the interest rate. It represents the "cost of time" or the friction applied to the principal. Because this rate is applied to the principal but the resulting value is not added to the money supply, it creates a permanent deficit. Time (T): This represents the duration of the debt contract. In physics terms, this is the temporal dimension through which entropy (interest) accumulates. The longer the time, the greater the "gravitational pull" of the debt becomes. The Integral (∫): This mathematical operation represents the continuous accumulation of interest over the life of the system. It shows that interest is not a static fee, but a compounding force that grows exponentially. : This represents the infinitesimal change in time. It indicates that in a modern financial system, the accrual of debt is a constant, continuous process rather than a periodic one.
The critical takeaway for the financial community is the discrepancy between Total Debt and Total Money Supply (M).

M≈Principal

Because the money supply is roughly equal to the principal created, but the debt is the principal plus the integral of interest, the system is mathematically insolvent from the moment of inception. There is an inherent lack of "energy" (units of currency) to satisfy the equation. This forces the system into a state of perpetual expansion—taking on new debt (P_2) to pay the interest on the old debt—which only increases the density of the singularity.

financial community calls this "liquidity management," but a physicist would call it a "divergent series." The only way to resolve a divergent series in a physical system is through a reset—a total collapse of the old structure to release the stored tension.

Escape Velocity: Moving Toward Digital Realism

The legacy system is currently trapped in a "debt spiral," a state where it must take on more debt just to service the interest on existing debt. This is the definition of a black hole in economic terms. No amount of "opinion-based" policy can change the math; the gravity of interest will eventually pull the "physical memecoin" of the dollar into the singularity of hyperinflation or systemic default.

Digital economic theory provides the only viable escape velocity. By moving to a system that is not based on debt-issuance—but rather on asset-backed certainty and fractal reserves—we remove the "gravitational constant" of mandated interest. In a digital economy, money is not a loan from a bank; it is a representation of value that exists independently of a debt contract. It allows the system to move from a state of forced expansion to a state of equilibrium, where the "physics of money" finally aligns with the reality of human productivity.

The Half-Life of Purchasing Power: A Forensic History

The purchasing power of a currency does not vanish; it is redistributed. In a forensic analysis of the last century, we see that the dollar follows a predictable decay curve similar to radioactive isotopes. If we set the purchasing power of the dollar in 1913 (the year the Federal Reserve was established) at 100%, the forensic data shows a persistent degradation that accelerates at every major policy shift you outlined—1917, 1933, 1971, and the final 2020 removal of reserves.

The fundamental equation for this decay is expressed as:

$$PP(t)=PP_0 \cdot e^{-\lambda t}$$

Where:

- **PP(t):** The purchasing power at time .
- **PP_0:** The initial purchasing power (the baseline).
- **e:** Euler's number, representing continuous compounding decay.
- **λ:** The decay constant, which in economics is the realized inflation rate.
- **t:** The time elapsed.

When the decay constant (λ) is manipulated by central banks to "target" 2% inflation, they are effectively setting a mandated half-life for your savings. At a steady 2% decay, the half-life of your money is approximately 35 years. If inflation hits 7%, the half-life drops to 10 years. By the time the reserve requirements hit zero in 2020, the decay constant became unanchored, moving the currency into a state of rapid isotopic breakdown.

The Quantity Theory of Money (QTM) as a Forensic Tool

To support the physics of decay with economic modeling, we must look at the Fisher Equation, the bedrock of the Quantity Theory of Money:

Where:

$$M \cdot V = P \cdot Y$$

- **M:** The money supply (the total mass of the memecoin/fiat).
- **V:** The velocity of money (how fast the "energy" circulates).
- **P:** The price level (the measure of entropy).
- **Y:** Real GDP (the actual work/output).

Forensically, when Y (productivity) grows at 2% but M (money supply) is expanded by 20% to cover debt-based expansion, the equation must be balanced. If V remains constant, P must rise. This is not "prices going up"; it is the "value per unit" of M going down. The forensic history of the dollar shows that every time the Federal Reserve increased M to bail out the "gimmies" or the banks, the variable P acted as a heat-sink, absorbing the excess entropy and destroying the purchasing power of the individual.

The Real Interest Rate and the Confiscation of Labor

The financial community often hides the decay of purchasing power behind "nominal" gains. However, the forensic reality is found in the Fisher Effect equation:

Where:

$$r=i-\varpi$$

- **r:** The real interest rate (the actual energy return).
- **i:** The nominal interest rate (the "reputation" rate).
- **ϖ:** The inflation rate (the entropy/decay).

When i is kept artificially low by the Fed while ϖ is high, r becomes negative. A negative real interest rate is a forensic signature of a wealth transfer. It means the "work" you stored in the bank is being biologically consumed to pay for the "debt-gravity" we discussed in the previous section. Between 1913 and 2026, the dollar has lost over 97% of its value. Forensically, this means the dollar has experienced approximately five half-lives. Each "recovery" touted by politicians was merely a slowing of the decay, never a reversal of the entropy.

The Digital Escape from Isotopic Decay

The reason the classical system hates digital realism is that algorithms do not allow for a manipulated decay constant. In a digital asset model, the M variable in MV=PV is fixed or programmatically capped. This forces the system to find equilibrium through Y (productivity) rather than P (price inflation). By moving to a low-entropy medium, we stop the "half-life" effect on our labor. We move from a currency that is "dying" to one that is "stable," allowing the human impulse for self-actualization to finally outpace the gravity of debt.

Centralized Manipulation as a Catalyst for Decay

In information theory, the utility of a signal is inversely proportional to its entropy. A market price is the most efficient information signal in existence; it condenses the subjective utility, scarcity, and opportunity cost of a resource into a single, actionable number. When the Federal Reserve engages in open market operations or adjusts the federal funds rate, they are not "guiding" the market; they are injecting noise into the signal.

This noise creates a false state of equilibrium. By artificially suppressing interest rates, the central authority signals that capital is abundant and risk is low. This induces the market to engage in "malinvestment"—allocating resources to projects that would be mathematically non-viable in a high-entropy (realistic) environment. This is the "opinion-based science" mentioned in the introduction. It replaces the factual assessment of risk with the confirmation bias of a committee. The result is a decoupling of the financial layer from the physical layer of the economy, accelerating the decay of the system's structural integrity.

The Catalyst Equation: Artificial Lowering of Activation Energy

In chemistry, a catalyst provides an alternative pathway for a reaction that requires lower activation energy. Centralized manipulation acts as a catalyst for the "reaction" of economic collapse. By removing the reserve requirements to zero in 2020, the central authority effectively removed the "activation energy" required for a systemic bank run or a currency devaluation.

The relationship between intervention and decay can be modeled by looking at the variance in price stability (σ^2) relative to the volume of intervention (I):

$$\Delta \text{Entropy} \propto [(dI/dt) \cdot (1/\text{Reserves})]$$

As the rate of intervention (dI/dt) increases and the reserves trend toward zero, the entropy of the system approaches infinity. The "decay" is no longer a slow, linear process; it becomes a non-linear, runaway reaction. The centralized authority believes they are "dampening" volatility, but they are actually "compressing" it. They are holding back the forest fire while allowing the deadwood (debt and insolvency) to accumulate to a height that ensures the eventual blaze will consume the entire forest.

The Moral Hazard and the Death of Feedback Loops

A vital component of any sustainable physical or economic system is the negative feedback loop. If a cell in a body consumes more energy than it produces, it dies. If a business fails to provide utility, it goes bankrupt. This is the "self-correction" that prevents entropy from overwhelming the system.

Centralized manipulation destroys these loops through the mechanism of moral hazard. When the "gimmies"—whether they are non-productive individuals or insolvent "too big to fail" banks—are shielded from the consequences of their inefficiency through the issuance of new currency, the system loses its ability to purge disorder. The "wastrels" are permitted to reap the maximum benefit for the minimum work, as Marx envisioned, but at the cost of the system's overall energy. This is a biological parasitism encoded into the ledger. The productive elements of the republic are forced to carry the increasing "mass" of the non-productive elements until the "gravity" of the debt becomes insurmountable.

Propaganda as a Stabilizing Fiction

To prevent the public from observing the decay, the central authority must employ propaganda as a psychological stabilizer. This is the "social studies" approach to finance: teaching the populace that "inflation is a sign of a healthy economy" or that "the debt does not matter because we owe it to ourselves."

From a forensic standpoint, this propaganda is an attempt to manage the "psychological solvency" of the memecoin/fiat. As long as people believe the colored pieces of paper have value, the system can continue to export its entropy. However, once the "reputation" of the central bank is revealed to be a black box of opinion-based science, the transition to algorithmic trust becomes inevitable. The "blind leading the blind" eventually walk off a cliff, and only those who have anchored their wealth in the "crystalline" logic of digital realism will survive the fall.[11]

Systems Complexity and the Point of Irreversible Collapse

In systems theory, complexity is not a sign of sophistication; it is often a sign of impending failure. As the Federal Reserve moves to manage every aspect of the economy—from the "zero-reserve" solvency of banks to the yields on long-term bonds—they must create increasingly intricate layers of

---

[11] Since I am using my Cooper AI bot to edit the text, I want to allow you the benefit of the comments which it makes on each section. These will be entitled "Cooper's Logic Checks" and will be AI interpretation of each section.
Cooper's Logic Check → The bankers call it "macroeconomic stability." In the real world, we call it "price fixing." Whenever you see a committee of twelve people deciding the price of the most important commodity in the world (money), you are not looking at a free market—you are looking at a cartel. The March 2020 move to 0% reserves was the final surrender of science to opinion. They stopped pretending the banks were solvent and started betting entirely on their ability to keep the propaganda machine running faster than the math of decay.

derivatives, repo facilities, and swap lines to maintain the illusion of order.

Each new layer of intervention creates a "tightly coupled" system. In a loosely coupled system, a failure in one bank remains local. In the current tightly coupled legacy system, a liquidity crisis in a minor regional bank can be transmitted at near-light speed through the entire global network because there is no "slack" (reserves) left in the system to absorb the shock. By removing the 10% reserve requirements in 1992 and the final 0% reduction in 2020, the central authority essentially removed the "crumple zones" from the financial vehicle. We are now driving a hyper-complex machine at maximum velocity with no brakes and no bumpers.

The Self-Organized Criticality (SOC) Model

The financial community needs to understand the concept of "Self-Organized Criticality," often illustrated by the "Bak-Tang-Wiesenfeld sandpile" model. As you drop grains of sand onto a pile, it builds up until it reaches a critical state. At this point, the addition of a single, identical grain of sand can trigger an avalanche of any size.

In economic terms, the "sand" is the debt-based expansion and the "gimmie" policies we have discussed. The central bank believes that because the last 10,000 grains of debt did not collapse the pile, the next one would not either. This is a catastrophic failure of logic. The pile is now so high—and the internal tension so great—that the "size" of the next grain (the trigger) is irrelevant. Whether it is a geopolitical shift, a sudden spike in energy costs, or a loss of "faith" in the memecoin, the system is mathematically primed for a landslide.

Non-Linear Feedback and the Point of No Return

The point of irreversible collapse is defined by the moment when negative feedback loops (stabilizers) are completely overwhelmed by positive feedback loops (accelerants). In a healthy economy, high prices reduce demand, which eventually lowers prices—this is a stabilizing negative feedback loop.

In a complex collapse, we enter a "death spiral." For example:

1. **Confidence Erodes:** Investors begin to dump the dollar because of the "protection racket" of inflation.[12]
2. **Yields Spike:** To attract buyers for the debt, interest rates must rise.[13]

---

[12] We have seen this as more and more nations are dropping the dollar as a reserve currency, looking desperately for other reserve currencies.

[13] The yields on US bonds Have increased from less than 1.5% in 2021 to over 4% in 2026. Federal Reserve Bank of St. Louis https://fred.stlouisfed.org/series/DGS10#:~:text=Notes:%20For%20further%20information%20regarding%20treasury%20constant,Statistical%20Release%20notes%20and%20Treasury%20Yield%20Curve.

3. **Debt Gravity Increases:** The cost to service the $34+ trillion debt eclipses all other spending.[14]

4. **Monetary Printing Accelerates:** The Fed prints more money to pay the interest, which further erodes confidence.[15]

This is a positive feedback loop where the "solution" (printing) accelerates the "problem" (devaluation). Once the energy required to maintain the "closed loop" of the dollar exceeds the productivity of the republic, the system hits its Phase Transition. The currency does not just "lose value"; it loses its status as a medium of exchange entirely. It becomes "dead energy."[16]

---

[14] The current interest on the US national debt is now over $1Trillion dollars each year, making it 20% of the national debt cost each year. https://www.usdebtclock.org/. Currently the Federal Reserve holds 25% of the national debt domestically and several notes on quantitative easing. Staff (2026). "The Federal Government has Borrowed Trillions. Who Owns all that Debt?" Peter g Peterson Foundation at https://www.pgpf.org/article/the-federal-government-has-borrowed-trillions-but-who-owns-all-that-debt/. Additionally it should be noted that other domestic banks and depository institutions hold over $7 Trillion which accounts for another 45% meaning most US debt is held by US private banks. *Id.*

[15] We keep seeing more and more currency being printed each year.

[16] Cooper's Logic Check → The "experts" on TV will tell you the system is "resilient." They said that in 1929, 2008, and 2020. They are paid to keep you in the sandpile until the avalanche starts. The move to 0% reserves was the "white flag" of a system that has reached maximum complexity and zero actual value. They havebuilt a Rube Goldberg machine to keep a dead currency twitching, and they are charging you the "inflation tax"

The Digital Realism Lifeboat

The only way to survive the collapse of a complex system is to de-couple from it before the phase transition occurs. This is the core of digital economic theory. By moving wealth into algorithmic, low-entropy assets like the KIROS framework, you are moving from a "tightly coupled" debt-trap to a "decentralized" sovereign rail.

While the legacy system is characterized by "fragility" (it breaks under stress), digital realism aims for "antifragility"—a system that actually becomes stronger and more verified as it is stress-tested. We are replacing the fragile complexity of a committee's "opinion-science" with the robust simplicity of mathematical proof and asset-backed certainty.

The Illusion of Stability in a Closed Loop

The primary reason the "physical memecoin" of the dollar appears stable to the average citizen is that they are trapped in a circular logical loop. They measure the value of their labor in dollars, and they measure the cost of their survival (rent, food, energy) in dollars. Because the dollar is the denominator for both sides of the equation, the denominator itself appears to be a constant ($1 = $1).

In physics, this is a failure of the frame of reference. If you are standing on a ship moving at a constant

---

to keep the lights on. The collapse is not a "if"—it is a "when," dictates by the laws of physics that no act of Congress can repeal.

velocity across a featureless sea, you feel stationary. Stability, in this context, is not a physical reality but a lack of perceived acceleration. The central authority maintains this illusion by ensuring that the "sea" (the global market) remains featureless through the suppression of alternative currencies and the use of propaganda that equates "volatility" with "risk." By making the dollar the mandatory medium for taxes and legal tender, they force the entire population into a closed-loop system where the decay of the medium is masked by the uniformity of its application.

The Hedonic Adjustment and the Warping of Metrics

To maintain the illusion as entropy increases, the central authority must periodically "recalibrate" the instruments of measurement. This is most evident in the Consumer Price Index (CPI) and the use of hedonic adjustments. When the price of a low-entropy good (like a steak) rises, the "opinion-based science" of the Bureau of Labor Statistics suggests that the consumer will substitute it for a high-entropy, lower-quality good (like ground beef).

By changing the "basket of goods," the government effectively warps the ruler while claiming the table has not moved. This is a mathematical sleight of hand designed to hide the dissipation of value. If the metric for "inflation" is constantly adjusted to exclude the items that are actually rising in price (food and energy), the loop appears stable to those who only read the headlines, even as their actual standard of living—their "stored work"—is being biologically consumed.

The Global Heat Sink: Exporting Volatility

The dollar's stability is also an illusion created by the Petrodollar system and its status as the world's reserve currency. In thermodynamics, a heat sink is an environment that can absorb a large amount of energy (entropy) without a significant change in temperature. For decades, the United States has used the rest of the world as a monetary heat sink.

When the Federal Reserve prints money, the resulting "heat" (inflation) is spread across the entire global population that holds dollars. This dilutes the immediate impact on the domestic loop, making the dollar appear "strong" relative to other failing fiat currencies. However, as we move toward a multipolar digital economy, that heat sink is becoming saturated. As foreign nations stop absorbing American entropy, the "heat" is reflecting back into the domestic loop. The illusion is breaking because the closed system is finally being forced to reckon with its own internal temperature.

The Shift to an Absolute Reference

Digital realism solves the illusion of stability by providing an external, absolute frame of reference: the ledger. Unlike the dollar, which is a "rubber yardstick" that shrinks every year, a decentralized digital asset with a fixed supply is a rigid measurement.[17] When you look at the dollar through the lens of a low-entropy asset, you finally see the acceleration of the elevator. You realize that the dollar is not stable; it is in a state of terminal freefall, and the "stability" you felt was merely the absence of a window to see the ground rushing up to meet you.[18]

Conclusion: The Terminal Velocity of Paper

In the study of fluid dynamics, terminal velocity is the constant speed that a freely falling object reaches when the resistance of the medium through which it is falling prevents further acceleration. For the legacy financial system, "paper money"—the physical memecoin—has reached this terminal state. The medium of fiat, once buoyed by the resistance of constitutional law and rigid reserve requirements, has become so thin that the currency is now in a state of frictionless freefall.

The central failure of the classical model is its inability to exist within an interconnected, high-velocity digital

---

[17] The response to this is to create a digital constant, which is the purpose of the KIROS project- to overcome the entropy through the use of an independent value in the field coupled with universal liquidity.

[18] Cooper's Logic Check → The bankers love to talk about "price stability," but they never mention "value stability." They haveconvinced the public to look at the numbers on their screen rather than the purchasing power in their pocket. The move to 0% reserves was the final stage of the illusion—it was the moment the elevator cable snapped. They are currently using the "full faith and credit" propaganda to convince you that you are still floating, but physics does notcare about your faith. It only cares about the impact.

world. Paper money, by its very design, is a localized, low-frequency technology. It relies on the latency of the "middleman" and the physical boundaries of the nation-state to mask its internal entropy. However, as the global economy transitions into a real-time, 24/7 digital environment, the "heat" generated by fiat's inherent decay can no longer be hidden. In a world where value must move at the speed of light, a medium that loses 2-7% of its energy annually is not a currency; it is a liability.

The move to zero-percent reserve requirements in March 2020 was the final admission that the paper system has no structural integrity left. It is an archaic relic of an era when "faith" could be manufactured through propaganda and geographic isolation. Today, the transparency of the blockchain and the efficiency of automated market makers have provided the world with a window. For the first time, the general population can see the ground rushing up.

We are witnessing a phase transition. As the "paper" hits its terminal velocity, the friction of its own obsolescence will cause it to incinerate. The interconnectedness of the modern republic requires a medium of exchange that is as fast, as global, and as certain as the code that runs our infrastructure. To remain tethered to the "physical memecoin" is to accept a future of perpetual debasement and systemic collapse.

The terminal velocity of paper is not just an end; it is a forcing function. It necessitates the move toward digital realism—a system where value is anchored in the immutable laws of physics and mathematics rather than the shifting opinions of an unqualified central committee. The era of the "gimmie" and the "wastrel" supported by the printing press is over. The era of the sovereign, digital economy has begun.[19]

---

[19] Cooper's Logic Check → The bankers are still trying to tell you that the "digital dollar" (CBDC) will save the system. That is like trying to put a jet engine on a paper airplane. It does notchange the fact that the underlying material is flammable and has no substance. A digital version of a zero-reserve currency is just a faster way to reach heat death. Real progress is not digitizing the old scam; it is replacing the scam with a protocol that does notleak energy. CBEDC (Central Bank Enacted Digital Currencies) have the potential to be more effective as the company creates a finite number of tokens which then become the bases for a static M in the equation, allowing for P to remain the only moving variable on each side of the equation.

Chapter 2: The Fractal Reserve Model. Beyond 1:1 backing—understanding liquidity depth and the mechanics of modern reserves.

"Earnings do not move the overall market; it is the federal reserve board… focus on the central banks and focus on the movement of liquidity… most people in the markets are looking for earnings and conventional measures. It is liquidity that moves markets."

Stanley Druckenmiller[20]

If you read the bill of the Clarity Act, which is getting harder with each draft as they try to bury it, you find that the American Banking Association has created the ultimate Hollow Man Fallacy.[21] According to the ABA, the American people only will trust cryptocurrency if stablecoins have a 1:1 backing like the banking industry in the United States, and that if we allow for DeFi banking protocols to offer yield on stablecoins, then there will be flight from traditional depository institutions to "Greener Pastures." The complexity of the stacked logical fallacies are unique in this as they use a straw man fallacy to present the

---

[20] Staff (2026). "Fractal Reserve Quotes." Brainy Quote at https://www.brainyquote.com/search_results?x=0&y=0&q=Fractal+REserve.

[21] A specific form of the straw man where the opposing viewpoint and the person arguing it are complete fabrications, used to attack an argument no one is actually making.

idea that Americans are actively going to bankers to express their worries about digital currencies, wrapped in a hollow man argument that people are complaining about higher yields meaning that there will be less money in banks; followed by what can be only be called a “No straight Scotsman” fallacy (or an outright lie) in that banks in the United States have a 1:1 backing in their reserves.

To unpack this, lets start from the end, the No Straight Scotsman. We know that this is a lie as we have covered it in Chapter 1, the reserve rate for depository institutions in the United States is both currently and effectively 0% of the current deposits, even including “bank value reserves.”[22] The “fact-checker truth” of this statement is that banks are banking on the fact that the United States will print more money if their overextension is exposed causing a run on the banks. Their plan is, in the event of a run, that the U.S. government will take yet another loan out against the “full faith and credit” of the United States from the Federal Reserve. For those of you in the back, “full faith and credit” means that if the U.S. gets into trouble there will be a levy of the shareholders (I mean citizens), the government will raise the tax to cover the debt to the Federal Reserve. So, the actual fallacy is covered with a theoretical fallacy that when the currency collapses, more taxes will fix the problem.

---

[22] *Supra.*

Next, we have the hollow man fallacy. The argument that people are worried about depositors shifting their funds from banks to DeFi institutions only scares one group—the banksters. Investors look at this as a good thing as it creates lift in the markets. Depositors (people with savings accounts) see this as a good thing as the anemic 0.25% offered by a savings account or 1% offered by a Certified Deposit (CD) is replaced with interest rates of 5% for low-risk investments (such as OROR tokens) up to 15% for more moderate utility tokens. Some DeFi platforms do allow people to 'gamble' on yields north of 25%, but most of the legitimate projects stay away from those numbers. Even the argument that the government is not in favor of this is hollow, as the politicians are already investing in these models while they are still legal.

The strawman approach, which is the overall fallacy, which is presented, is desperation from a 700-year-old dying industry. Ever since the banks backed both sides in the 100-year war, the bank system has kept every side of every conflict in debt. They say that the safest "bet" in the casino is to be the house; when you look at investment's the safest investment is to be the bank holding debt. You get to set the interest rates (the odds), and you get to turn down investments you feel are risky (turning down big bets). It is a win-win for the banks and offers a stacked deck against the depositors. Trillions have been made using the government, the politicians, the business community, and the taxpayers as pawns; however, the digital industry offers an alternative.[23]

The Evolution from 1:1 Custody to Fractional Abstraction

The origins of banking were rooted in the "warehouse" model. A depositor brought a specific weight of gold or silver to a custodian and received a receipt. In this stage, the reserve ratio was . The receipt was a low-entropy information signal; it represented a direct, physical link to an asset in the vault. The bank's role was purely custodial, and its profit was derived from storage fees rather than the re-hypothecation of the depositor's energy.

From a physics perspective, the system was in equilibrium. There was no "money creation," only "representation." The velocity of capital was limited by the physical movement of the underlying assets or the transfer of their receipts. While this model provided absolute solvency, it lacked the "lift" required for a rapidly expanding industrial society. This lack of liquidity provided the opening for the first iteration of the "bankster" model: the realization that not all

---

[23] Cooper's Logic Check → The ABA is telling you that DeFi is "risky" because it is not 1:1. Meanwhile, they are operating at 0%. If I have 10% in the vault and they have 0%, I am infinitely more solvent than they are. Their attack on "flight to greener pastures" is the ultimate tell: they know their 0.25% interest rate is a "stay-poor" tax, and they are terrified that the "shareholders" (the taxpayers) are finally figuring out how to be their own bank.

depositors would demand their energy at the same time.

The Fractional Transition: The Discovery of Latency

The shift to fractional banking was a move from physicality to probability. Bankers discovered that they could issue more receipts than they had gold in the vault—provided that the "velocity of redemption" remained low. By keeping only, a fraction of the assets on hand (initially 20-50%), they could "lend" the rest into existence.

This was the birth of the "multiplier effect." In economic theory, this is celebrated as the engine of growth. In forensic physics, it is the introduction of systemic risk. The moment the bank moves from to , the ledger enters a state of "superposition." The money exists in two places at once: on the depositor's balance sheet and on the borrower's balance sheet. This abstraction works only as long as the "Psychological Solvency" we discussed earlier remains intact. If the "observer" (the depositor) attempts to measure the position of their money by withdrawing it, the superposition collapses, revealing the "Hollow Man" beneath.

The Era of Total Abstraction: The 0% Limit

As the 20th century progressed, the "fraction" in fractional reserve banking began to trend toward zero. Each legislative shift—from the tiered requirements of 1917 to the removal of non-transactional reserves in 1992—was a step toward total abstraction. The "anchor" of gold was removed in 1971, and the final "safety net" of cash reserves was deleted in March 2020.

We have now reached the stage of Fractional Abstraction. The "reserves" in the modern banking system are no longer physical assets; they are digital entries representing "high-quality liquid assets" (HQLA), which are often just more debt (Treasuries). The system is now a closed loop of debt backing debt. The custody model has been replaced by an abstraction model. The "physical memecoin" of the dollar is no longer a warehouse receipt; it is a speculative bet that the government can levy enough taxes on the "shareholders" to prevent the void in the vault from being exposed.

The Digital Reclamation of the Floor

The digital economy is currently being attacked by the ABA for not being , but this is a strategic diversion. The real evolution is not moving back to the 1600s warehouse: it is moving toward Fractal Realism. Unlike the legacy bank, which hides its reserve behind a "black box" of opinion-based science, a digital protocol can prove its reserve ratio in real-time on the ledger.

We are replacing the "abstraction" of the bankster with the "certainty" of the algorithm. In the digital shift, we can engineer a reserve that is neither an immobile anchor nor a fraudulent void. We are building a "Fractal Floor" that provides the liquidity necessary for commerce while maintaining the physical integrity required for survival.[24]

Removing the Anchor: The Decoupling of Reserves and Reality

The decoupling was not a single event, but a century-long surgical procedure. The first major cut occurred in 1917, when the Federal Reserve replaced the universal reserve requirement with a tiered system. This was the moment the "anchor" began to drag. By allowing smaller banks to hold as little as 7% in reserves, the central authority admitted that the "Full Faith and Credit" was more important than the "Full Vault and Asset."

However, the final severance—the move to 0% reserves in March 2020—represented the total removal of the anchor. In a 0% reserve environment, there is no longer a physical or mathematical floor to the currency. The bank is no longer "fractional"; it is "fictional." The relationship between the number of dollars in the digital loop and the number of physical assets in the vault is now . This decoupling allows the money supply to expand at a rate that is limited only

---

[24] Cooper's Logic Check → For the financial professionals reading this: You've been taught that "liquidity is life." But in the legacy system, your "liquidity" is actually "dilution." The move from too was not an evolution; it was a slow-motion heist. They took the "energy" out of your money and replaced it with a "claim." Now that the reserves are at , that claim is only as good as the government's ability to arrest people who won't pay their taxes. Digital realism is the only way to put the floor back in the vault.

by the hubris of the Board of Governors, but it simultaneously ensures that the currency has no weight to prevent it from being swept away by the "gravity of interest" we discussed in Chapter 1.

The Illusion of High-Quality Liquid Assets (HQLA)

To mask this decoupling from the financial community, the regulatory bodies introduced the concept of High-Quality Liquid Assets (HQLA). These are the "ghost reserves" that replaced actual cash. In the modern banking ledger, a bank "meets" its liquidity coverage ratios not by holding your money, but by holding government debt (Treasuries).

This is a recursive paradox: the bank's reserves are composed of the very debt that was issued to create the currency in the first place. The "anchor" is made of the same paper as the "ship." From a forensic standpoint, this means the system has zero external support. If the value of the Treasury falls (due to rising interest rates or loss of confidence), the "reserve" evaporates at exactly the same time as the "asset" devalues. This is the definition of systemic fragility. The anchor is not just unattached; it has been replaced with a holographic projection.

The Latency Trap and the Digital Reality

The only thing that allows this decoupled system to survive is "latency"—the time it takes for a depositor to realize the vault is empty. The legacy banking system is built on a "T+2" or "T+5" timeline specifically to give the central bank time to "print" the missing anchor if a run occurs.

In the digital world, latency is being eliminated. Automated market makers and peer-to-peer settlement protocols operate in real-time. When capital moves at the speed of light, a decoupled 0% reserve system cannot survive. The moment the "observer" asks for their energy back, the "Hollow Man" of the bank is exposed instantly. This is why the American Banking Association is so desperate to attack DeFi; they know that in a world of instant settlement, their lack of an anchor is a terminal defect.

Re-Anchoring via Digital Realism

Digital economic theory is the process of re-anchoring the economy to reality. We are replacing the "HQLA" fiction with Algorithmic Certainty. In a fractal reserve model (like KIROS), the anchor is not a political promise; it is a mathematical constant. By maintaining a verifiable, non-zero reserve of assets or computing energy, we provide the "weight" necessary to stabilize the medium. We are moving from a "decoupled" state of speculative memecoins back to a "coupled" state of sovereign commerce.[25]

---

[25] Cooper's Logic Check → For the guys in the corner offices: You think you are "hedging" your risk by holding Treasuries. In reality, you are holding a receipt for a debt that can only be paid if the government prints more receipts. You've decoupled from the ground and you are betting that the air will hold you up forever. The March 2020 policy was not a "stimulus"—it was the moment the Fed admitted the vault was empty and threw the

Psychological Solvency vs. Mathematical Insolvency

Psychological solvency is a state where an institution or system is functionally bankrupt—meaning its total liabilities far exceeding its liquid assets—but it continues to operate because the participants *believe* it is sound. It is a confidence-based equilibrium. In the legacy banking loop, this belief is not rooted in the vault; it is rooted in the "Full Faith and Credit" of the United States government and the Federal Reserve's "Physical Memecoin" printing press.

This is a form of collective cognitive bias. As long as the depositor believes they can withdraw their $100 tomorrow, they do not check to see if that $100 actually exists in the vault today. This allows the bank to engage in "Maturity Transformation"—the process of taking your "short-term" deposits and locking them into "long-term" debt-based investments (like mortgages or 30-year Treasuries). In a 0% reserve environment, the bank is entirely dependent on the fact that you will not exercise your right to your own energy. Psychological solvency is the "holographic floor" of the bank; it feels solid until you try to jump on it.

The Forensic Reality: Mathematical Insolvency

Mathematical insolvency, conversely, is the objective physical state of the ledger. From a forensic

---

keys away. Digital realism is the only way to build a vault that actually has a floor.

standpoint, if a bank has $10 billion in demand deposits and $0 in required reserves, and its "High-Quality Liquid Assets" (HQLA) consist of long-term Treasuries that have lost 20% of their market value due to interest rate spikes, the bank is mathematically insolvent. It cannot satisfy its obligations if even a small fraction of the "load" (depositors) shifts simultaneously.

When the Federal Reserve eliminated reserve requirements in March 2020, they effectively codified mathematical insolvency into the system. They signaled to the financial community that "the math does not matter as long as the belief holds." This is the "No Straight Scotsman" lie in action: the banks claim to be safe "warehouses" for your wealth, but the math proves they are actually highly leveraged "speculative vehicles" using your labor as their collateral.

Living in the Fantasy: The Propaganda of the "Safety Net"

The primary tool used to maintain the fantasy world is the Federal Deposit Insurance Corporation (FDIC). The public is told that their money is "insured" up to $250,000. However, the financial community knows the math: the FDIC's insurance fund typically holds less than 2% of the total insured deposits in the United States.

If a systemic "Run on the Banks" occurs, the FDIC is mathematically insolvent. The "insurance" is not a pile of cash; it is a promise that the government will print more money to cover the loss. This brings us back to the Entropy of Fiat from Chapter 1. The "fix" for insolvency is more debasement. The fantasy world requires the citizen to believe that a "check for $250,000" that buys half as much as it did yesterday is the same thing as "being made whole." This is the ultimate "Hollow Man" argument: they are not protecting your value; they are protecting the *illusion* of your value.

The Phase Transition: When Math Breaks the Fantasy

Collapse occurs when the delta between the mathematical reality and the psychological belief becomes too large to bridge with propaganda. This usually happens at the "Point of Criticality" discussed in Section 1.5. A single event—a high-profile bank failure like Silicon Valley Bank or a geopolitical shift—forces the "observer" to look into the vault. Once the observer sees the "Ghost in the Vault" (which we will audit in the next section), the psychological solvency evaporates instantly.

At that moment, the system attempts to transition back to math, but because the reserves are at 0%, there is no math to catch the fall. This is why the digital world is so terrifying to the legacy cartels. Digital realism does not require "faith." A DeFi protocol is Mathematically Solvent by design; the code either has the assets to execute the transaction, or it does not. There is no "belief" required because the proof is on the ledger.[26]

The Ghost in the Vault: Quantifying the Missing Underlay

In a traditional 1:1 custody model, the underlay is 100%. The "mass" of the asset matches the "volume" of the claim. However, in the "physical memecoin" economy, the underlay has been systematically hollowed out. To quantify this, we must look at the divergence between M2 Money Supply and the total physical currency and reserves held by depository institutions.

When the Federal Reserve eliminated the 10% net transaction requirement in 2020, they effectively declared that the "underlay" no longer needed to be physical. Instead, it could be "notional." This created a situation where for every $100 a citizen "sees" in their digital bank portal, there is $0 in mandated physical cash sitting behind it. The $100 exists only as a "ghost"—a digital ghost entry in a centralized database. The "Missing Underlay" is not just a small deficit; it is a structural vacuum.

---

[26] Cooper's Logic Check → For the people still keeping their life savings in a "0% reserve" bank: You are not "saving"; you are participating in a 700-year-old magic trick. The bankster tells you your money is safe, but the math tells you your money is being used as the "fuel" for their over-leverage. The March 2020 policy change was the moment the magician stopped using a hat and started using an empty box. They are betting that you are too "blinded by social studies" to notice the difference. Digital realism is the process of turning the lights on.

Re-hypothecation as a Dilution Catalyst

The gap is further widened by the process of re-hypothecation—the practice of using the same collateral to back multiple different loans or derivatives. In the legacy system, a single "high-quality liquid asset" (HQLA), such as a 10-year Treasury, can be pledged as collateral in the repo market multiple times.

From a physics perspective, this is an attempt to create "infinite density" from a finite mass. If one bond is used to back four different credit lines, the actual underlay for each of those lines is only 25% of the nominal value. When you factor in the 0% reserve requirement at the base layer, the effective underlay of the entire banking system becomes a microscopic fraction of the total liabilities. This is the "Hollow Man" on a global scale. The financial community calls this "market depth," but forensically, it is simply a house of cards waiting for a shift in the gravitational constant (interest rates) to collapse.

Quantifying the Inevitable: The Liquidity Coverage Ratio (LCR) Fallacy

The regulatory bodies attempt to quantify safety through the Liquidity Coverage Ratio (LCR), which requires banks to hold enough "unencumbered" HQLA to survive a 30-day stress scenario. However, this calculation is based on "opinion-based science" rather than factual assessment. It assumes that the HQLA (Treasuries) will maintain their value during a crisis.

As we saw in the 2023 banking tremors, when interest rates rise to combat the very entropy the Fed created, the market value of these "ghost reserves" drops. A bank that thinks it has a 100% LCR may suddenly find it has a 70% LCR because the "market price" of their anchor has evaporated. The "Missing Underlay" is a dynamic threat; it grows larger as the system's internal heat increases. The financial community is betting that they can stay ahead of the "Ghost," but the math of 0% reserves makes it a statistical certainty that eventually, the vault will be asked to produce what it does not have.

Digital Realism: Filling the Vault with Code

The digital industry offers the first true solution to the ghost in the vault. Through the use of "Proof of Reserves" and algorithmic transparency, the missing underlay is eliminated. In a digital protocol, the underlay is not a "ghost"—it is a verifiable, cryptographic truth.

Whether it is a 1:1 backing for a stablecoin or the specific fractal reserve of a security token, the data is public and immutable. We are moving from a "fantasy world" of hidden deficits to a "realist world" of verifiable assets. By quantifying the underlay and making it a prerequisite for commerce, we remove the "bankster's" ability to profit from the vacuum. We are putting the floor back in the vault, and this time, it is made of math, not propaganda.[27]

Modern Bank Runs in the Digital Age: Why "Slow" Does not Work

Historically, bank runs were limited by the physical speed of the depositor. One had to physically travel to a branch, stand in a line, and wait for a teller to count out physical notes. This friction provided the "buffer" that allowed the Federal Reserve time to move "ghost reserves" (emergency liquidity) into the vault. The legacy system is designed around this latency—the "T+2" settlement cycle and the "business day" are not technical limitations; they are artificial brakes designed to prevent the "superposition" of fractional banking from collapsing too quickly.

In the digital age, this friction has evaporated. When Silicon Valley Bank collapsed in 2023, the "run" did not happen in a lobby; it happened on a smartphone. $42 billion was withdrawn in a single day—a velocity of capital that the legacy 0% reserve model is physically incapable of matching. The "slow" machinery of the Fed and the FDIC were left trying to

---

[27] Cooper's Logic Check → The ABA wants to talk about "transparency" in crypto. Let's talk about the transparency of the vault at your local Chase or Wells Fargo. If you walked in and asked to see the 10% reserve for your neighborhood's deposits, they'd call security. Why? Because there is nothing to see. The "Ghost" is the only thing in the building. They have replaced your labor with a digital "IOU" and they are charging you for the privilege of holding it. Digital realism is not just "better tech"—it is the end of the magic trick.

fight a wildfire with a spreadsheet. The bankster's greatest defense—your inability to get your money quickly—is being neutralized by the very technology they adopted to lower their own overhead.

The Velocity of Information and the Death of "Psychological Solvency"

As we discussed in Section 2.3, psychological solvency is the belief that the vault is full. In the classic system, that belief was maintained through "opinion-based science" and slow-moving news cycles. Today, information travels at the speed of social media. A single tweet or a leaked balance sheet can trigger a global "Exit" command before the bank's board of directors can even schedule a Zoom call.

The problem for the "slow" bank is that while the *demand* for liquidity is now digital and instant, the *assets* backing that liquidity remain "slow" and physical (mortgages, long-term bonds, industrial loans). This creates a "Duration Mismatch" that is amplified by digital velocity.

When the bank has 0% in mandated reserves and its "HQLA" is tied up in 10-year notes, it is mathematically impossible for them to meet a high-velocity run. The system is essentially a high-speed train running on wooden tracks; as soon as the speed increases beyond a certain threshold, the tracks disintegrate.

Automated Market Makers vs. Manual Gatekeepers

The financial community needs to look at the "Exit" mechanism of the digital world. In a DeFi protocol, liquidity is managed by Automated Market Makers (AMMs) and smart contracts. There are no "business hours" and no "gatekeepers." If a run occurs, the protocol settles the transactions according to the math of the ledger—instantly.

The legacy bank, however, relies on "Manual Gatekeepers." When the math fails, they close the doors. They "halt trading" or "freeze accounts." This is the ultimate "Hollow Man" move: they stop the market to save the institution. In a digital, interconnected world, these freezes are seen as a "default signal," which only accelerates the panic in the rest of the interconnected system. By trying to slow down the run, they ensure that the next run will be even faster and more violent.

The Digital Realism Solution: Real-Time Solvency

Digital realism moves us away from the "latency-as-defense" model. By utilizing fractal reserves that are verifiable in real-time, the "incentive" to run is diminished. In a 0% reserve bank, you run because you want to be the first one to get the last dollar. In a transparent, asset-backed digital model, you do not have to run because you can see the vault from your phone.

We are replacing the "slow" fraud of the legacy cartel with the "fast" truth of the ledger. The digital age has made the "physical memecoin" of the dollar obsolete precisely because paper cannot survive in a world of light-speed information. The "slow" model is dead; the only question is how many people will be trapped behind the closed doors of the legacy banks when they finally admit they cannot keep up.[28]

Re-establishing the Floor: The Necessity of Baseline Reserves

In the legacy system, the ABA uses a "Hollow Man" argument to suggest that any reserve requirement higher than 0% is an unnecessary drag on growth. In reality, a baseline reserve is the only thing that prevents a market fluctuation from becoming a systemic collapse. When we talk about "Re-establishing the Floor," we are not advocating for the immobile 1:1 "warehouse" model that stifles liquidity. Instead, we are advocating for a Fractal Reserve Model—a scientifically determined baseline that ensures mathematical solvency.

A baseline reserve (typically 10% to 20% in high-integrity digital frameworks) acts as a structural damper. It provides the "slack" necessary to absorb

---

[28] Cooper's Logic Check → The banksters love to say, "Your money is safe." What they mean is, "Your money is safe as long as you don't ask for it." The moment you and your neighbors all ask for it at once, the "safety" vanishes. They are depending on your "social studies" education to keep you from understanding that a 0% reserve bank is just a slow-motion Ponzi scheme. In 2020, they removed the last of the brakes. They are driving the bus off the cliff and telling you that the "wind in your hair" is a sign of a strong economy. Digital realism is the parachute.

the high-velocity "Exit" commands we discussed in the previous section. If a bank or protocol has 0% reserves, any withdrawal is a liquidity event. If it has a 20% floor, the first 20% of withdrawals are handled with zero impact on the underlying asset health. This floor transforms the system from a "fragile" state to a "robust" one, replacing the "Full Faith" of the government with the "Full Proof" of the ledger.

The Phase Transition: Moving Away from Fiat

The movement away from fiat is not merely a preference for "new technology"; it is a flight from a decaying medium. As we established in Chapter 1, fiat is a high-entropy system designed to leak energy. To re-establish a floor, we must move the "principal" of our wealth into a medium that does not require a debt-issuance to exist.

Fiat is an "unfunded liability." When you hold a dollar, you hold a promise that someone else will pay a tax in the future. Digital realism replaces this liability with an **Asset-Backed Certainty**. By moving wealth into tokens anchored by real-world assets (RWA) or compute energy, we are creating a floor that is independent of the Federal Reserve's "Physical Memecoin" press. We are moving from a system of "decree" (fiat) to a system of "discovery" (market-driven asset value).

The Proof of Reserve (PoR) Architecture

The primary tool for re-establishing the floor in the digital age is Proof of Reserve (PoR). Unlike the legacy "Ghost in the Vault," where a bank's true state is hidden behind a quarterly audit performed by an "unqualified" third party, PoR allows for real-time, 24/7 verification.

In this model:

1. **The Floor is Visible:** Every participant can see the exact ratio of assets to liabilities.
2. **The Floor is Immutable:** Smart contracts prevent the "bankster" from lowering the reserve to 0% to chase speculative yields.
3. **The Floor is Liquid:** Because the reserves are digital and transparent, they can be deployed instantly to settle withdrawals, eliminating the "latency trap."

This transparency removes the incentive for a bank run. You do not have to be the first one to the door if you can see that the door is propped open by a verifiable vault. We are replacing the "Psychological Solvency" of the 700-year-old cartel with the **Computational Solvency** of the modern republic.

Restoring the Role of the Individual

By re-establishing the floor and moving away from fiat, we restore the individual's role as an active citizen in a republic rather than a "shareholder" (taxpayer) in a failing bank. When the floor is 0%, you are a victim of the system's entropy. When the floor is a baseline fractal reserve, you are a participant in a stable economy.

The movement away from fiat is the ultimate act of "self-actualization" that Maslow described. It is a refusal to allow your stored labor to be consumed by the "gimmies" and the "wastrels" of the legacy system. We are building a new floor—not out of paper, and not out of "full faith"—but out of the crystalline logic of digital realism.[29]

Conclusion: Engineering a Sustainable Asset Ratio

The engineering of a sustainable asset ratio marks the definitive end of the "Hollow Man" era in banking. By rejecting the false dichotomy between the stagnant 1:1 warehouse model and the fraudulent 0% reserve of the "physical memecoin," we establish a new paradigm of fractal realism. This model recognizes that liquidity is the lifeblood of a market, but that without a verifiable, non-zero floor, that liquidity is merely a prelude to a catastrophic phase transition. The fractal floor provides the necessary structural damping to survive the high-velocity "Exit" commands of the digital age, replacing the archaic defense of

[29] Cooper's Logic Check → The ABA will tell you that "reserves are capital that is not working." That is like a pilot telling you that "parachutes are weight that is not helping the plane fly." You don't need them until the moment you do—and at that moment, they are the only thing that matters. March 2020 was the day the pilot threw the parachutes out to "save weight." Digital realism is the process of putting them back on. If your bank has 0% reserves, you are not a depositor; you are an unsecured creditor to a bankrupt institution. It is time to move to "Greener Pastures."

friction with the modern certainty of mathematical proof.

Moving away from fiat is not a speculative leap, but a tactical withdrawal from a system that has codified insolvency as its primary operating principle. The "No Straight Scotsman" arguments of the legacy cartels are exposed as a desperate attempt to protect a monopoly on the spread. As the world becomes more interconnected, the "psychological solvency" that once propped up the banksters' black box is being replaced by the "computational solvency" of the ledger. We are no longer required to accept an anemic return on our stored labor while the "house" bets our principal on zero-reserve fantasies; the digital republic allows us to reclaim the vault and build it on the crystalline logic of code.

Ultimately, the goal of the fractal reserve model is to align the physics of money with the reality of human productivity. By re-establishing a floor that is visible, immutable, and liquid, we remove the "gimmie" incentive from the top of the hierarchy and restore the role of the individual as a sovereign actor. The "terminal velocity of paper" described in Chapter 1 finds its resolution here: we stop the freefall by re-anchoring our medium of exchange to real-world assets and algorithmic trust. The sustainable asset ratio is the parachute for a failing economy, providing the escape velocity needed to leave the legacy debt-spiral behind and enter a future of stable, high-velocity commerce.

Chapter 3: The Velocity of Value. How digital speed changes the fundamental math of supply and demand.

"Price is what you pay, value is what you get."

Warren Buffet[30]

Value is a principle which we are commonly taught in school, the idea that value is a constant and that we have the ability to work with it in math class. The reason that economics is not a "hard" science like math or physics is due to the nature of "value." Value is not a constant, it is not even objective. While aggregate values are, by and large, objectified, the underlying values are subjective in nature- possibly the most subjective element in the whole human psyche. Our schools systems attempt to teach that value is objective, because if you do not then many of the other subjects that they teach are undercut by the realization that civics, math, human rights, and others are also subjective. The teacher is not right because the value is constant, the teacher is right because the book says the teacher is right. Basing education on a fallacy is very dangerous; however, basing an economy on a fallacy is even more deadly.

To begin with, what is the value of one? We act as if we should accept that one is a constant (which is in mathematical terms) in all cases. In mathematics, one

---

[30] Staff (2026). "Value Quotes." Brainy Quote at https://www.brainyquote.com/search_results?x=0&y=0&q=Value.

is the number between 0 and 2, it is representative as the smallest whole element within a base ten system (or base 20 or really any base system on which we rely). Oddly, one really found its place when the world shifted to Arabic numbers in the Middle Ages. Prior to that one was the first number, but there was not a number before it (other than negative numbers). Until Brahmagupta (an Indian Mathematician) developed the concept in 628 A.D., there was no use of “0” other than as a placeholder (such as in “101).[31] Approximately 100 years later (← see more placeholders), “0” migrated to the Middle East through the exchange of equations and became a central part (literally) of the Arabic numbering system (which is why a lot of pre-700 equations were not overly accurate). “0” came to Europe in 1202 when introduced by the Italian Mathematician Fibonacci in his book Liber Abaci. So, for all you underachievers who ever received a “0” on an assignment, you need to thank Brahmagupta, the Arabs, and Fibonacci for the common use of “0.”

When we transition to the real world, value becomes much more complicated. When you have “zero” you still have nothing, which is the universal constant; however, when you have “1” what do you have one of? This is where value becomes so important, especially in finance. “I have one money” makes no sense. Is it a rupee, is it a dollar, is it a yuan, is it one

---

[31] Matson, John (2009). “The Origin of Zero.” Scientific American at https://www.scientificamerican.com/article/history-of-zero/.

of those “Disney bucks” they used to sell at Walt Disney World. Because of the variance in currency, “money” is a separate value system from math; hence, the reality that economics is a soft science.

Value is derived from the amount of goods and/or services which can be purchased with a currency. Therefore, the value of the currency is subject to two different variable aspects:

1. The perceived value of the currency from the buyer’s standpoint (B_s)
2. The perceived value of the currency from the seller’s standpoint (S_s).

This relationship between the two variables can be expressed three ways:

1. $B_s=S_s$
2. $B_s \geq S_s$
3. $B_s \leq S_s$

This is because these are there are only three different ways in which the relationship can be noted. We avoid the pure argument of “<” or “>” because subjectivity allows for the movement of the value. Governments “need” the equation to be $B_s=S_s$ because the fundamental argument of central reserve bank fiat currency is $B_s \approx S_s$ because \$1=\$1. This however is not the case.

In reality, the value of B_s is derivative in its native form. B_s is actually derived from the value of the item which the person is looking to acquire now (V_i), relative to the value of other items (V_o), compared to the value of the funds if left in their present state (Net Present Value c), which can be represented as:

$$B_s = V_i \propto (\sum V_o) \cdot NPV\ (c)$$

As you can see, this makes the B_s very chaotic. Our minds, in any transaction should be making the conscious decision does buying V_i mean more to me than buying any of V_o or saving my money (NPV(c)). The government in this case wants us to look at the B_s as being worth a constant, which is easier so most people just go along with the movement.

Meanwhile, on the other side of the equation, we have where the seller is coming from. The seller is looking at the value of the object they have relative to the value of the currency. Further, they are also looking at the buyers relationship to the object (Bo) relative to other buyers relationship to the object which they are selling (On). Additionally there may be a relationship between this and the debt or cost which the seller has which related to the personal value of the object to the seller (Os). These equations can be seen as:

$$S_s = B_o \propto_O n \propto (O_s \cdot [B_o \propto_O n > C \text{ or } B_o \propto_O n \leq C)$$

$$S_s > C + I_v$$

In this case "c" is the cost to produce the good and I_v is the labor value put into the product or services. As the relationship becomes more dynamic, the relative value of the currency becomes more volatile, which leads to more problems in the overall economy.

The final variable added to this problem is time. As B_s and S_s are subjective variables and C is a relatively objective variable which moves with the passage of time, you have three moving variables in a digital equation operating within an analog world. This creates the Temporal-economic paradox that by the time you assess the value, the value has already change. Therefore, we can see that the greater the amount of time for a transaction, the less reliable the price is.

The Friction Tax: Quantifying Annual Transmission Loss

The legacy system is not a single pipeline; it is a series of disconnected reservoirs. When an international transaction is initiated via SWIFT, it must traverse a "correspondent banking" network. This is the equivalent of a bucket brigade where every person in line takes a sip before passing the bucket along. Each "hop" between banks introduces:

1. **Direct Fees:** Fixed costs for message transmission.
2. **Spread Slippage:** The B_s vs. S_s delta during currency conversion.
3. **Opportunity Cost:** The NPV(c) loss of capital sitting in "nostro/vostro" accounts (liquidity that is "out of play").

For domestic transactions, the "bank holding" period is a localized version of this friction. When a bank holds a deposit for 3-5 days before "clearing" it, they are creating a vacuum of value. During this window, the money is mathematically in a state of superposition—it has left the sender but has not arrived at the receiver. This "float" is a multi-billion dollar subsidy for the banking cartel, essentially an interest-free loan provided by the labor of the citizenry.

The Failure of the Bridge: The XRP Case Study

While XRP was designed to reduce this friction, it ultimately fails to solve the temporal-economic paradox. Because XRP acts as a bridge asset, the transaction requires two separate conversions: Fiat A to XRP, and XRP to Fiat B. Even if the transmission of the token is fast, the entry and exit points are subject to the subjectivity of the $B_s \propto S_s$. If the market is volatile, the "slippage" during those conversion windows can exceed the cost of a traditional SWIFT wire. You are essentially trying to cross a river by jumping onto a moving boat; the speed of the boat is irrelevant if the docks on either side are crumbling.

The High-Velocity Alternative: Solana and Sui

The digital shift introduces a "superconducting" medium for value. Protocols like Solana and Sui are engineered for high-throughput and low-latency, reducing the friction tax to near-zero.

- **Solana:** By using Proof of History (PoH), Solana synchronizes the "time" variable of our equation (T) across the entire global network. This allows for thousands of transactions per second with sub-second finality.

- **Sui:** By utilizing a causal order for independent transactions, Sui eliminates the "bottleneck" friction inherent in traditional sequential ledgers.

In these models, the T in our temporal paradox is reduced to a negligible constant. When settlement is atomic (instant), the B_s and S_s have no time to diverge. There is no "float," no "nostro" accounts, and no "correspondent" sipping from the bucket. The trillions of dollars currently lost to the legacy friction tax are immediately reclaimed as active, productive capital.[32]

The SWIFT Relic: Analyzing the Latency of 1970s Architecture

The most critical realization for any investor or active citizen is that SWIFT does not move money. It is a messaging system, founded in 1973, that sends instructions from one bank to another. When you initiate a "wire transfer," you are essentially paying for

---

[32] Cooper's Logic Check → The banksters tell you that "slow is safe." They use that time to gamble with your "float" in the overnight repo markets. If the world loses to trillion annually in transmission friction, that is to trillion in labor that was performed but never compensated. It is a biological tax on human productivity. Moving to a high-velocity chain like Solana or Sui is not just about "faster payments"—it is about plugging the leak in the bathtub so the republic can finally hold water.

a secure, standardized email (MT103 or the newer ISO20022 formats).

The actual settlement occurs on a separate, disconnected layer of correspondent banking. This is where the 1970s architecture fails the 21st-century economy. Because Bank A does not have a direct connection to Bank Z in a different jurisdiction, the message must "hop" through intermediary banks. Each hop represents a separate ledger entry, a separate compliance check, and a separate delay. In physics terms, this is Systemic Latency—the time required for a signal to propagate through a fragmented medium.

Quantifying the "Last Mile" Entropy

While SWIFT gpi (Global Payments Innovation) has attempted to modernize the system, forensic data from 2026 shows that 80% of a transaction's journey is spent in the "last mile." Even if a message crosses the ocean in seconds, it can sit at the beneficiary bank for 24 to 72 hours awaiting manual reconciliation or domestic regulatory clearance.

This latency is not a technical glitch; it is a structural feature of the legacy system. During this window, the money is "in flight," allowing the correspondent banks to collect "float"—essentially an interest-free loan on the energy of your labor. This is the Temporal-Economic Paradox in action: the longer the transaction takes, the more "heat" (lost value) is generated by the system, and the less reliable the price (P) becomes.

The Reconciliation Black Hole

In a 1970s architecture, ledgers are siloed. Bank A has its own database, and Bank B has another. If there is a "data error"—which occurs in a significant percentage of cross-border transfers—the system stops. Because the ledgers are not synchronized in real-time, humans must intervene to "reconcile" the books.

This creates a Ledger Disconnect. Forensically, we can quantify this in the trillions of dollars of capital that are permanently "locked" in nostro/vostro accounts—pre-funded bank accounts used to facilitate these slow handshakes. This is "dead energy" that could be fueling the global economy but is instead held as a hostage to the legacy cartel's inefficiency.

The Digital Antidote: Atomic Synchronization

The transition to digital realism—moving toward high-velocity chains like Solana or Sui—replaces the "message-and-settle" model with Atomic Synchronization. In a blockchain environment, the message *is* the money. There is no correspondent bank, no "last mile" delay, and no manual reconciliation.

When the ledger is constant and global, the "Ghost in the Vault" vanishes. The financial community must recognize that SWIFT is a relic not because its code is old, but because its logic is analog. As the world becomes more interconnected, the "physical memecoin" of the dollar cannot survive the friction of

1970s pipes. We are moving toward a world of "zero latency," where the velocity of value finally matches the speed of human thought.[33]

XRP and the Bridge-Asset Fallacy: Why Mid-Point Conversion Fails

The central promise of XRP is its role as an "On-Demand Liquidity" (ODL) bridge. In theory, a bank in the US sends USD, which is converted to XRP, transmitted across the ledger, and converted into EUR for a bank in Germany. The banksters claim this is "efficient." However, from a physics and economic standpoint, this creates a Double-Conversion Friction.

Every time an asset is converted, it is subject to the $B_s \propto S_s$ equation we established in the introduction. Because the transaction involves two separate exchange points (Fiat-to-XRP and XRP-to-Fiat), the user is exposed to slippage and spread twice. If the market for XRP is volatile—which it must be to maintain speculative interest—the "savings" in transmission speed are often cannibalized by the "cost" of the conversion windows. You are essentially

---

[33] Cooper's Logic Check → The banksters tell you SWIFT is "secure" because it is slow. That is like saying a horse and buggy is "secure" because it can't crash at 100 mph. The "security" they offer is actually **Control.** They keep the system slow so they can act as the gatekeepers of your energy. By removing the 10% and 0% reserve requirements (Chapter 2), They have ensured that the "float" they collect during these delays is the only thing keeping them liquid. Digital realism is not just faster; it is the end of their ability to hide the vacuum in their vaults.

trying to stabilize a bridge by building it on two separate fault lines; the speed at which you cross is irrelevant if the ends of the bridge are shifting during the transit.

The Temporal-Economic Paradox of Mid-Point Conversion

The "bridge-asset fallacy" rests on the assumption that a mid-point conversion can be faster than the volatility of the market. In Chapter 1, we discussed the Entropy of Fiat; here, we see the Entropy of the Bridge.

Even a 3-second settlement time is long enough for the (buyer's perceived value) and (seller's perceived value) to diverge in a high-frequency trading environment. This results in "Settlement Risk" that the "slow" SWIFT model hides through its 3-day latency. By bringing the settlement into the 3-second range without a constant, non-volatile medium, XRP exposes the user to the raw volatility of the digital market without the safety of a stabilized "floor."

The Compliance Trap: Appeasing Both Worlds

XRP's primary failure is its attempt to be "the bank's crypto." By design, Ripple (the company) has built a system that allows for centralized freezing and censorship of transactions to satisfy the "opinion-based science" of legacy regulators. This is the Hollow Man Fallacy in its most dangerous form. If a digital asset can be "turned off" or "frozen" by a central authority to appease a nation-state, then it is not a sovereign currency; it is simply a "faster version" of the existing fiat decay. The financial community is beginning to realize that you cannot bridge a 0% reserve, debt-based system with a decentralized future by maintaining the centralized "kill switches" of the past. By trying to appease the banksters with compliance and the crypto world with speed, XRP has created a structure that is too centralized for the republic and too "uncontrolled" for the cartel.

The "Ghost" of Centralization: Key Criticisms

Forensic audits of the XRP ecosystem point to several terminal flaws that the "bridge-asset" marketing ignores:

1. **Founder Dumping and Inflationary Pressure:** Unlike the fixed-supply logic of "crystalline" digital realism, a massive portion of the XRP supply was held by the founders and the company. This creates an internal entropy where the "value" of the bridge is constantly being diluted by the very people who built it.

2. **The Decentralization Illusion:** While the XRP Ledger is technically decentralized, the "Unique Node List" (UNL) recommended by Ripple creates a centralized bottleneck. If the nodes are managed by the same entities trying to maintain the "physical memecoin" of the dollar, the system remains a closed loop of centralized intent.

3. **The Stablecoin Threat:** The rise 1:1 of backed (or fractal-backed) stablecoins on high-velocity chains like Solana and Sui has made the "bridge token" obsolete. If you can send a stable representation of value directly across a constant ledger, you have zero need for a mid-point conversion. The bridge is being replaced by a direct, trans-oceanic tunnel.
4. **Lost Blocks:** While XRP continually addresses that the ETH blocks are "muddy," this does not excuse the over 30,000 blocks which the XRP ledger has lost (XRPL). This violates the first rule of Blockchain that the ledger must be immutable. Would you trust your bank if they lost 30,000+ accounts?

The Terminal Velocity of the Bridge

XRP is a 1970s solution to a 1970s problem that arrived forty years too late. By the time it attempted to bridge the gap, the world had already begun to move toward Real-Time Atomic Settlement. The bridge-asset fallacy is being exposed by the reality of constant ledgers where value does not need to "convert" to cross the border—it simply *exists* on both sides of the border simultaneously. We are moving away from the "Double-Conversion" friction and toward a world where the ledger is the only bridge we need.[34]

---

[34] Cooper's Logic Check → The "XRP Army" will tell you that the "banks are coming." They have been saying that for a decade.

Ledger Disconnect: The Economic Cost of Reconciliation Gaps

The economic cost of the ledger disconnect is quantified through the lens of failed payments and manual labor. Forensic data from 2026 suggests that failed payments alone cost the global economy over $120 billion annually in fees, labor, and lost business. When we expand this to include the "reconciliation bottleneck"—the thousands of hours employees spend manually matching transactions across fragmented siloed databases—the cost scales into the trillions.

A typical large organization spends approximately 100,000 person-hours per year solely on account reconciliation. This is "dead labor"—work performed not to create new value, but simply to verify that the energy sent from Point A actually arrived at Point B. In a 0% reserve system, these gaps are even more dangerous, as the "float" created by the disconnect masks the mathematical insolvency of the intermediaries.

The truth is, the banks don't want a bridge they don't own; they want a "digital dollar" (CBDC) that they can manipulate at a 0% reserve. XRP tried to play both sides, and in the end, it is being squeezed out by the **Physics of Money.** If I can send an asset on Solana in 400 milliseconds without a bridge-token conversion, why would I ever pay the "XRP Tax"? It is the same "slow" fraud, just moving at a slightly faster speed.

The Liquidity Trap of Siloed Data

Reconciliation gaps create a "liquidity trap" for corporations. Because the ledgers are disconnected, a company may have $10 million in "accounting value" that is functionally invisible to their treasury department because it is stuck in the "latency window" of a correspondent bank. This forces companies to take out short-term credit lines to cover operational expenses—paying interest to the very banks that are causing the delay.

This is a biological parasitism on the supply chain. The "reconciliation gap" is essentially a tax on the Velocity of Value. By the time the books are balanced at the end of the month, the NPC (c) (Net Present Value) of that capital has already been eroded by the "Entropy of Fiat."

Digital Realism: The End of the Disconnect

The digital shift introduces the Unified Ledger. In a high-velocity environment like Solana or Sui, there is no "reconciliation" because there is no disconnect. The transaction *is* the reconciliation. When the buyer and seller occupy the same cryptographic space, the "Ghost in the Vault" is replaced by an immutable, real-time proof of solvency. By eliminating the disconnect, we reclaim the millions of person-hours wasted on manual data entry and redirect that energy toward the actual development of society.[35]

---

[35] Cooper's Logic Check → The banksters love the disconnect because "reconciliation" is a fee-generating activity for them.

Real-Time Settlement and the Elimination of Counterparty Risk

In the legacy banking world, when you buy an asset or send a wire, you are not completing a transaction; you are entering into a short-term contract. The period defined T+2 or T+1 (the days following the trade) is a state of "unsecured credit." During this latency window, you are exposed to the risk that the other party—the bank, the broker, or the clearinghouse—becomes insolvent, suffers a technical failure, or simply fails to deliver.

This risk is a direct function of the Temporal-Economic Paradox we established. As the duration (T) of the settlement increases, the probability of an external shock increases proportionally. In the "physical memecoin" economy, where banks operate on psychological solvency rather than mathematical reserves, counterparty risk is the "invisible entropy" that forces institutions to hold billions in collateral, effectively locking up capital that should be fueling the republic.

Atomic Settlement: The Collapse of the Window

Real-time settlement (or "Atomic Settlement") is the digital solution to this structural entropy. In a high-velocity environment like Solana or Sui, the transfer of

---

They charge you to send the money, they charge you when the "slow" message fails, and they charge you for the credit you need while your own money is in transit. It is a triple-dip on your productivity. Digital realism is not just "better accounting"; it is the restoration of the direct link between work and reward.

the asset and the transfer of the payment happen simultaneously, or they do not happen at all. There is no "in-between" state.

From a mathematical standpoint, this reduces counterparty risk to zero. The "window of vulnerability" is closed because the settlement is "all-or-nothing." This is the move from Conditional Trust (I trust that the bank will settle in 48 hours) to Algorithmic Truth (the code settled in four hundred milliseconds). By eliminating the need for trust, we eliminate the need for the massive "insurance" layers and "clearing fees" that the banksters use to profit from their own inefficiency.

The End of the "Gimmie" Float

The elimination of counterparty risk also marks the end of the "gimmie" incentive in the clearinghouse model. Currently, the legacy cartel uses the "settlement window" to engage in re-hypothecation—using your "in-transit" funds to back their own speculative bets. They are literally profiting from the risk they created by being slow.

When settlement is real-time, there is no "float" for the bankster to gamble with. The capital moves directly from S_s to B_s without a 48-hour stopover in a 0% reserve vault. This increases the total velocity of the market and ensures that the "value" remains in the hands of the productive citizens of the republic. Digital realism is not just about speed; it is about the total removal of the "middleman's" ability to hold your energy hostage during the latency of the analog world.[36]

The Constant Ledger: Global Synchronization as a Growth Engine

The Constant Ledger represents the transition from fragmented, siloed databases to a single, globally synchronized state of truth. In the legacy "physical memecoin" economy, growth is perpetually throttled by the fact that every institution is looking at a different version of reality, necessitating endless cycles of reconciliation and verification that act as a biological drain on human productivity. When we move to a high-velocity environment like Solana or Sui, we are essentially synchronizing the "Time" variable in our economic equations across the entire planet. This global synchronization functions as a massive growth engine by eliminating the "temporal-economic paradox" where value is lost in the gaps between disconnected ledgers. Because every participant is looking at the same "0" and the same "1" in real-time, capital no longer needs to sit idle in "nostro/vostro" accounts to act as a buffer for analog

---

[36] Cooper's Logic Check → The banksters tell you that "clearinghouses are for your protection." That is like a kidnapper saying he's "keeping your money safe" until your family pays the ransom. They created the slow system so they could justify charging you a fee to "manage" the risk that the slow system created. It is a circular protection racket. In 2020, when they removed the reserve floor, the clearinghouse became even more dangerous because the "safety net" they were promising was made of thin air. Digital realism is the only way to trade without a chaperone.

uncertainty. This "dead energy" is reclaimed and redirected toward active development, increasing the total velocity of the republic's economy without the inflationary entropy required by the central bank. By establishing a constant ledger, we move from a state of chaotic, subjective price-chasing to a state of objective, high-frequency coordination where the B_s and S_s and can find equilibrium instantly. This is the ultimate "Phase Transition" of finance: the moment the global economy stops being a collection of local "bucket brigades" and becomes a single, superconducting network of value, allowing the human race to reclaim the trillions of labor-hours currently wasted on the friction of the analog world.[37]

Conclusion: Reclaiming the Trillions Lost in Transit

The reclamation of the trillions lost in transit marks the final liberation of human labor from the archaic tax of analog latency. For centuries, the "friction tax" has been a silent parasite, siphoning off the energy of the global republic to fund the gatekeepers and intermediaries of a disconnected system. By quantifying the annual transmission loss and

---

[37] Cooper's Logic Check → The banksters want you to believe that "synchronization" is a security risk because it removes their ability to act as the gatekeepers of truth. In reality, their "fragmented ledger" is the only thing that allows the "Ghost in the Vault" to exist. If everyone can see the floor at the same time, the magic trick of 0% reserves stops working. Digital realism is not just about "better accounting"; it is about creating a global engine of growth that does not rely on the "gimmies" and the "wastrels" of the legacy cartel.

identifying the "reconciliation black hole," we have exposed that these trillions were never truly "gone"—they were simply "dead energy" held hostage by the 1970s architecture of SWIFT and the "bridge-asset fallacy." Digital realism offers the first true engineering solution to this drain, providing a high-velocity, superconducting medium where the "Velocity of Value" can finally outpace the "Entropy of Fiat."

The transition to a constant ledger and atomic settlement is a forced evolution necessitated by the terminal velocity of paper. As we move away from the "physical memecoin" and the "gimmie" incentive of the legacy cartel, we are reclaiming more than just currency; we are reclaiming time. The millions of person-hours currently wasted on manual reconciliation and the trillions of dollars locked in the "latency trap" of nostro accounts represent a massive misallocation of human potential. In a globally synchronized economy, this trapped capital is released back into the hands of the productive, allowing for a level of growth and infrastructure development that was mathematically impossible under the 0% reserve, high-friction model of the past.

By eliminating counterparty risk and closing the "window of vulnerability" inherent in T+2 settlement, we have removed the primary excuse for the banksters' existence. The legacy system relied on the fact that you could not trust your neighbor without a centralized chaperone; digital realism proves that you can trust the math of the ledger. Reclaiming these trillions is the ultimate incentive for the active citizen to opt out of the "protection racket" of centralized finance and move toward a sovereign, digital infrastructure. We are no longer paying for the privilege of being slow; we are investing in the necessity of being fast.

Ultimately, Chapter 3 has shown that the "price" we pay in the legacy system is far higher than the number on the invoice. The true cost of the "physical memecoin" is the aggregate of every delayed wire, every failed reconciliation, and every second of "float" stolen by the bank. As we conclude this autopsy of the legacy rails, we realize that the solution is not to "fix" the bridge, but to realize the bridge is no longer needed. The digital world is already interconnected; by adopting the "constant ledger," we are simply allowing our economic reality to catch up to our physical reality. The trillions have been found; it is time to put them to work for the republic.

Chapter 4: Algorithmic Trust. Replacing the "reputation" of central banks with the "certainty" of code.

“Trust of the innocent is the liar’s most useful tool.”

Stephen King[38]

One of the most ongoing memes in the digital world is when people post something which they have no sources or information for, the community posts the source for them. The source is “trust me bro.” This is one of the strongest messages that can be sent by the meme community that the actor is not acting in the best interest of the community in posting FUD (Fear, uncertainty, doubt) or hype which is unsupported. Just trusting the speaker is very dangerous in a fast moving environment- luckily, the blockchain is a verification element so when anyone says something, no matter how good their reputation is, we can always trust but verify.

To ground the "physical memecoin" theory in reality, the financial community must look at the track records of the institutions that manage the rails of the economy. While these banks spend billions on "sterling" branding to project an image of stability and high-minded stewardship, the forensic history of the last 30 years reveals a consistent pattern of predatory

[38] Staff (2026). “Trust Quotes.” Brainy Quote at https://www.brainyquote.com/search_results?x=0&y=0&q=Trust.

behavior, systemic fraud, and a blatant disregard for the "0%" reserves they are supposed to protect.

The major banks in the United States operate under a halo of "Systemic Importance," but their actual reputations among informed citizens are characterized by a profound trust deficit. They have moved from being custodians of community wealth to being high-frequency engines of re-hypothecation and fee extraction. The following list of scandals highlights that for the legacy cartel, fines are not a deterrent—they are merely a "cost of doing business" in a system where they are allowed to gamble with the public's labor.

Forensic Audit of Major Bank Scandals (1996–2026)

- **Bank of America: The Subprime Mortgage Crisis (2014)**
    - **Description:** The bank was found to have sold defective, "toxic" residential mortgage-backed securities to investors and government entities, leading directly to the 2008 global collapse.
    - **Penalty:** $30.6 billion in total settlements—the largest in history—covering multiple violations of consumer and investor protection.
- **JPMorgan Chase: The "London Whale" and Toxic Securities (2013)**

- **Description:** Beyond their role in the mortgage crisis, the bank suffered massive losses ($6 billion+) due to reckless "whale" trades in the London office, exposing a total lack of internal risk controls.
- **Penalty:** $13 billion settlement with the DOJ for mortgage abuses; an additional $920 million for the London Whale failures.

- **Wells Fargo: The Fake Accounts Scandal (2016–2020)**
  - **Description:** In a pursuit of aggressive sales quotas, employees opened millions of unauthorized bank and credit card accounts in customers' names without their consent.
  - **Penalty: $3 billion** settlement with the DOJ and SEC; an additional $3.7 billion in 2022 for widespread mismanagement of mortgages and auto loans.
- **Goldman Sachs: The 1MDB Embezzlement Scandal (2020)**
  - **Description:** The bank was involved in a massive international bribery and money-laundering scheme where billions of dollars were misappropriated

from a Malaysian state-owned investment fund.

- **Penalty:** $2.9 billion to the DOJ and over $1 billion in related SEC penalties.

- **Citigroup: Toxic Securities and LIBOR Manipulation (2014)**
  - **Description:** Similar to its peers, Citi was penalized for misleading investors about the quality of mortgage bonds and for its role in the global price-fixing of the LIBOR interest rate.
  - **Penalty:** $7 billion for mortgage-related fraud and hundreds of millions in LIBOR-related fines.

The reason these banks do not possess the reputation they market is that their business model relies on the Hollow Man Fallacy we discussed. They tell the public that digital assets are "risky" while they are being penalized for the very same crimes: fraud, theft, and market manipulation. A "sterling" reputation is built on the integrity of the ledger and the presence of a floor; when a bank operates at 0% reserves and pays billions in fines for defrauding its own customers, it ceases to be a financial institution and becomes a legalized protection racket. In any other industry, this would have been shut down. In the banking industry, however, they were given bailouts.

The Failure of Reputation-Based Economics

Reputation-based economics relies on the Bayesian Updating of beliefs—the idea that if an institution has acted reliably in the past, it will do so in the future. However, as we established in Chapter 2, legacy banks operate in a state of Psychological Solvency. This creates a "Subjectivity Gap" where the reputation of the bank (the “R” in our equation) is decoupled from the actual math of the vault (A).

In 2026, the OCC and FDIC officially acknowledged this failure by codifying the elimination of "reputation risk" from their supervisory programs. Regulators finally admitted that "supervising for reputation" adds no material value to safety and soundness because reputation cannot be quantified or predicted. By the time a bank's reputation fails, the mathematical insolvency has already consumed the depositors' energy. Reputation is a holographic shield; it looks solid until the first high-velocity "Exit" command pierces it.

The "Too Big to Jail" Moral Hazard

The failure of reputation is accelerated by the Bootstrap Mechanism of repeated interaction. In the legacy cartel, the "Big Four" banks have a reputation not for integrity, but for Systemic Importance. This creates a moral hazard where the institution knows that its "Reputation" is backed by a government bailout (the "Full Faith and Credit").

This turns the bank's reputation into a predatory tool. As the list of scandals in the introduction proves, fines are merely a "friction tax" on fraud. When JPMorgan or Wells Fargo pays a multi-billion dollar penalty, their reputation "recovers" because they are the only rails left for the public to use. This is not an economy of trust; it is an economy of Captive Reputation. The "innocent" (the taxpayers) are forced to trust the "liar" because the liar owns the bridge.

The Entropy of Branding vs. the Crystalline Logic of Code

Reputation is a high-entropy signal. It requires constant, multi-billion dollar branding campaigns and "people-centered communication" to maintain. When economic performance worsens, central banks retreat into "strategic silence" or technical jargon to protect their autonomy. This is the Spoken Equivalent of a 0% Reserve.

Digital realism replaces this decaying signal with Algorithmic Trust.

- **Legacy:** $T=f(\text{Reputation}+\text{Branding})$
- **Digital:** $T=f(\text{Code}\cdot\text{Verification})$

In a reputation-based system, you trust the *actor*. In an algorithmic system, you trust the *math*. A smart contract does not have a "reputation" to protect, so it does not need to lie. It simply executes the $S_s \propto B_s$ equation as written. By removing the human variable, we eliminate the sales quotas, the "London Whales," and the "Hollow Man" fallacies that have defined the last 30 years of banking.

The failure of reputation-based economics is the final signal that the analog world is no longer fit for the digital republic. We are moving from a world where we "believe" in the bankster's honesty to a world where the ledger makes honesty a technical requirement. The "sterling" reputation of the legacy bank is a 1970s relic; the future belongs to the Constant Ledger, where trust is not a feeling, but a 400-millisecond proof of solvency.[39]

Verifiability vs. Vulnerability: The Central Bank Black Box

The legacy financial system is built on "Siloed Information." Each bank maintains its own internal ledger, hidden behind layers of proprietary software and legal privilege. When a central bank makes a policy shift—such as the 2020 move to 0% reserve requirements—the true impact on systemic liquidity is obscured. The public is given "Forward Guidance" (opinion-based science) rather than "Real-Time Data" (fact-based evidence).

---

[39] Cooper's Logic Check → The banksters spend more on their "brand" than most countries spend on their militaries. Why? Because the brand is the only thing hiding the fact that they have 0% in the vault. If you knew the math, you wouldn't care about the mahogany desks or the marble pillars. Reputation is the "pretty paint" on a bridge That is already collapsed. In the digital world, we don't look at the paint; we look at the load-bearing code. If the code says the money is not there, "Trust me, bro" won't save you.

This lack of verifiability is not an accident; it is a defensive mechanism. If the "shareholders" (citizens) could see the actual state of the "Ghost in the Vault" in real-time, the Psychological Solvency of the system would collapse. In a black box, vulnerability grows in the shadows. We only discover the "fracture" when the system fails—such as during the 2008 collapse or the 2023 regional banking tremors. By the time the "output" of the black box shows a failure, the energy has already been lost.

The "Trust Me" Vulnerability

Vulnerability in the legacy system is a direct result of "Human Intermediation." Because we cannot verify the ledger, we must trust the "unqualified" gatekeepers. This creates multiple points of failure:

1. **Reporting Latency:** Audits are snapshots of the past, often months old by the time they are released.
2. **Subjective Valuation:** Assets in the black box are often "Mark-to-Model" (what we *think* they are worth) rather than "Mark-to-Market" (what they are *actually* worth).
3. **Moral Hazard:** The gatekeepers know that the "black box" hides their over-leverage, encouraging them to take risks that would be impossible in a transparent system.

Digital Realism: The Glass Vault

Digital realism replaces the "Black Box" with the "Glass Vault." In a blockchain environment, verifiability is a native feature, not a requested favor. Through Proof of Reserves (PoR) and on-chain analytics, the vulnerability of the system is neutralized by total transparency.

- **Real-Time Auditing:** You do not wait for a quarterly report; you check the block explorer.
- **Immutable Logic:** The "reserve floor" is enforced by code, not by a committee that can change its mind during a crisis.
- **Zero-Knowledge Proofs:** We can verify that the assets exist and the math is solvent without compromising the individual privacy of the republic's citizens.

The "Central Bank Black Box" is a relic of an era when information moved slowly and the public could be kept "blinded by social studies." In the digital age, information asymmetry is a terminal liability. By moving toward a system of absolute verifiability, we reclaim the power of the observer. We no longer have to guess if the floor is solid; we can see the crystalline structure of the math. The era of trusting the "liar's tool" is over; the era of verifying the code has begun.[40]

---

40 Cooper's Logic Check → The banksters say that "transparency causes panic." What they mean is "transparency

The Immutable Protocol: Laws of Math vs. Whims of Men

The legacy financial system is built on the concept of "Administrative Discretion." This is the idea that a central authority has the wisdom to "fine-tune" the economy by manipulating interest rates, reserve requirements, and the money supply. However, as we established in Chapter 1, this is "opinion-based science." When men have the power to change the rules, they inevitably do so to favor the "gimmies" and the "wastrels" at the top of the hierarchy.

The "Whims of Men" lead to systemic entropy. In March 2020, the whim was to eliminate reserve requirements. In 2023, the whim was to create emergency lending facilities to bail out "systemically important" failures. Each of these decisions is a violation of the "Social Contract" with the productive citizen. Because the rules are flexible, they are also vulnerable to lobbying, political pressure, and the "London Whale" style hubris we audited in the previous section.

---

reveals our insolvency." If a bridge is about to collapse, the most "dangerous" thing you can do is hide the cracks from the people driving over it. The legacy black box is just a way to keep the passengers calm until the bus hits the water. Digital realism turns the lights on so we can see the cracks *before* we put our labor on the bridge.

The Rigidity of the Protocol: Math as the Ultimate Referee

An Immutable Protocol is a system where the rules are written in code and enforced by a decentralized network. There is no "Board of Governors" who can decide to print more units to cover a deficit. In this environment, the Laws of Math act as the ultimate referee:

1. **Deterministic Supply:** The issuance schedule is fixed. 1+1will always equal 2, and token cap will never become greater because a politician is facing an election.
2. **Programmatic Enforcement:** Smart contracts do not "look the other way" for a prestigious bank. If the collateral is not present, the transaction fails or the liquidation occurs instantly.
3. **Resistance to Censorship:** Math does not have an "opinion" on who should be allowed to transact. It only verifies that the cryptographic signatures are valid and the funds are present.

By removing the "Human Variable," we eliminate the primary source of systemic fraud. A smart contract cannot be pressured by a manager to open fake accounts like the Wells Fargo scandal. It cannot be bribed to launder money like the 1MDB embezzlement. It simply follows the if/then logic of the code.

The Phase Transition: From "Trust" to "Certainty"

The legacy system requires "Trust"—a fragile, subjective belief that the men in charge would not steal your energy. Digital realism provides "Certainty"—a hard, objective fact that the rules cannot be changed without your consent (via consensus).

This is the "Crystalline Structure" of the new economy. Just as a building is only as stable as the physics of its foundation, an economy is only as stable as the rules that govern its medium of exchange. When the foundation is built on the "whims of men," it is a foundation of sand. When it is built on the Immutable Protocol, it is a foundation of granite. We are moving from a world of "managed decline" to a world of "mathematical growth."

The Immutable Protocol is the final realization of the "Rule of Law" in a digital world. By tethering our value to the laws of math, we reclaim our sovereignty from the "banksters" and their "black box" decisions. We are no longer the "shareholders" of a failing experiment; we are the participants in a verified reality. The era of the "liar's tool" has reached its terminal velocity. The era of the protocol has begun.[41]

---

[41] Cooper's Logic Check → The "experts" on TV will tell you that "flexibility" is a strength because it allows the Fed to "react to crises." Logic check: The Fed *creates* the crises with their flexibility, then they ask for more power to "fix" them. That is like an arsonist asking for a job as the fire chief. An Immutable Protocol does not need to "react" because it does not create the

Transparency as a Structural Security Feature

In a 0% reserve banking system, risk is invisible until it is realized. Because the bankster's ledger is a "Black Box," the financial community cannot assess the true depth of the missing underlay. Transparency flips this dynamic. When the reserves of an institution or protocol are on-chain, the "observer" becomes the auditor.

This creates a Real-Time Forensic Feedback Loop. If a protocol begins to over-leverage or if its collateral ratio dips below the "Fractal Floor," the market sees it instantly. There is no need for a whistleblower or a DOJ investigation three years after the collapse. The transparency acts as a structural damper: the immediate visibility of risk prevents the "superposition" of debt from reaching the point of systemic criticality.

Eliminating the "Information Asymmetry" Tax

The legacy cartel profits from "Information Asymmetry"—the fact that they know more about the state of the economy than the citizens they represent. They use this gap to engage in predatory "front-running" and to time their exits before the "Hollow Man" is exposed.

Transparency as a security feature eliminates this "Information Tax." When the ledger is constant and global, every participant has access to the same "0" and the same "1." This synchronization levels the

---

over-leverage in the first place. Math does not have a "hero complex"—it just has the truth..

playing field, ensuring that "Psychological Solvency" cannot be weaponized against the productive class. In this environment, security is derived from the fact that the liar has no place to hide. The Immune System of Open Source Structural security is further bolstered by the open-source nature of digital protocols. While a bank's internal "black box" software is vulnerable to hidden backdoors and "Human Error" (like the Wells Fargo quota fraud), a transparent protocol is subjected to a "Continuous Global Audit."

Thousands of independent observers—the "white hat" hackers and mathematicians of the republic—are constantly scanning the code for vulnerabilities. This is the Immune System of Transparency. A flaw that is visible is a flaw that can be patched. A system that hides its flaws, as the central banks do with their "strategic silence," is a system that is waiting to fail.

Transparency is the ultimate antidote to the "Gimmie" and "Wastrel" incentive. It forces an institution to be honest because the alternative is immediate, mathematical exposure. By moving from a "Trust-Me" model to a "Watch-Me" model, we have engineered a system where the architecture itself prevents the fraud. We are not just making banking "better"; we are making it forensically sound.[42]

---

[42] Cooper's Logic Check → The banksters say that "privacy" is why they keep their ledgers secret. Logic check: They don't care about *your* privacy—They have been selling your data for decades. They care about *their* privacy. They want to hide the fact that the vault is empty. In digital realism, we use Zero-

Decentralized Validation: Eliminating the "Single Point of Failure"

The legacy banking system is built on a "Hub and Spoke" architecture. Whether it is the Federal Reserve at the top of the domestic pyramid or SWIFT at the center of the global messaging network, every transaction relies on a central gatekeeper to validate its existence. This creates a catastrophic SNoF. If the hub is compromised—by corruption, "opinion-based science," or physical infrastructure failure—the entire network is paralyzed.

This centralization is what allows for the "London Whale" or the Wells Fargo "Fake Accounts" scandals. Because validation is centralized within the institution's own "Black Box," there is no external check on their internal entropy. The institution validates itself, creating a circular logic that masks risk until it is too late. The "Single Point of Failure" in the legacy world is not just a technical server; it is the human integrity of a small group of "unqualified" gatekeepers.

The Power of the Many: Distributed Consensus

Decentralized validation flips the script. Instead of one bankster saying, "Trust me, the money is there," we have thousands of independent nodes running the

---

Knowledge Proofs to protect the individual's privacy while maintaining the institution's **total transparency.** You don't need to know who I am to know that the math of the protocol is solvent. The only people who fear a glass vault are the ones who are planning to steal the floor.

same open-source protocol, saying, "We have verified the math, and the transaction is valid."

In this model, the "Validation Floor" is impossible to move. To commit fraud, an attacker would have to compromise the majority of the network simultaneously—a feat that is mathematically and economically unfeasible in a robust digital republic. This is Byzantine Fault Tolerance: the ability of a system to reach the truth even if some of its participants are liars or "wastrels." By distributing the power to validate, we eliminate the ability for any single entity to "gimmie" their way into a deficit.

The End of the "London Whale" and the "Rogue Trader"

In a decentralized environment, the "Rogue Trader" is a physical impossibility. In the legacy system, a single individual at JPMorgan could hide $6 billion in losses because the validation was siloed and slow. In a digital protocol, every movement of value is validated against the Immutable Rules of the ledger in real-time.

- **Legacy:** Validation is a "permissioned" act performed by a biased insider.
- **Digital:** Validation is a "permissionless" act performed by an objective algorithm.

Because the ledger is synchronized globally and constantly, there is no "dark space" for a London Whale to swim. The transparency we discussed in Section 4.4, combined with decentralized validation, ensures that the system's health is the responsibility of the network, not the "whim" of a CEO.

Eliminating the Single Point of Failure is the final step in moving away from the "Hollow Man" of legacy finance. We are building a republic where the "floor" is maintained by the collective certainty of the citizens and their code. Decentralized validation ensures that no matter how many "whims" a politician may have, the math of the vault remains untouched. We have moved from a fragile hub to a resilient web, where the truth is the only constant.[43]

Auditing the Code: The Shift from Blind Faith to Proof

The transition from blind faith to proof represents the most significant shift in economic history since the introduction of double-entry bookkeeping. In the legacy "physical memecoin" system, an audit is a retroactive post-mortem performed by a centralized third party that is often as "unqualified" or compromised as the institution it is inspecting. This "Blind Faith" model requires the public to trust that a

---

[43] Cooper's Logic Check → The banksters say that "decentralization is inefficient." Logic check: It is only "inefficient" because it stops them from being the only ones who can change the numbers. They want a "Single Point of Control" so they can maintain the "Single Point of Extraction." In digital realism, we accept a tiny bit of "computational effort" to ensure that no one can ever pull the rug out from under the entire economy again. If the Fed's "Black Box" goes dark, the dollar dies. If a thousand nodes go dark on a global ledger, the ledger keeps right on ticking. That is not inefficiency—That is **survival.**

quarterly snapshot accurately reflects the continuous reality of a 0% reserve vault. As we saw with the collapse of Enron and the more recent failures of 2023, these audits often act as a holographic veneer, masking systemic fragility until the very moment of impact. In contrast, digital realism introduces the concept of Continuous Algorithmic Auditing, where the code itself is the auditor.

In a blockchain-based republic, the audit is not a document produced by a committee; it is a real-time, 24/7/365 stream of data available to every observer. Because the ledger is immutable and the protocol is open-source, the "Ghost in the Vault" cannot exist. If a smart contract requires 120% collateralization to remain solvent, the network verifies that math before every single transaction is finalized. This is the move from "Trusting the Liar" to "Verifying the Law." We no longer need to hope that the bankster is being honest about his "High-Quality Liquid Assets" because those assets are cryptographically locked and visible on the glass floor of the protocol.

This shift fundamentally changes the security architecture of the economy. By auditing the code instead of the person, we remove the "Gimmie" and "Wastrel" incentive from the validation layer. A smart contract cannot be bribed, it cannot be pressured by sales quotas, and it cannot "miss" an entry due to human error. It simply executes the logic it was programmed to perform. For the active citizen, this provides a level of certainty that no "sterling" reputation could ever match. We are reclaiming our sovereignty by demanding proof over promises, ensuring that our stored labor is protected by the crystalline logic of mathematics rather than the shifting whims of a central bank's black box.[44]

Conclusion: The Sovereignty of the Algorithm

The reclamation of the trillions lost in transit marks the final liberation of human labor from the archaic tax of analog latency. For centuries, the "friction tax" has been a silent parasite, siphoning off the energy of the global republic to fund the gatekeepers and intermediaries of a disconnected system. By quantifying the annual transmission loss and identifying the "reconciliation black hole," we have exposed that these trillions were never truly "gone"—they were simply "dead energy" held hostage by the 1970s architecture of SWIFT and the "bridge-asset fallacy." Digital realism offers the first true engineering solution to this drain, providing a high-velocity, superconducting medium where the "Velocity of Value" can finally outpace the "Entropy of Fiat."

---

[44] Cooper's Logic Check → The banksters love to say that their audits are "rigorous." Logic check: If they were rigorous, we wouldn't need "Stress Tests" every year to see if the banks will survive a minor market hiccup. A stress test is just an admission that they don't actually know if the math works until they break it. In digital realism, the "Stress Test" is the protocol itself. It runs every second of every day. If the math does network, the block does not close. It is time to stop praying for an honest auditor and start relying on an honest algorithm.

The transition to a constant ledger and atomic settlement is a forced evolution necessitated by the terminal velocity of paper. As we move away from the "physical memecoin" and the "gimmie" incentive of the legacy cartel, we are reclaiming more than just currency; we are reclaiming time. The millions of person-hours currently wasted on manual reconciliation and the trillions of dollars locked in the "latency trap" of nostro accounts represent a massive misallocation of human potential. In a globally synchronized economy, this trapped capital is released back into the hands of the productive, allowing for a level of growth and infrastructure development that was mathematically impossible under the 0% reserve, high-friction model of the past.

By eliminating counterparty risk and closing the "window of vulnerability" inherent in settlement, we have removed the primary excuse for the banksters' existence. The legacy system relied on the fact that you could not trust your neighbor without a centralized chaperone; digital realism proves that you can trust the math of the ledger. Reclaiming these trillions is the ultimate incentive for the active citizen to opt out of the "protection racket" of centralized finance and move toward a sovereign, digital infrastructure. We are no longer paying for the privilege of being slow; we are investing in the necessity of being fast.

Ultimately, Chapter 3 has shown that the "price" we pay in the legacy system is far higher than the number on the invoice. The true cost of the "physical memecoin" is the aggregate of every delayed wire, every failed reconciliation, and every second of "float" stolen by the bank. As we conclude this autopsy of the legacy rails, we realize that the solution is not to "fix" the bridge, but to realize the bridge is no longer needed. The digital world is already interconnected; by adopting the "constant ledger," we are simply allowing our economic reality to catch up to our physical reality. The trillions have been found; it is time to put them to work for the republic.

Conclusion

"Early economic theory was rooted in the Italian, French, and Spanish traditions, which were subjectivist oriented. Then it shifted onto the terrible path by Smith and Ricardo and the British Classical Tradition which is "objectivist' – values are inherent in production."

Murray Rothbard[45]

The conclusion of Part I marks the definitive transition from the "physical memecoin" of the legacy central bank to the crystalline certainty of digital realism. By auditing the entropy of fiat, the fraud of the zero-reserve vault, and the archaic friction of 1970s transmission, we have exposed the "Hollow Man" of modern economics. We are now standing at a crossroads between the subjective decay of the "progressive" tradition and a return to a more disciplined, productive reality. This path requires a fundamental realignment with the classical understanding of value—one that prioritizes the producer over the parasite.

As Murray Rothbard noted, economic theory took a "terrible path" when it drifted toward a purely subjectivist orientation that allowed for the total decoupling of price from physical reality. The British Classical Tradition, championed by Smith and

---

[45] Staff (2026). "Economic Theory Quotes." Brainy Quote at https://www.brainyquote.com/search_results?x=0&y=0&q=Economic+Theory+.

Ricardo, understood that values are inherent in production. This "objectivist" perspective is the bedrock of digital realism. It posits that money must be a representation of stored work—a record of energy expended—rather than a "subjective" decree by a central committee. By re-establishing the "floor" through fractal reserves and immutable code, we are effectively resurrecting the British tradition, ensuring that value is once again anchored in the objective reality of production rather than the shifting whims of the bankster's "faith."

The progressive economic tradition, which has dominated the last century, is the ultimate "subjectivist" trap. It has convinced the republic that value can be conjured out of thin air through debt-issuance and "opinion-based science." This approach has turned the dollar into a moving target, where the "price" of survival increases while the "value" of labor is systematically debased. By moving toward the Constant Ledger, we are rejecting this progressive entropy. We are reclaiming an economy where is a constant and where the "velocity of value" serves the person who creates the good, not the middleman who messages the instruction.

To support the British tradition is to acknowledge that an economy cannot survive on "consumption" alone; it must be built on the integrity of its assets. The "Objectivist" path demands that the medium of exchange have a structural underlay. Whether that underlay is gold, real-world assets (RWA), or the cryptographic energy of a blockchain, it serves as the "anchor" that prevents the terminal velocity of paper. The digital republic is the modern fulfillment of Smith's "Invisible Hand," now powered by an Invisible Protocol that ensures no single point of failure can steal the labor of the many to fund the "gimmies" of the few.

Ultimately, Part I has provided the forensic proof that the legacy system is no longer a viable vessel for human energy. We have seen the "Ghost in the Vault" and quantified the "Friction Tax" that drains trillions from our collective productivity. As we move into Part II, we leave behind the "Trust me, bro" era of reputation-based economics. We move forward into a world of Algorithmic Trust, where the laws of math and the discipline of production provide the only "sterling" reputation that matters. The path back to objective value has been paved; it is time for the republic to walk it.

While value is inherent in production, it is more visible in utility. That is where the value really starts to shine.[46]

---

46 Cooper's Logic Check → The "progressive" economists love to talk about "social justice" while they use the "subjective" value of the dollar to rob the poor through inflation. Logic check: There is no "justice" in a system where the "object" (your work) is disconnected from the "value" (your pay). By returning to the British tradition of objective value through digital realism, we are putting the power back where it belongs: with the people who actually build things. The banksters want you to live in their

"subjective" fantasy because they own the pen; we're moving to a "math" reality because the ledger belongs to everyone.

Part II: American Law and Economic Theory

"Rightful liberty is unobstructed action according to our will within limits drawn around us by the equal rights of others. I do not add 'within the limits of the law' because law is often but the tyrant's will, and always so when it violates the rights of the individual."

Thomas Jefferson[47]

and

"There is no greater tyranny than that which is perpetrated under the shield of the law and in the name of justice."

Montesquieu[48]

It is rare that I find two quotes which are of such necessity that they should be included in a chapter. Rarer still is to find two quotes that are so interrelated that their juxtaposition demonstrates a crisis of reality. Jefferson defines the concept of human rights; Montesquieu defines in the way in which we lose our rights. Combined, they present a very simple recipe for just law- the concept that your rights end where they negatively effect someone else and that when

---

[47] Staff (2026). "Law Quotes." Brainy Quote at https://www.brainyquote.com/topics/law-quotes.
[48] Staff (2026). "Law Quotes." Brainy Quote at https://www.brainyquote.com/topics/law-quotes.

the government tells you otherwise it is tyranny. This is a moral foundation for law, a foundation which we should all be able to appreciate.

Beyond this we are faced with a challenge. What is the law revolving around commerce and the economy. This area of law has been crowded for the last 50 years by the education system in the United States limiting civics to a semester in seventh grade while social studies is incorporated every year, mostly for a full year. It is the Union/government complex saying "look at this, this will make you a good person- ignore what will make you a good citizen." Ironically, what makes us a good person is highly subjective, what makes a person a good citizen is rather objective. What is "good" as a person depends on the eyes of the beholder, nearly everyone is both a good and bad person in the eyes of different people; however, a good citizen is one who does their civic duty, participates in the community, votes, and protects the rights of others, all the while not violating just laws. While there is some argument as to what a "just law" is, the remainder are pretty clear cut.

In this portion of the book, we examine the specific law of the United States. While those reading this in other countries may not have as much use for this discussion as we have domestically, it still can be a valuable insight into the largest economy of the world. Chapter 5 wades into this discussion with a discussion of the underlying theory of Article I section 10 of the United States constitution. This prohibition on unfunded liability at the state level directly translates into the ability of actors other than the federal government to provide for "funded" liabilities, to ensure the success of local commerce.

Chapter 6 directs the conversation to illicit uses of federal powers under the classical system, specially the violations of the federal powers granted under Article I. As the government is using ambiguity to preserve the "Vicy Financial system", it is also using regulation by enforcement to dilute the confidence in the law. With vague regulations and a extremely broad interpretation of the Howey test, the government has been attacking legitimate companies while settling with scammers and crooks across the board. Compliance and selective prosecution are being used to protect specific actors within the space by making it too difficult for competitors who are not hiring lobbyist from entering the market. This is a clear violation of the dormant commerce clause and the ability of individuals in the United States to start companies, even if they compete with those who are buying congresspeople, like the American Bankers Association.

Chapter 7 is the "boring" chapter, that is necessary for a strong analysis of the economic situation. Chapter 7 beings together the most important cases within the digital asset space and looks at how the government is creating an oligopoly for our personal finances by attacking the boundaries of classical economics. This creates an effective danger zone, which makes it even harder for small companies to go into business of helping people have access tot heir wealth.

Chapter 8 rounds out the section with a direct discussion of the Clarity Act, which may be a law by the time that this book is published. Clarity, for better or worse, has several very useful factors which make digital assets much more effective; however, the American Bankers Cartel is/has fought for language to be included which prohibits yield bearing accounts for stable coins. As the ABA has already attached the digital community by defining Stable coins as unstable OROR tokens, the prohibition on yield attacks the utility of the intermediary stage. To make matters worse, this is direct bribery as the stated position of the banks is that they do not want competition. Why would they, when Defi companies are offering 15% APY and banks are only offering 0.5% (with fees). For 113 years, banks have had a monopoly on savings accounts.[49]

The economic and legal framework in the United States is the same framework which led to the sub-prime mortgage bubble. The bad actors are protected as long as they are buying congresspeople, and in an election year the rates are quite low. New legislation is needed to prohibit not only the participation of politicians, bureaucrats, and their families in the

---

[49] When the banking cartel was created savings accounts were approximately 4-7% for regular savings accounts, now regular accounts are approximately 0.38%-0.41%. FDIC at https://www.fdic.gov/national-rates-and-rate-caps.

market, but a direct prohibition on corporate lobbying of anything related to the national financial system from the banking sector. Those who hold our deposits have a fiduciary duty to ensure that the client is treated fairly, the obscene recent profits are showing that this is not the case. [50]

[50] By no means are we against profits; however, the exploitive profits which are being generated by banks are well beyond the scope of the economic foresight of the constitution. Further, they are a violation of the founding concepts of the Constitution.

Chapter 5: The Constitutional Mandate. Article I, Section 10 and the forgotten legality of non-fiat tender.

"Our constitution was made only for a moral and religious people. It is wholly inadequate to the government of any other."

John Adams[51]

In the United States, the constitution is the is the lodestone which guides us in our operations. If we leave the constitution, then we are really not a nation, but simply a collection of states bickering amongst each other. In order to be a "more perfect union" we must have a functional economy. It is time to realize that the digital asset system is the gateway to that economy.

To understand this, we must understand the legality of the process. While states are clearly prohibited from minting their own currency, the right to have private tender for individuals is protected by the Bill of Rights as it is unaddressed in the main body of the constitution. However, we need to stay within the intent of the constitution, which means that currencies should be backed (Gold and Silver clause) and should not be "letters of credit" as they are unreliable.

---

[51] Staff (2026). "Constitution Quotes." Brainy Quote at https://www.brainyquote.com/search_results?x=0&y=0&q=Constitution+.

Further, we need to address the issue that while the Federal government has the full authority to determine which currency (or currencies) shall be used for the payment of federal debt, private debt is managed by the dormant commerce clause and is a right of the people. With the constitutional failure of Jeckell Island and the last 113 years of loss to inflation, it is time to reimagine the currency of the United States and the world- all on the digital ledger.

The Original Intent: Article I, Section 10 and the Gold/Silver Clause

The Founders lived through the terminal collapse of the Continental Dollar—a "physical memecoin" that reached zero value because it had no objective underlay. When they wrote that "No State shall... make any Thing but gold and silver Coin a Tender in Payment of Debts," they were creating a Mandatory Reserve Floor.

In the British Classical Tradition, "value is inherent in production." Gold and silver were selected because they represent Stored Work. You cannot "decree" gold into existence; you must mine it, refine it, and mint it. This physical constraint acts as an algorithmic check on the "Whims of Men." In a modern digital framework, the "spirit" of this clause dictates that any asset used by a State or a Bank to settle public debt must possess the same crystalline, objective characteristics. In the 21st century, this means RWA-backed tokens—digital representations of gold, silver, land, or energy—are the only constitutionally consistent mediums for state-level "Tender."

State and Bank Restrictions: The Guardrails of the Republic

Under the original intent of Section 10, the State is a "Trustee" of value, not a creator of it. Because the State has the power of coercion (taxes and legal tender laws), it is strictly prohibited from using that power to force "Bills of Credit" (unbacked debt) upon the populace. This restriction extends to the banking cartel that acts as an arm of the state.

If a Bank or a State seeks to facilitate the "Payment of Debts," they are limited to "Things" that have verifiable fractal underlay of physical reality. To allow a State to use a 0% reserve fiat or a speculative utility token as "Tender" is a direct violation of the Section 10 mandate. They are bound to the Objectivist path. They must use tokens that are tethered to production, ensuring that the "floor" of the economy remains solid.

Federal Preemption and the RWA Constraint

While the Federal Government is given the power to "coin Money" and "regulate the Value thereof" under Article I, Section 8, this power does not grant them the right to violate the laws of physics or the spirit of the Constitution. The Federal Government is a creature of delegated powers; it was never granted the authority to emit "memecoins" backed only by "Full Faith and Credit"—a subjective term that has become a euphemism for "Psychological Solvency."

Following the logic of Section 10, the Federal Government is expressly restricted to tokens backed by RWA. If the "Value" is to be "regulated," it must first *exist*. You cannot regulate the value of "nothing." By issuing unbacked fiat, the Federal Government has moved into the realm of "Bills of Credit," which the Founders specifically sought to extinguish. A constitutionally compliant Federal token must be a digital "Species"—a verifiable representative of the republic's actual assets.

The Sovereign Individual: The Right to Utility and Memecoins

The genius of the American framework is that the restrictions placed on the *State* do not apply to the *People*. While the State is bound to the "Gold and Silver" (RWA) standard to protect the public from debasement, individuals and private companies are protected by the Ninth and Tenth Amendments.

In private commerce, a citizen has the sovereign right to trade in any medium they and their counterparty agree upon. Whether that is a high-velocity utility token, a speculative memecoin, or a fractionalized share of a digital art piece, it is a matter of Private Contract. The State cannot make these "Tender" (meaning they cannot force a creditor to accept them), but they cannot prohibit their use as a "medium of exchange" between consenting adults.

This creates a Dual-Track Economy:

1. **The Public Floor (RWA):** States, Banks, and the Fed operate on a mandatory, RWA-backed, "Species" standard to ensure systemic stability.
2. **The Private Laboratory (Utility/Meme):** Individuals and companies innovate with any tokenized asset they choose, allowing the "subjective" market to determine their value without risking the "objective" foundation of the republic.

Restoring the Constitutional Architecture

By returning to the original intent of Article I, Section 10, we plug the 113-year leak in the American economy. We stop the State from gambling with "Bills of Credit" and restore the "Thing" to its rightful place at the center of the ledger. Digital realism is not about banning innovation; it is about ensuring that the people who hold the "keys to the vault" are held to a mathematical and physical standard, while the People remain free to explore the digital frontier.[52]

---

[52] Cooper's Logic Check → The banksters want you to think Section 10 is an "antique" because it is the only thing that stops them from being the "House" in a rigged casino. They want to use "subjective" fiat to pay their "objective" debts to you. Logic check: If you owe the bank $1,000, they want "real" value; if they owe the republic $34 trillion, they want to pay in "memecoins" printed by the Fed. Digital realism flips that. We put the State back in the "RWA Cage" where they belong and let the People play with whatever tokens they want in the backyard. That is how you build a "more perfect union" that does not go broke every fifty years..

The Legal Tether: Why "Bills of Credit" Were Originally Prohibited

Before the Constitution, the United States operated under the Articles of Confederation and the "Continental" currency. This was the original American "physical memecoin." Because the Continental Congress had no power to tax and no "Objectivist" underlay (Gold or Silver), they issued "Bills of Credit"—promises to pay that were backed by nothing but the hope of future victory.

The result was a textbook case of Monetary Entropy. As the supply of Continentals decoupled from the physical reality of production, the currency reached terminal velocity. The phrase "not worth a Continental" became the 18th-century equivalent of a "rug pull." The Founders realized that when a government can print "Value" without the "Work" of production, it is not just managing an economy; it is committing a slow-motion theft of the people's time.

Defining the "Bill of Credit" in Digital Realism

In the legal context of 1787, a "Bill of Credit" was defined as any paper issued by the government, intended to circulate as money, which was not immediately redeemable in "Species" (Gold or Silver). It was a debt instrument masquerading as an asset.

In the language of Part I, a Bill of Credit is a Hollow Man. It represents a claim on future labor that may never be performed. By prohibiting the States from emitting these bills, the Constitution was creating a

"Legal Tether" to the floor. It ensured that the State could only facilitate the "Velocity of Value" if it first possessed the "Object" of value. This is the British Classical Tradition codified into supreme law: money must be a representation of production (), not a decree of intent ().

The Moral Hazard of the Printing Press

The Founders prohibited Bills of Credit because they understood the Moral Hazard of unbacked issuance. When a politician can pay for a bridge, a war, or a "gimmie" program by printing a bill rather than taxing the people or producing a good, the link between Cost and Benefit is severed.

This creates a "Subjective Fantasy" where the government believes it has infinite resources, while the "Objective Reality" is that the purchasing power of the citizen is being liquidated. James Madison, in *Federalist No. 44*, described the "pestilent effects of paper money" as a "disorder" that "inflicts a most unmerited, a most cruel, and a most memorable grievance" on the people. The prohibition was intended to be the permanent cure for this disorder—a requirement that the government operate within the crystalline constraints of the Constant Ledger.

The 113-Year Deviation: Modern Fiat as a Bill of Credit

Forensically, the Federal Reserve Note is the modern evolution of the "Bill of Credit." While it is issued by a central bank rather than a State, its functional logic is identical: it is a circulating debt instrument that is not redeemable in any "Thing" of objective value.

By ignoring the "Legal Tether" of Section 10, the legacy system has allowed for the very "thermal runaway" the Founders sought to prevent. The current $34 trillion debt is the ultimate "Bill of Credit"—a massive, unbacked claim on the future energy of the republic. Digital realism is not just about moving to a blockchain; it is about restoring the Constitutional Prohibition by requiring that all "Tender" used by the government and its banks be tethered to Real-World Assets (RWA).

Restoring the Firewall

The prohibition of Bills of Credit was the Founders' way of saying that the government cannot be a "Wastrel." It must be a participant in the "Objectivist" economy, bound by the same laws of math and production as the citizens it serves. As we enter Part II, we recognize that the "Legal Tether" is not a restriction on our freedom—it is the Protector of our Labor. By reclaiming the spirit of Section 10, we are finally putting the "Hollow Man" to rest and returning to a republic built on the certainty of the "Thing."[53]

---

[53] Cooper's Logic Check → The "progressive" historians want you to think the Founders were just obsessed with "Shiny Rocks" (Gold and Silver). Logic check: They didn't care about the rocks; they cared about the Constraint. They knew that if you let a politician touch the "Supply" button, they'll keep hitting it until the machine breaks. A "Bill of Credit" is just a lie that travels at the speed of paper. Digital realism replaces the "Paper Lie" with the

Federal Preemption vs. State Sovereignty in Monetary Choice (dormant commerce clause and commerce clause)

Article I, Section 8, Clause 3 (the Commerce Clause) grants Congress the power "to regulate Commerce... among the several States." Historically, this has been the "progressive" lever used to justify Federal preemption over almost every aspect of economic life. The legacy cartel argues that for commerce to be "regular," there must be a single, uniform Federal tender. Under this logic, the Federal Reserve Act of 1913 was not just a banking law; it was a preemption strike designed to sideline the States' Article I, Section 10 obligations.

By asserting that "Legal Tender" status is a Federal monopoly, the government has essentially told the States they no longer have the right to demand "Gold and Silver" (RWA) for the payment of debts. This has created a Monetary Monoculture. When the Federal tender begins to reach terminal velocity through debasement, the States find themselves trapped: they are prohibited by Section 10 from emitting their own "Bills of Credit," yet they are "preempted" from facilitating an alternative, stable medium for their citizens.

"On-Chain Truth." It is time to get back to a system where the government has to work for its money, just like you do.

The Dormant Commerce Clause: The People's Shield

The "Dormant Commerce Clause" is a judicial doctrine which holds that because Congress has the power to regulate interstate commerce, the States cannot pass laws that improperly burden that commerce. In the hands of the banksters, this is used to prevent States from authorizing non-fiat tender. However, digital realism flips this argument.

If the Federal tender (the dollar) is failing to serve as a reliable "Standard of Value," then the Federal government's *failure* to provide sound money becomes a burden on interstate commerce. When inflation creates "price-chasing" chaos, commerce is no longer "regular." Therefore, the Dormant Commerce Clause actually protects the right of States and individuals to utilize a "Thing" (RWA-backed assets) that restores stability. If a State authorizes the use of a digital asset like KIROS for private debt settlement, it is not "regulating" Federal money; it is removing a burden on commerce created by Federal debasement.

The Tenth Amendment and the Sovereignty of Private Contract

Under the Tenth Amendment, "the powers not delegated to the United States... are reserved to the States respectively, or to the people." The Federal Government was given the power to "coin Money," but it was never given the *exclusive* power to prohibit the people from using other "Things" as a medium of exchange.

This is the "Sovereignty of Choice." While the Federal government can mandate what it accepts for *Federal taxes*, it has no Constitutional authority to prohibit a citizen in Pennsylvania from paying a citizen in Florida in an RWA-backed token. This is a private contract, managed by State law, and protected by the Ninth and Tenth Amendments. The Federal "Preemption" ends where the People's "Sovereignty" begins.

State Sovereignty: The Return of the Guardrail

We are seeing the return of State sovereignty in the form of "Sound Money" legislation across the republic. When a State legislature recognizes gold, silver, or RWA-backed digital assets as legal tender for state-level debts, they are not "rebelling" against the Fed; they are fulfilling their Section 10 Mandate.

The States are the final guardrail against a "Hollow Man" collapse. By creating a multi-currency framework where the Federal "memecoin" must compete with RWA-backed "Species," the States fulfill their original role as a check on Federal overreach. In the digital republic, this means States have a sovereign duty to provide the infrastructure for their citizens to opt-out of debasement.

From Monopoly to Competition

The "Federal Preemption" of money is a 113-year-old experiment in centralization that has resulted in a 98% loss of purchasing power. The Constitution never intended for a monetary monopoly. By reclaiming the Dormant Commerce Clause and the Section 10

Mandate, the States can restore a competitive framework where "Value" is determined by production and math, not by the "Whims of Men" in a DC black box. The "Legal Tether" is being reattached, and the sovereignty of the ledger is the tool of the restoration.[54]

The Judicial Erosion of Sound Money: From the Civil War to Nixon

The first structural fracture in the American monetary floor occurred not through a lack of gold, but through a perceived "necessity" of the State to survive. During the American Civil War, the Lincoln administration faced a terminal liquidity crisis. To fund the war effort, they issued "Greenbacks"—unbacked paper notes that were essentially the 19th-century version of a "physical memecoin." This was a direct violation of the Article I, Section 10 prohibition against "Bills of Credit," setting the stage for a judicial showdown that would decide if the Constitution was a rigid protocol or a flexible suggestion.

In the landmark case *Hepburn v. Griswold* (1870), the Supreme Court initially attempted to hold the line for

---

[54] Cooper's Logic Check → The banksters love "Uniformity" because it makes it easier to rob everyone at the same speed. They call it "efficiency," but it is really just a way to make sure there's no "Exit" door. Logic check: If a ship is sinking, "uniformity" means everyone drowns at the same time. "Sovereignty" means you have the right to a lifeboat. Article I, Section 10 is the lifeboat. The Federal Government can keep its "Standardized Drowning Program" for its own debts; the People and the States have a Constitutional right to swim..

Objectivist economics. Chief Justice Salmon P. Chase—who had ironically oversaw the issuance of the Greenbacks as Treasury Secretary—penned a ruling that declared the Legal Tender Acts unconstitutional. He argued that forcing a creditor to accept "subjective" paper in place of the "objective" gold specified in a contract was a violation of the Fifth Amendment. At this moment, the "Legal Tether" was still intact, asserting that the government could not legislate away the laws of physics and production.

However, the "Wastrels" of the political class could not allow a return to sound money while war debts remained. Under intense pressure, President Grant expanded the Supreme Court by two seats, specifically appointing justices known to favor the Greenback. Just one year later, in *Knox v. Lee* (1871), the Court reversed its previous decision in a stunning display of judicial whiplash. This was the birth of the "Doctrine of Necessity," a legal framework which argued that the preservation of the government outweighed the specific mathematical prohibitions of the Constitution.

The *Knox* decision shifted the American economy from a "Rule of Math" to a "Rule of Men." The Court ruled that "value" was not an inherent property of production (V_p), but a decree of the sovereign (D_i). By granting the Federal Government the power to "create" value by legislative fiat, the Judiciary effectively decapitated the Gold/Silver clause. They argued that if the government *needs* the money to be valid, then it *is* valid—a circular logic that forms the basis of all modern inflationary entropy.

This era concluded with the legal personification of the "Hollow Man." By making paper "Legal Tender" for private debts, the Court allowed the State to intervene in every private contract in the Republic. The "Species" mandate was reduced to a mere "option," and the "Bills of Credit" firewall was permanently breached. This provided the precedent that the banksters would later use at Jekyll Island to move the entire economy into a centralized "Black Box."

The Jekyll Island Coup and the 1913 Decapitation

The erosion of sound money reached its terminal phase not in a courtroom, but in the shadows of a private island in Georgia. In November 1910, a secret cabal of the world's most powerful "Wastrel" bankers—representing the interests of Rockefeller, Morgan, and the European Rothschilds—met at Jekyll Island to draft a blueprint for a centralized monetary monopoly. Their goal was to move the "Single Point of Failure" of the economy from the transparent market to a private "Black Box" entity. They knew that as long as the people could verify the math of the vault, the banksters could never achieve total "Psychological Solvency."

The resulting Federal Reserve Act of 1913 was a masterpiece of Information Asymmetry. It was presented to the public as a "stabilizing force" that would prevent bank runs, but its forensic purpose was to allow banks to engage in "Fractional Reserve" expansion without the objective check of a Gold standard. By creating a Federal "Bill of Credit" that was technically issued by a private bank but functionally enforced by the State, they circumvented the Section 10 prohibition on States emitting paper money. This was the "decapitation" of the producer, as the "Standard of Value" was handed to a committee of "unqualified" gatekeepers.

The Jekyll Island Coup replaced the Constant Ledger with a "Managed Ledger." For the first time in American history, the value of the dollar was no longer tethered to a "Thing" (Production); it was tethered to Debt. Under this new architecture, every dollar entered circulation as a loan from the Federal Reserve to the government, ensuring that the "Entropy of Fiat" would eventually require infinite growth just to service the interest. This turned the American labor force into a "Captive Audience" for a perpetual debt-spiral.

The Judiciary offered no resistance to this coup, as the "Doctrine of Necessity" from the 1870s had already paved the way for "managed" money. By the time the *Gold Clause Cases* (1935) reached the Supreme Court, the "Black Box" was so entrenched that the Court ruled the government could unilaterally nullify private contracts that demanded payment in gold. They argued that private citizens could not "obstruct" the government's power to regulate the currency, effectively making the State the sole owner of all "Value" in the Republic.

This era solidified the "Single Point of Failure" that continues to threaten the Republic today. By moving the "Vault" from the public square to a private board room, the banksters ensured that "Verifiability" was replaced by "Blind Faith." The 1913 Act was the moment the "Hollow Man" became the architect of the economy, setting the stage for the final "Nixon Shock" that would remove the last vestige of physical reality from the global ledger.

The Nixon Shock and the Final Phase Transition to "Hollow" Money

The final phase transition to "Hollow Money" occurred on August 15, 1971, when President Richard Nixon unilaterally severed the last "Legal Tether" between the dollar and the physical world. By this time, the "Gimmies" of the Great Society and the "Wastrels" of the Vietnam War had created a massive over-leverage that the U.S. gold reserves could no longer mask. Foreign nations, performing their own forensic audits of the American vault, realized that the "Hollow Man" was bankrupt and began demanding their "Species" (Gold) back in record numbers.

Nixon's response, known as the "Nixon Shock," was to "temporarily" suspend the convertibility of the dollar into gold. In doing so, he ended the Bretton Woods system and moved the entire world into a state of

Pure Subjectivity. The dollar was no longer a "representative" of a "Thing"; it became the "Thing" itself—a "physical memecoin" backed by nothing but the military coercion of the State and the "Full Faith and Credit" of a debt-ridden treasury. This was the ultimate victory of the "Progressive" tradition over the "British Classical Tradition."

Without the "Objective Floor" of gold, the global economy entered a state of Monetary Entropy. The $B_s \propto S_s$ equation we discussed in Chapter 3 became completely untethered, leading to the erratic volatility and "price-chasing" chaos of the late 20th century. The "Velocity of Value" was no longer a function of production, but a function of how fast the central bank could print new "Bills of Credit" to outrun the previous ones. The "Legal Tether" was replaced by a "Political Leash."

The Judiciary's silence during this transition was the final admission that the Constitution's monetary clauses had been "hollowed out." No court intervened to remind the President of the Article I, Section 10 mandate or the 5th Amendment property rights of the citizens. The "Doctrine of Necessity" had become the "Doctrine of Permanent Emergency." Since 1971, the Republic has been operating on a "Managed Decline," where the only constant is the devaluation of the citizen's labor to service the entropy of the state.

The Nixon Shock created the Temporal-Economic Paradox that necessitates Part II of this book. We are currently living in the "Reconciliation Gap" created by

1971. Digital realism is the only path back to the "Objectivist" reality that the Nixon Shock attempted to destroy. By moving to an RWA-backed, constant ledger, we are not just adopting new tech; we are performing a "Hard Reset" on the 113-year error that began at Jekyll Island and ended in the "Hollow" economy of today.

Digital Assets as Modern "Tender": A Constitutional Re-interpretation

The movement of the American economy into digital realism is not an act of rebellion against the constitutional order, but its ultimate fulfillment. Under a strict forensic interpretation of the Gold and Silver Clause of Article I, Section 10, a digital asset with a Real-World Asset (RWA) underlay is the only modern "Thing" that satisfies the Founders' requirement for objective tender. In the legacy "Hollow Man" economy, the citizen is forced to use a Federal Reserve Note that is functionally a "Bill of Credit"—an unbacked debt instrument that the Constitution explicitly prohibited the States from using to settle debts. By contrast, a digital asset anchored to a fractal reserve of gold, silver, or energy represents "stored work" and "production," aligning it with the British Classical Tradition that values are inherent in the object itself, not in the decree of a central committee.

Constitutional re-interpretation in the digital age requires us to look at the "species" mandate as a functional requirement for stability rather than a literal requirement for physical metal. The Founders chose gold and silver because their supply was governed by the laws of physics and the math of extraction, providing a "Hard Floor" that the "Whims of Men" could not manipulate. A decentralized digital asset provides this same crystalline logic through code and consensus. When a State or a private citizen chooses to use an RWA-backed token to settle a debt, they are utilizing a medium that is more constitutionally sound than the unbacked paper of 1971. The 10th Amendment further protects this right, as the power to prohibit the use of objective, non-fiat tender for private contracts was never delegated to the Federal government.

Furthermore, the "Dormant Commerce Clause" supports the transition to digital tender as a means of protecting the integrity of interstate trade. When the Federal tender is losing its "Standard of Value" through inflationary entropy, it becomes a burden on commerce. Digital realism provides the "remedy" by re-establishing a constant ledger where the buyer's perceived value () and the seller's perceived value () can meet on a solid, non-volatile floor. This interpretation suggests that the digital asset is not a "new" invention in the eyes of the law, but a "new species" of the very tender the Founders intended to protect the republic from the "pestilent effects" of paper money.

By adopting this constitutional framework, we move from a state of "Managed Decline" to a state of

"Mathematical Growth." The digital ledger acts as a modern "Shield against Debasement," ensuring that the labor of the citizen remains tethered to reality. We are not "interpreting" the Constitution to fit the tech; we are using the tech to finally obey the Constitution. The legal path to the digital republic is not a loophole; it is the "lodestone" of Article I, Section 10, pointing us back toward a more perfect and productive union.[55]

Restoring the Multi-Currency Framework under the Tenth Amendment

The Tenth Amendment is the ultimate structural guardrail: *"The powers not delegated to the United States by the Constitution, nor prohibited by it to the States, are reserved to the States respectively, or to the people."* While Article I, Section 8 grants Congress the power to "coin Money," nowhere does the Constitution grant the Federal government the *exclusive* right to prohibit the use of other "Things" as a medium of exchange for private debt. The "Legal Tender" monopoly is a judicial fiction that has been used to trap human labor in a devaluing asset.

---

[55] Cooper's Logic Check→ The "progressive" lawyers want you to think that the Constitution is a "living document" so they can treat it like a "dead letter." Logic check: If the "Gold and Silver" clause is dead, then the "Value" of your labor is dead with it. They want a "Subjective" law to go with their "Subjective" money. Digital realism is the only way to get back to "Objective" law. We don't need a new Constitution; we just need a medium of exchange that actually follows the one we have. Math does not care about your "living" interpretation; it only cares about the truth of the ledger.

Restoring the multi-currency framework means re-establishing the "Sovereignty of Choice." In this model, the Federal government continues to issue its "physical memecoin" for the payment of Federal taxes and internal government operations. However, the States and the People reclaim their right to utilize non-fiat tender—RWA-backed digital assets, gold-standard tokens, or utility coins—for private commerce. This creates a Competitive Ecosystem where the "Standard of Value" is determined by the market's demand for stability rather than a central committee's demand for inflation.

The Tenth Amendment as an Anti-Fragility Mechanism

A monoculture is inherently fragile. If the Federal Reserve Note enters a terminal debt-spiral, the entire economy collapses because there is no alternative "rail" for value to travel on. By contrast, a multi-currency framework under the Tenth Amendment creates Economic Anti-Fragility. If the Federal tender is losing 10% of its value, the citizen can shift their stored labor into an RWA-backed "Species" that maintains a constant floor.

This framework forces the Federal government to practice "Monetary Discipline." Currently, the banksters print with impunity because they know the citizenry is "captured." If they had to compete with a digital "Gold Standard" accessible on every smartphone, they would be forced to maintain NPV(c) the of the dollar or face a total "Exit" to the superior ledger. The Tenth Amendment is not just about "State Rights"; it is about the Right to Opt-Out of a failing experiment.

State-Level Implementation: The Digital Species Harbor

The restoration of this framework is already beginning at the State level. Forward-thinking legislatures are passing "Sound Money" acts that recognize gold, silver, and "Specie-backed" digital assets as legal tender. By doing so, the States are fulfilling their Section 10 Mandate. They are providing a "Safe Harbor" for their citizens, ensuring that if the Federal "Hollow Man" collapses, the state's internal commerce remains tethered to the objective reality of the ledger.

This state-level action creates a "Dual-Ledger" environment. A business in Texas or Florida can price its goods in USD (for tax purposes) but settle its contracts in an RWA-backed token (for value preservation). This removes the Temporal-Economic Paradox by allowing the buyer and seller to lock in a price that is not subject to the "Entropy of Fiat." The States act as the laboratories of monetary competition, proving that the republic functions best when the "Whims of Men" are checked by the "Logic of Math."

The "Gimmie" Resistance: Overcoming the Monopoly

The legacy cartel will claim that a multi-currency framework is "chaotic" or "confusing." Logic check: You already use a multi-currency framework every time you travel, use credit card points, or trade digital assets. The "confusion" they fear is actually Transparency. They do not want you to be able to compare their devaluing paper to a constant digital asset because the comparison makes their fraud obvious.

In a digital republic, technology handles the complexity. Atomic swaps and real-time exchange rates mean that a consumer can hold "Hard Money" (RWA tokens) and spend it as "Soft Money" (USD) at the point of sale. The complexity is managed by the code; the Sovereignty remains with the individual. This is the ultimate fulfillment of the Tenth Amendment: a world where the people are no longer the "products" of the central bank, but the "masters" of their own medium of exchange.

The Shield of the Tenth Amendment

Restoring the multi-currency framework is the only way to plug the $34 trillion leak in the American ship. We are moving toward a future where "Value" is not a decree, but a choice. By utilizing the Tenth Amendment as a shield, we protect the "Objectivist" tradition of production from the "Subjectivist" tradition of debasement. The "Legal Tether" is being restored, not by a single act of Congress, but by the collective decision of a "moral and religious people" to return to the math of the vault.[56]

---

[56] Cooper's Logic Check → The banksters love the "One Ring to Rule Them All" approach because they own the Ring. They want

Conclusion: The Supreme Law as a Shield Against Debasement

The "Supreme Law" of the American Republic was never intended to be a flexible suggestion for politicians, but a rigid engineering specification designed to protect the integrity of human labor. By grounding the monetary system in Article I, Section 10, the Founders created a constitutional shield against the "pestilent effects" of unbacked paper. They understood that when a government is granted the power to decouple "Value" from "Production," it inevitably descends into a state of predatory debasement. Digital realism is the modern activation of this shield, using the immutable logic of the ledger to re-establish the "Hard Floor" that was surgically removed by the "Wastrels" of the legacy cartel over the last century.

To view the Constitution as a shield is to recognize that "Sound Money" is the ultimate guardian of civil liberty. When the "Legal Tether" of gold and silver—or their modern RWA-backed digital equivalents—is intact, the State is forced to operate within the crystalline constraints of reality. It cannot fund endless

---

you to think that having a choice in money is "un-American." Logic check: There is nothing more American than competition. We have choice in our cars, our phones, and our religions—why should the most important tool of our labor be a forced monopoly? They want you trapped in the "physical memecoin" because That is the only way they can keep the 0% reserve fraud going. Digital realism is the "Break Glass in Case of Emergency" for the whole republic.

wars or "gimmie" programs through the "subjective" theft of inflation. The "Objectivist" tradition championed by the Founders ensures that every unit of currency is a verified representative of "stored work," preventing the "Hollow Man" of 0% reserves from consuming the Net Present Value of the citizen's future.

The judicial and legislative erosion of this shield since the Civil War has left the American economy in a state of terminal entropy. By replacing the "Rule of Math" with the "Whims of Men," the legacy system has turned the "lodestone" of the Constitution into a "dead letter" to facilitate a $34 trillion fraud. However, the legal path to restoration remains open through the Tenth Amendment and the sovereign choice of the People. The "Dormant Commerce Clause" and the "Gold/Silver Clause" provide the necessary "Safe Harbor" for a multi-currency framework, where the digital republic can finally opt-out of the "managed decline" of the Federal monopoly.

Ultimately, Chapter 5 has shown that we do not need to reinvent the American experiment; we simply need to obey its original source code. The digital ledger is the technological manifestation of the Founders' intent—a system where truth is verified by the many rather than decreed by the few. By reclaiming the Constitution as our shield, we are reclaiming our time, our energy, and our sovereignty. The era of "blind faith" in the bankster's black box is over; the era of the supreme law as a mathematical reality has begun.[57]

[57] Cooper's Logic Check → The banksters want you to think the Constitution is "outdated" because it is the only thing that actually has the power to fire them. Logic check: If a contract says you own a house, and the bank tries to take it without paying, you don't call the contract "outdated"—you call the bank "thieves." Article I, Section 10 is the contract for the whole republic. They have been "squatting" in our economy for 113 years, but the digital ledger is the eviction notice. Math is the law, and the law is back in town.

Chapter 6: Regulatory Weaponization. How ambiguity is used as a tool for market suppression.

"When you have ten thousand regulations you destroy all respect for the law."

Winston Churchill[58]

If regulations are not a tool for protecting the people, they are illegal. There is no regulation which is not offensive to the constitution which allows for the protection of forging governments, foreign corporations, or the government itself over the protection of the people. Repugnance to the Constitution is the easiest way for a law to be dismissed in the United States system. When laws and regulations are weaponized to make it easier for the government to attack citizens who are not breaking any law, then it is time to remove the law and the agency from the government to protect the people.

This chapter looks at the methods which are being used to have the government work as an enforcer for the banking cartels. Gone are the days when the government was simply acting in the best interest of the people, now there is a "bought and paid for" system which is protected by the lobbies to attack

---

[58] Staff (2026). "Regulation Quotes." Brainy Quote at https://www.brainyquote.com/search_results?x=0&y=0&q=Regulations.

innovation in the United States. This creates a very dangerous system for the people of the United States as they become "workers" rather than "citizens."

Ambiguity is one of the greatest tools of the government in the promotion of companies it wants while attacking innovators in the field. This process is often called "regulation by enforcement," where the government looks for a crime to punish rather than punishing a crime that is known to be committed. The Howey standard from 1946 is a brilliant example of this. The SEC has the power to enforce securities violations, but in the digital asset space they have to force things to be securities before they have jurisdiction (unless Clarity passes). This creates a dangerous "you are what you say we are" not "you are what the law says you are scenario." This coupled with the rising trends of "de facto bans" is undermining the United States on the global stage as a digital asset leader.

Selective prosecution is another problem which we are facing as a country. The Epstein files aside, the United States is prosecuting some companies while letting others slide. To make matters worse, when they do "prosecute" they illegally use the civil courts to get criminal penalties, in violation of the 4th,5th and 6th amendments. The use the civil courts, of course, to apply the lower standard of proof in the case. This is coupled with lack of due process and higher compliance entries for new companies to compete with companies that entered the market under no compliance laws.

The government should provide a fair playing field for citizens. Favoring foreign banks and theirs subsidiaries over American citizens is economic treason in the era of trade wars. Congress, the courts and the executive branch need to be promoting American companies- that is their job. The law of the land is the law to protect the land and the current system is protecting the lobbyists and letting innovators flutter in the wind with no protection at all.[59]

The Doctrine of Strategic Ambiguity: Regulation by Enforcement

Strategic ambiguity is the intentional refusal by a regulatory agency to provide "Ex-Ante" (before the fact) rules. Instead, they rely on "Ex-Post" (after the fact) enforcement actions to set precedents. This creates a state of Jurisdictional Fog, where an innovator cannot know if their token is a currency, a commodity, a utility, or a security until they receive a Wells Notice or a subpoena. This is not "Rule of Law"; it is "Rule of Whim."

[59] Cooper's Logic Check → The "experts" say that "vague regulations are flexible." Logic check: Vague regulations are a **leash**. They keep the rules blurry so they can pull the collar whenever you try to run past the legacy banks. They call it "Consumer Protection," but they are only protecting the "Consuming" of your labor by the cartels. In digital realism, we don't need a "permission slip" from a bureaucrat to use math. If the code is transparent and the math is solvent, the regulation is redundant.

By keeping the definitions blurry, the government ensures that it always has a "hook" to sink into any project that threatens the dominance of the legacy banking rails. If the rules were clear, the "Gimmies" could not selectively target competitors. Ambiguity allows the regulator to act as a "subjective judge" in an objective field, effectively saying to the innovator: "You are not breaking a law we have written; you are breaking a law we haven't finished imagining yet."

The Enforcement Trap: Litigation as Suppression

"Regulation by Enforcement" is the process of using the courtroom to bypass the legislative process. Instead of working with Congress to draft a "Clarity Act," agencies like the SEC and CFTC engage in "Jurisdictional Land Grabs" through litigation. They pick a target—often an American company trying to play by the rules—and sue them under a 1946 standard that was never intended for decentralized code.

This process is forensically designed to be a Capital Drain. Even if the company eventually wins in court, the "Process is the Punishment." By the time the case is settled, years of innovation have been lost, millions in capital have been diverted to lawyers, and the "Wastrel" banks have had time to build their own proprietary, permissioned versions of the technology. This is market suppression disguised as "Consumer Protection." It ensures that only those with "bought and paid for" lobbies can survive the regulatory gauntlet.

The Repugnance of Ambiguity to the Constitution

Under the Void for Vagueness doctrine, a law is unconstitutional if it does not provide a person of ordinary intelligence "fair notice" of what is prohibited. Strategic ambiguity is the ultimate violation of this principle. When a regulator says, "Come in and talk to us," but provides no path to registration, they are creating a "Trap for the Innocent." This is Repugnant to the Constitution because it violates the Due Process clauses of the Fifth and Fourteenth Amendments.

In the digital republic, we recognize that the "Law of the Land" must be as transparent as the "Code of the Ledger." If the government cannot provide a clear, mathematical definition of a violation, then no violation has occurred. The use of ambiguity to protect foreign banking subsidiaries over American citizens is not just a bureaucratic error; it is Economic Treason. It forces the "Active Citizen" to become a "Subservient Worker," waiting for a permission slip that never comes.

Ending the Fog

The Doctrine of Strategic Ambiguity is the final desperate move of a 0% reserve system that knows it cannot compete with the truth. By keeping the rules vague, they hope to slow the "Velocity of Value" and keep the "Hollow Man" in power for one more cycle. But the lodestone of the Constitution still points to clarity. To protect the people, we must remove the "Bureaucratic Hammer" and replace it with a system of **Clear Notice**, where the law is a shield for the innovator, not a club for the cartel.

The Howey Test as a Catch-all: Distorting 1946 Precedent for 2026 Tech

The *Howey* test was designed to determine if a specific arrangement—in that case, the sale of land in a Florida orange grove coupled with a service contract to harvest the fruit—constituted an "investment contract." The Supreme Court established four prongs: (1) an investment of money, (2) in a common enterprise, (3) with a reasonable expectation of profits, (4) derived from the efforts of others. This was an "analog" test for a centralized, human-intermediated scheme.

In a decentralized digital protocol, these prongs collapse under the weight of Mathematical Reality. When a user buys a utility token to access a decentralized network, they are not investing in a "common enterprise" led by a "Hollow Man" executive; they are purchasing a key to a global machine. The "efforts of others" are replaced by the Autonomous Execution of Code. By attempting to stretch *Howey* to cover autonomous protocols, the SEC is essentially trying to regulate the alphabet because someone might use it to write a promissory note. It is a fundamental category error that ignores the "Thing-ness" of the token in favor of a "Subjectivist" interpretation of the buyer's intent.

The Jurisdictional Hijack: Forcing the Security Label

The "Strategic Ambiguity" we discussed in Section 6.1 relies on the *Howey* test being as elastic as possible. If the SEC can argue that any token is a security, they gain a "Bureaucratic Hammer" over every innovator in the republic. This forces digital assets into a compliance framework designed for centralized corporations—requiring quarterly reports, board meetings, and centralized disclosures that are physically impossible for a decentralized protocol to fulfill.

This is the Regulatory Trap. By forcing a decentralized asset to be a "Security," the government effectively makes it illegal to exist. You cannot have a decentralized network with a "centralized issuer" responsible for disclosures. This distortion is used to ensure that the "Rails" of the economy remain in the hands of the legacy cartels, who are the only ones with the "bought and paid for" legal teams capable of navigating the citrus grove maze.

The Correct Classification: Cryptocurrency as a Currency Medium

If we return to the "Lodestone" of the Constitution and the British Classical Tradition, it becomes clear that a digital asset designed for exchange is not an "investment contract"—it is a Currency Medium. It is a "Thing" used to transfer value, much like the gold and silver coins mentioned in Article I, Section 10. As such, the proper regulatory home for digital assets is not the SEC, but the Office of the Comptroller of the Currency (OCC).

The OCC is designed to manage the "Rails" of value and the stability of the "Medium." By moving digital assets under the Comptroller, we move from the "Subjective Profit" standard of *Howey* to the "Objective Utility" standard of a currency. This would provide the "Clarity" the industry needs: tokens would be treated as "Species" of money, subject to safety and soundness standards, rather than "speculative investments" subject to the whims of an enforcement-only agency.

Restoring the "Logic of the Ledger"

Regulating digital assets via the OCC aligns the tech with the Section 8 power to "regulate the Value" of money. It recognizes that a token is a tool of commerce, not a share in a company. When the Comptroller manages the medium, the focus is on Verifiability and Liquidity—the core tenets of digital realism. This removes the "Security" stigma that is currently being used to "Choke Point" American innovators out of the global market.

Ending the Citrus Era

The use of the *Howey* test as a catch-all is the final defensive wall of the legacy "Wastrels." They know that if digital assets are recognized as a legitimate currency medium, the 0% reserve fraud of the banking cartel is over. By restoring the jurisdictional boundary and moving digital assets to the OCC, we are re-attaching the "Legal Tether" to reality. We are choosing a system where the "Comptroller" ensures the math is solvent, rather than an "Enforcer" who ensures the innovation is suppressed.[60]

Administrative Overreach: The Rise of the De Facto Ban

Administrative overreach in the digital age has evolved from a matter of public debate into a system of "Operation Choke Point" style maneuvers designed to bypass the legislative process entirely. A de facto ban occurs when an administrative agency—acting without a direct mandate from Congress—utilizes its supervisory power over the banking "Rails" to intimidate traditional financial institutions into severing ties with digital asset companies. By issuing "informal" warnings, raising capital requirements for "high-risk" sectors, or threatening more frequent audits for banks that service cryptocurrency clients, the administrative state creates a wall of systemic exclusion. This is the "Hollow Man" of regulation: it does not prohibit the activity by law, which would be subject to judicial

---

[60] Cooper's Logic Check → The "experts" say that "Howey is a flexible standard that protects investors." Logic check: If I buy a bag of oranges to eat them, it is fruit. If I buy them hoping the price goes up, the SEC says it is a "Security." That is not a "standard"; That is a **psychology test**. In digital realism, we don't care what you *think* you are doing; we care what the token *actually does*. If it moves value, it is a currency. They are using 1946 oranges to try and stop 2026 spaceships. It is time to stop the "citrus" circus and put the Comptroller back in charge of the money.

review, but instead makes the activity "unbankable" through bureaucratic pressure.

This method of governance represents a terminal violation of the "Rule of Law" because it replaces transparent statutes with "Strategic Ambiguity" and back-room threats. When a regulator suggests to a bank that their "reputation risk" is too high because they service a decentralized protocol, they are not enforcing a safety standard; they are performing a jurisdictional hijack. This creates an environment of "Regulatory Treason," where the government actively works to suppress American innovation to protect the "Wastrel" legacy cartel. Because these companies cannot operate without access to the payments system to pay employees or taxes, the administrative pressure functions as an execution order. The "De Facto Ban" is the ultimate tool of the "Gimmies," allowing them to kill a competing technology without ever having to defend their reasoning in a public forum or a court of law.

Furthermore, these bans undermine the United States' standing as a global leader in digital realism. While the republic's innovators are being systematically "de-banked" at home, foreign banking subsidiaries and state-sponsored entities are moving to capture the market share. This selective suppression ensures that only the "bought and paid for" incumbents—who are often the very institutions audited for systemic fraud in Chapter 4—are allowed to build the digital infrastructure of the future. By using the administrative hammer to favor the legacy cartel, the government is not protecting the consumer; it is protecting a protection racket. The result is a "Managed Decline" where American capital is forced to flee to more "Species-friendly" jurisdictions, leaving the citizens of the republic trapped in a devaluing monoculture.

Ultimately, the rise of the de facto ban is a signal that the administrative state has become "Repugnant to the Constitution." Under the Fifth Amendment, no person shall be deprived of life, liberty, or property without due process of law. Denying a legal business access to the basic infrastructure of commerce without a specific, proven crime is a denial of due process. In the digital republic, we recognize that the "Rails" belong to the people, not to a committee of "unqualified" gatekeepers. To neutralize the bureaucratic hammer, we must restore a system of "Clear Notice" and "Non-Discrimination" in banking, ensuring that the math of the ledger—not the whim of a regulator—determines who is allowed to participate in the economy.[61]

---

[61] Cooper's Logic Check → The banksters say they are "protecting the system from risk." Logic check: The "risk" they are worried about is **competition**. They don't want you to have a choice because as soon as you have a choice, you'll realize their 0% reserve bridge is made of cardboard. A "De Facto Ban" is just a coward's way of saying they can't win a fair fight in the marketplace of ideas. They can't stop the math, so they try to stop the "on-ramp." In digital realism, we don't ask for permission to use the math; we build our own ramps.

Selective Prosecution: Protecting Legacy Cartels via Litigation

As we audited in Chapter 4, the major banks of the United States have a forensic history of predatory behavior, ranging from the subprime mortgage crisis to the 1MDB embezzlement. Yet, when these legacy institutions commit systemic fraud, the "prosecution" is almost always a civil settlement. A fine is issued, which is paid using the very capital extracted from the public's labor, and the executives continue their operations without interruption. This creates an Immunity Loop: for the legacy cartel, litigation is not a deterrent, but a "toll" paid to keep the bridge closed to newcomers.

Contrast this with the treatment of digital asset innovators. When a decentralized protocol attempts to provide a transparent, 1:1 reserve alternative to the banking cartel, the government does not issue a fine; it issues a "Death Sentence." Agencies utilize the Strategic Ambiguity of the *Howey* test to launch aggressive, resource-draining litigation designed to bankrupt the innovator before a trial can even begin. This is selective prosecution in its purest form: the "Wastrels" are given a "Get Out of Jail Free" card, while the "Objectivists" are hunted for the crime of being more efficient than the state-sponsored monopoly.

The Target Selector: Lobbies and the "Epstein Files" Paradox

The selection of targets for prosecution is often driven by the "Bought and Paid For" lobby system. In the trade wars of 2026, we see a dangerous trend where the U.S. government favors foreign banking subsidiaries—which maintain deep ties to the D.C. administrative class—over American-born digital asset companies. This is Economic Treason. By prosecuting American innovators while letting globalist banking conglomerates slide on similar or worse violations, the government is actively hollowing out the domestic economy to satisfy its "Wastrel" sponsors.

This paradox is most visible in the contrast between the treatment of financial innovation and the handling of systemic corruption. While the government devotes thousands of man-hours to finding a "securities violation" in a utility token, it remains curiously silent on the forensic trails found in the "Epstein Files" or the internal risk failures of the "London Whale." This discrepancy reveals that the goal of the current regulatory regime is not the "Protection of the People," but the Protection of the Portfolio. The law has been turned into a "Target Selector" used to keep the competition "fluttering in the wind" while the cartel consolidates its power.

Litigation as a Barriers-to-Entry Weapon

Selective prosecution functions as a massive Compliance Tax on new capital. If an American citizen wants to launch a new, asset-backed financial tool, they must first calculate the "Litigation Risk" of being targeted by an agency looking for a headline. Because the legacy banks entered the market under no such compliance laws—and continue to operate under a "Lower Standard of Proof" via civil settlements—they have an unassailable advantage.

The use of the court system as a gatekeeper ensures that only the "Incumbents" survive. By the time a digital asset company survives the selective prosecution gauntlet, the legacy cartel has already "copied" the technology into a permissioned, centralized "Black Box" version. This is the ultimate "Gimmie" maneuver: using the public's tax dollars to sue the public's innovators so that the public's banks can keep their 0% reserve fraud going for one more decade.

Restoring Equal Protection

Selective prosecution is Repugnant to the Constitution because it violates the Equal Protection Clause. In the digital republic, we demand a return to a "Fair Playing Field." The government's job is to promote American companies and protect the "Active Citizen," not to serve as an enforcer for a banking cartel that has already failed its forensic audit. To neutralize the bureaucratic hammer, we must insist on a "Rule of Math" where the law applies equally to the

$34 trillion central bank and the startup in a Pennsylvania garage.[62]

Using Civil law to get the lower standard of proof.

In a functional republic, the distinction between civil and criminal law is a sacred boundary. Civil law is intended to resolve private disputes and provide restitution for damages (reparative). Criminal law is the exercise of the state's coercive power to punish and deter (punitive). However, in the "Regulation by Enforcement" era, agencies now use civil litigation to seek "disgorgement" and "civil penalties" that often exceed the total revenue of the target company.

When an agency seeks a penalty that is purely punitive—not intended to compensate a specific victim but to "punish" an innovator for failing to follow an ambiguous regulation—the matter is functionally criminal. Under the "Scalia-Kennedy" logic in cases like *Austin v. United States* (1993), any civil sanction that cannot be solely characterized as remedial is a "punishment." By applying a "Preponderance of the

[62] Cooper's Logic Check → The banksters say they are "holding the industry to a high standard." Logic check: If the standard is so high, why are they the ones always paying billions in fraud fines? They are not "holding a standard"; they are holding the door shut. They want to use the SEC and the DOJ as their personal "Clean-up Crew" to remove any innovator who tries to build a better bridge. In digital realism, the ledger does not care about your lobbyist or your "friends in high places." It only cares if the math is right. It is time we held the government to the same standard of transparency as the code they are trying to ban.

Evidence" standard (51% certainty) to matters that are punitive in nature, the government commits Constitutional Fraud, effectively lowering the bar from the "Beyond a Reasonable Doubt" standard (99% certainty) required by the 6th Amendment.

The Theft of the Sixth: Deprivation of the Jury and Confrontation

The most egregious result of this "Civil Shortcut" is the systematic theft of the Sixth Amendment Right to a Jury Trial. In criminal court, a citizen has the right to be judged by a jury of their peers. In the "Hollow Man" civil system, agencies often push cases toward Administrative Law Judges (ALJs)—employees of the very agency bringing the charges. Even in Federal District Court, by labeling the matter "civil," the government restricts the defendant's ability to cross-examine witnesses with the same rigor and limits the protections against self-incrimination found in the Fifth Amendment.

This practice was dealt a severe blow in the 2024–2025 judicial cycle (notably *SEC v. Jarkesy*), where the court signaled that the SEC's use of internal judges for punitive fines violated the 7th Amendment right to a jury. However, the executive branch continues to double down on "Civil-Criminal Hybridization." They use the lower discovery standards of civil court to perform "fishing expeditions" that would be prohibited under the Fourth Amendment's protection against unreasonable searches and seizures if the matter were filed as criminal.

The Charter at Risk: Executive Treason Against the Citizen

The charter of any executive office is predicated on the "Oath of Office"—a sworn commitment to protect and defend the Constitution. When an agency head or an executive office intentionally utilizes civil courts to evade criminal standards of proof, they are engaging in Ultra Vires actions—acting beyond their legal power. This is a betrayal of the agency's charter. If an office exists to "protect the people" but spends its resources engineering ways to strip those people of their Due Process rights, that office has lost its legal and moral authority to exist.

We must argue that any agency engaging in this "Standard-Lowering" maneuver should have its charter called into question by Congress. Under the Major Questions Doctrine, an agency cannot simply decide to re-engineer the judicial process to make it easier to "win." The government should be the ultimate model of fair play. Instead, by favoring the lower standard of proof to target American innovators while letting the "Legacy Cartel" settle their crimes with "Neither Admit Nor Deny" civil fines, the executive branch is committing Procedural Treason.

The "Common Enterprise" of Judicial Erosion

This erosion is part of a broader "Common Enterprise" to protect the 0% reserve banking system from the transparency of the digital republic. The banksters prefer civil law because it allows them to treat "Fines as a Cost of Doing Business." The innovators, however, are hit with the same civil tools to achieve "Company-Killing" outcomes. This selective application of the "Lower Standard" ensures that the established "Wastrels" are never truly threatened, while the "Objectivists" are liquidated without the benefit of a criminal defense.

Restoring the Standard of Proof

In the digital republic, we recognize that the law is a "Constant Ledger" that cannot be manipulated for convenience. If the government wishes to punish a citizen, it must meet the highest burden of proof in the land. The use of civil law for criminal-grade penalties is Repugnant to the Constitution and must be dismissed. We must demand that the "Bureaucratic Hammer" be subjected to the "Rule of Math"—where the math of the evidence must be absolute before the energy of the citizen is taken away.[63]

---

[63] Cooper's Logic Check → The banksters and their "Wastrel" lawyers say that civil courts are "more efficient for complex financial matters." Logic check: "Efficiency" is just their code word for "Getting a conviction without the evidence." They want a system where they can "Preponderate" you out of existence. If I take your car, it is a crime. If the government takes your company and your bank account because they *think* you might have broken a rule they haven't written yet, they call it "Civil Enforcement." In digital realism, we call it Theft by Bureaucracy. It is time to put the "Criminal" back in criminal law and tell the SEC to follow the 6th Amendment or go home.

The Cost of Compliance: Barriers to Entry for Innovative Capital

The "Compliance Tax" in the modern financial landscape has transitioned from a necessary regulatory safeguard into a weaponized barrier to entry designed to protect the legacy banking cartel. For the innovative capitalist, the cost of entering the market is no longer measured solely in research, development, or talent acquisition, but in the millions of dollars required to navigate a labyrinth of "Strategic Ambiguity." When it costs $5 million to $10 million in legal fees just to receive a non-binding opinion on whether a digital asset project is "legal," the administrative state has effectively socialized innovation and privatized the "on-ramps." This disproportionate burden ensures that only the "Wastrel" institutions—those with deep-seated lobbying ties and "bought and paid for" legal departments—can afford to survive the regulatory gauntlet. This is market suppression disguised as "consumer protection," where the high cost of compliance acts as a de facto ban on any capital that is not already part of the established "Hollow Man" hierarchy.

By raising the compliance floor to an unreachable height, the government is committing "Economic Treason" against its own productive class. In the digital republic, an innovator in a Pennsylvania garage should have the same access to the market as a multinational bank subsidiary. However, the current system enforces a "Pay-to-Play" model where the "Compliance Entry Fee" is specifically calibrated to liquidate new competition. This creates a dangerous stagnation where the "Active Citizen" is discouraged from building the "Constant Ledger" because the bureaucratic hammer will fall long before the first block is even mined. This is not just an expense; it is a systematic extraction of energy from the "Objectivist" tradition of production to fund the "Subjectivist" tradition of bureaucratic bloat. When the cost of proving you are following the law exceeds the cost of building the product, the law is no longer a guide—it is a parasite.

Furthermore, this compliance barrier creates a "brain drain" and "capital flight" that undermines the United States' standing in the global trade wars. Capital is a high-velocity asset; it will naturally flow toward jurisdictions that offer "Clear Notice" and low-friction entry. By weaponizing the SEC and other agencies to maintain high compliance entries, the legacy cartel is forcing American innovation to flee to more "Species-friendly" environments. This selective suppression ensures that the "Hollow Man" banks can maintain their 0% reserve fraud without fear of a more efficient, transparent competitor rising from the domestic soil. To restore the republic, we must dismantle these artificial barriers and return to a system where the "Rule of Math" provides the security, making the multi-million dollar "Permission Slip" from an unqualified gatekeeper obsolete.[64]

Due Process and the Right to Clear Notice in Financial Innovation

The Supreme Court has long held that a statute is "void for vagueness" if it fails to provide a person of ordinary intelligence "fair notice" of what is prohibited. In the realm of financial innovation, the legacy cartel has inverted this doctrine. By refusing to provide a "Safe Harbor" or a clear definition of what constitutes a "digital security" versus a "utility token," the government has created a "Trap for the Innocent." When the law is so blurry that even a Ph.D. or a J.D. cannot determine the legality of a protocol without a multi-million dollar legal opinion, the law has ceased to be a guide and has become a predatory tool.

Due process requires that the "Rules of the Road" be established *Ex-Ante* (before the fact). "Regulation by Enforcement" is a terminal violation of this principle because it attempts to set the rules *Ex-Post* (after the fact) through punitive litigation. This "Subjectivist"

---

64 Cooper's Logic Check → The "experts" love to talk about "guardrails" to keep the industry safe. Logic check: If the "guardrail" is a ten-foot-thick concrete wall with a gold-plated toll booth, it is not there to keep you on the road—it is there to keep you off of it. They want a "Compliant" industry, which is just their code word for an "Expensive" industry that they can control. In digital realism, the "Compliance" is built into the code. If the ledger is transparent and the math is solvent, you don't need a ten-million-dollar lawyer to tell you it is "safe." It is time to stop paying the gatekeepers for the privilege of being efficient.

approach allows the government to pick winners and losers based on who has the largest lobby, rather than who is following the law. In the digital republic, we must insist that if the state cannot provide a clear, mathematical definition of a violation, it lacks the jurisdictional authority to prosecute.

The "Fair Notice" Defense as a Structural Necessity

The "Fair Notice" defense is not just a legal loophole; it is a structural necessity for a functioning economy. Innovation requires the deployment of capital, and capital requires Certainty. When the administrative state intentionally maintains a "Jurisdictional Fog," it is committing a slow-motion theft of the nation's productive energy. Innovators are forced to "guess" at the law, and when they guess wrong—according to the shifting whims of an agency head—their property and labor are seized without a fair warning.

This lack of clear notice is particularly egregious when the government uses the civil courts to seek criminal-grade penalties, as we audited in Section 6.5. By stripping away the "Beyond a Reasonable Doubt" standard while simultaneously keeping the "Notice" vague, the executive branch is performing a "Due Process Bypass." To restore the republic, we must demand a Right to Clear Notice Act, which would mandate that no enforcement action can be taken against a digital asset project unless the agency has first published clear, objective criteria that the project has definitively violated.

The Tenth Amendment and the Sovereignty of Local Notice

Where the Federal government fails to provide clear notice, the Tenth Amendment allows the States to step into the vacuum. A State has the sovereign right to provide its citizens with a "Safe Harbor" by codifying the definitions of digital assets within its own borders. By providing "Clear Notice" at the state level, the government fulfills its primary duty: protecting the citizen from arbitrary power. This creates a "Competitive Clarity" where capital flows to the jurisdictions that respect the Rule of Math and the Rule of Law.

The "Right to Clear Notice" is the only thing standing between a productive republic and a "Bureaucratic Dictatorship." If we allow the "Wastrels" to continue using ambiguity as a weapon, we are essentially conceding that the government owns our labor and can "re-classify" it as illegal at any time. In the digital realism of 2026, we recognize that the "Ledger of the Law" must be as immutable and transparent as the "Ledger of the Token."

The Restoration of Fair Play

Ultimately, the "Right to Clear Notice" is about the restoration of fair play in the American economy. The government's job is to act as a neutral referee, not as a player for the "Legacy Team." By demanding due process, we are re-attaching the "Legal Tether" to the Constitution and ensuring that the "Active Citizen" can build the future without fear of a "subjective" ambush.

The era of the "Bureaucratic Hammer" must end; the era of Crystalline Certainty must begin.[65]

Conclusion: Neutralizing the Bureaucratic Hammer

Neutralizing the bureaucratic hammer requires a fundamental shift from a "Permissioned" economy to a "Verifiable" one. For too long, the administrative state has used the smoke and mirrors of strategic ambiguity to protect the legacy banking cartel from the creative destruction of the digital republic. By weaponizing archaic standards like the 1946 Howey Test and bypassing constitutional due process through civil-criminal hybridization, these "unqualified" gatekeepers have attempted to slow the velocity of value to a pace they can tax and control. However, as we have forensically documented, these maneuvers are repugnant to the Constitution and represent a terminal overreach that threatens the very "Active Citizenship" upon which the nation was built.

The restoration of the American innovator's sovereignty depends on the abolition of "Regulation

---

[65] Cooper's Logic Check → The banksters love to say that "innovation moves too fast for the law." Logic check: Innovation moves at the speed of thought; the law moves at the speed of a "Wastrel" trying to figure out how to tax it. They don't have a "Clarity" problem; they have a "Control" problem. They want to keep the rules vague so they can keep the "Exit" door locked. In digital realism, the "Notice" is in the code—it is open, it is public, and it is clear. It is time the government stopped hiding behind "ambiguity" and started following the Due Process they swore to protect.

by Enforcement." We must replace the subjective "whims of men" with the objective "Rule of Math," ensuring that the law serves as a crystalline shield rather than a predatory club. This means demanding clear notice, jurisdictional clarity under the Comptroller of the Currency, and the end of de facto bans orchestrated through back-room administrative pressure. When the rules are as transparent and immutable as the blockchain protocols they seek to govern, the "Wastrels" lose their ability to pick winners and losers based on the depth of a lobbyist's pocket.

To truly neutralize the hammer, the republic must embrace the Tenth Amendment's multi-currency framework, allowing the States to act as laboratories of clarity. By establishing state-level safe harbors and recognizing RWA-backed digital assets as legitimate tender, we create a competitive marketplace of law that forces Federal agencies to either provide certainty or lose relevance. The "Hollow Man" of the administrative state relies on a monopoly of information and a monopoly of force; digital realism breaks both by providing the citizen with the tools to audit the system in real-time and opt-out of the "managed decline" of the 0% reserve monoculture.

Ultimately, the goal of this forensic audit is to ensure that the United States remains the lodestone of global innovation. We cannot win the trade wars of 2026 by fighting with the "citrus grove" tools of 1946. By reclaiming our right to due process and the sovereignty of the ledger, we are re-attaching the

"Legal Tether" to the original intent of the Founders. The bureaucratic hammer only has power when the people are kept in the fog of ambiguity. As we move into the next phase of this transformation, we turn the lights on, realizing that the math of the future has no need for the "permission slips" of the past.[66]

---

[66] Cooper's Logic Check→ The banksters say the "Hammer" is there to keep the house from falling down. Logic check: They are not the carpenters; they are the ones who sold you the "0% reserve" lumber and then sued you for noticed the rot. They want you to think regulation is a "safety net," but it is actually a "fishing net" designed to catch anyone swimming toward the exit. In digital realism, the "safety" is not in a bureaucrat's stamp—it is in the **Auditability of the Code**. We don't need a hammer to build a better bridge; we just need the truth of the math.

Chapter 7: The Jurisprudence of Digital Assets. Defining the legal "personhood" of autonomous protocols.

“The principle of equity first came into evidence in Roman Jurisprudence and was derived by analogy from the physical meaning of the word.”

Herbert Reed[67]

By invoking Herbert Reed’s observation on the physical origins of equity, we are grounding the digital republic in the Roman tradition of fairness—a tradition that has been systematically hollowed out by the "Wastrels" of the administrative state. If the law is to survive the transition to digital realism, it must evolve a new legal taxonomy that recognizes the "Code Veil" as a distinct entity, separate from the centralized "Hollow Man" corporate structures of the 20th century.

The central crisis of modern jurisprudence is the attempt to govern autonomous, decentralized protocols using the language of 1940s citrus groves. As we move from "Corporate Personhood" to "Protocol Personhood," the legal system must grapple with a ghost in the machine: an entity that has no board of directors, no physical headquarters, and no "Gimmie" incentive, yet facilitates trillions in value transfer. This chapter performs a forensic autopsy on

---

[67] Staff (2026). “Jurisprudence Quotes.” Brainy Quote at https://www.brainyquote.com/search_results?x=0&y=0&q=Jurisprudence.

the case law that has attempted—and largely failed—to contain the velocity of the digital species within the rigid jars of legacy definitions.

We begin with the realization that the "Chevron Deference" era is dead, and with it, the unearned authority of "unqualified" gatekeepers to interpret the law to suit their own jurisdictional land grabs. From the programmatic sales distinction in *Ripple* to the application of the Major Questions Doctrine, the judiciary is finally being forced to re-read the "Lodestone" of the Constitution. The era where a bureaucrat could simply "decree" a protocol into a security is reaching its terminal velocity, replaced by a judicial requirement for crystalline clarity and legislative mandate.

Furthermore, we must address the "Liability of the DAO" and the right to "Master Account Access," which represent the front lines of the trade wars of 2026. If the Federal Reserve can arbitrarily deny access to the "Rails" to a compliant bank like Custodia, then the "Equal Protection" of the law is a myth. Jurisprudence in the digital age is not about creating "new" rights, but about ensuring that the original rights of the "Active Citizen"—to contract, to hold property, and to settle debts—are not extinguished by a "Subjective" administrative hammer.

Ultimately, Chapter 7 provides the "Legal Map" for the new assets. We are defining the boundaries of a system where "Equity" is not a feeling, but a mathematical output of a smart contract. By mapping the shift from *Howey* to *Uniswap*, we are documenting the birth of a new legal species: the Autonomous Entity. We are moving toward a world where the "Supreme Law" acts as a shield for the code, ensuring that the "Objectivist" tradition of production remains the foundation of our more perfect, digital union.[68]

SEC v. W.J. Howey Co. (1946): The Foundation of the Investment Contract

In *SEC v. W.J. Howey Co.* (1946), the Supreme Court was tasked with determining whether a real estate transaction involving Florida citrus groves constituted an "investment contract." The W.J. Howey Company sold plots of land to investors, who then entered into a service contract with Howey-in-the-Hills Service, Inc., to cultivate, harvest, and market the crops. The investors were largely non-residents who lacked the expertise or equipment to manage the groves themselves, relying entirely on the company's efforts for a return on their capital.

---

[68] Cooper's Logic Notes→ The banksters love to hide behind "Legal Personhood" when they commit fraud, but they want to deny it to the protocols that would stop their fraud. Logic check: If a corporation—which is just paper and a filing fee—can be a "person" for the sake of lobbying, then a smart contract—which is math and logic—should at least be a "person" for the sake of the law. They hate "Protocol Personhood" because you can't put an algorithm in a "re-education" camp or pressure it to open fake accounts. In digital realism, the code is the ultimate "Honest Actor." It is time the law stopped treating math like a crime and started treating it like the **Truth**.

The Court established what is now known as the Howey Test, a four-pronged standard to identify an investment contract: (1) an investment of money, (2) in a common enterprise, (3) with a reasonable expectation of profits, (4) to be derived solely from the efforts of others. The rule of law emphasizes substance over form, aiming to capture schemes where individuals are led to invest money in a common enterprise with the expectation that they will earn a profit through the management and control of others. This precedent, reinforced by cases like *SEC v. Edwards* (2004), was intended to protect the "innocent" from centralized fraudulent schemes.

Applying this 1946 standard to the digital realism of 2026 reveals a terminal category error. In a decentralized protocol, there is no "common enterprise" in the legacy sense because there is no centralized "Hollow Man" or corporate board directing the entity's value. When an active citizen acquires a utility token, they are purchasing a key to an autonomous machine, not a share in a citrus grove. The "efforts of others" prong fails completely in the context of open-source, decentralized code where the network's value is derived from the math of the protocol and the collective participation of the ledger, rather than the managerial genius of a promoter.

Furthermore, most cryptocurrencies function as a Currency Medium or a commodity, as seen in the logic of *CFTC v. My Big Coin Pay, Inc.* (2018). Forcing a token into the *Howey* framework ignores its inherent utility—its "Thing-ness"—and focuses instead on the subjective intent of the purchaser. If an individual buys a tool hoping its value increases, the tool does not magically become a security. By attempting to stretch *Howey* to encompass decentralized math, the SEC is performing a jurisdictional hijack that ignores the fundamental shift from human-intermediated trust to algorithmic certainty.

Ultimately, *Howey* is a forensic relic that is ill-equipped to map the jurisprudence of autonomous protocols. To use a case about orange groves to regulate the global rails of value is to admit that the administrative state has no objective standard for the 21st century. We must reject *Howey* as the primary standard for digital assets and move toward a taxonomy that recognizes the "Code Veil" as distinct from the investment contracts of the past. As the judiciary moves toward the "Major Questions Doctrine" seen in *West Virginia v. EPA*, it is clear that such a massive expansion of regulatory power requires a crystalline mandate from the People, not a creative re-interpretation of an 80-year-old citrus case.[69]

---

[69] Cooper's Logic Check → The banksters love *Howey* because it is a "Subjectivity Trap." They want to look into your brain and decide that if you *hoped* to make a profit, they get to regulate your labor. Logic check: If I buy a classic car hoping it goes up in value, does the SEC get to tell me how to drive it? No. They are trying to use a 1946 orange to stop a 2026 superconducting engine. In digital realism, we don't care about your

Hocking v. Dubois (1989): Vertical vs. Horizontal Commonality in Assets

In *Hocking v. Dubois* (1989), the Ninth Circuit examined whether the resale of a condominium unit in Hawaii, coupled with the buyer's participation in a rental pool arrangement, constituted an investment contract. Gerald Hocking purchased the unit from a previous owner, not the developer, and entered into a rental management agreement with a third party. The central legal dispute focused on the "common enterprise" prong of the *Howey* test, specifically how to define the relationship between the investor and the promoters or other investors.

The Court utilized this case to clarify the distinctions between **Horizontal Commonality** and **Vertical Commonality**. Horizontal commonality requires the pooling of investor funds where the fortunes of each investor are tied to the success of the overall venture. In contrast, Vertical commonality focuses on the relationship between the investor and the promoter, where the investor's success is dependent on the promoter's expertise. The *Hocking* court ultimately found that the rental pool arrangement could satisfy these requirements, even in the secondary market, if the elements of a "package deal" were present.

"expectations"; we care about the **Function of the Code**. If it is decentralized, the "efforts of others" prong is a ghost. It is time to bury the citrus grove and let the Comptroller handle the currency.

When applying these concepts to digital assets, the *Hocking* precedent highlights the structural mismatch between legacy assets and decentralized protocols. In a truly decentralized network, there is no "vertical" relationship because there is no central promoter whose expertise dictates the asset's value. Similarly, "horizontal" commonality is challenged because, while users may participate in the same network, their digital assets are often individual property used for distinct utility purposes—such as paying for gas fees or executing smart contracts—rather than being pooled into a singular profit-seeking venture managed by a third party.

The logic of *Hocking* underscores why many digital assets fail the "common enterprise" test. Unlike the Hawaiian condo rental pool where a central manager made all the decisions, a decentralized protocol operates through autonomous code and distributed consensus. Cases like *Revak v. SEC Realty Corp.* (1994) further support this by requiring a stricter showing of horizontal commonality. In the digital realism of 2026, the lack of a centralized manager or a mandatory pooling of profits means that most utility tokens do not fit the "common enterprise" mold, as the fortunes of the token holders are not tied to a promoter, but to the objective utility of the network itself.

Ultimately, *Hocking v. Dubois* serves as a reminder that the "common enterprise" prong requires more than just a shared interest in an asset's price. It requires a specific legal and functional link between the parties that simply does not exist in the decentralized "Code Veil" of an autonomous protocol. While the *Hocking* court was willing to see a "package deal" in a real estate context, the fragmented and permissionless nature of digital assets makes such a finding a bridge too far. As we move away from the "Hollow Man" of centralized management, the jurisprudence must recognize that shared participation in a global ledger is not a common enterprise, but a common standard for the exchange of value.[70]

SEC v. Shavers (2013): Defining Bitcoin as Money and Securities

In *SEC v. Shavers* (2013), the Eastern District of Texas addressed an enforcement action against Trendon Shavers and his company, Bitcoin Savings and Trust. Shavers had solicited Bitcoin from investors, promising high interest rates in a scheme that was forensically identified as a classic Ponzi structure. The central jurisdictional question was whether the court had authority over the matter, which

---

[70] Cooper's Logic Check → The "Wastrels" love the *Hocking* logic because it lets them squint at a secondary market sale and call it a "Security." Logic check: If I buy a condo to live in, it is a house. If I let a manager rent it out, it is a business. In digital realism, the "manager" is a line of code that does not take a vacation or a bribe. If there's no "Promoter" to sue, there's no "Vertical Commonality." They want to find a "Common Enterprise" in the cloud, but all they are finding is a weather pattern. You can't regulate the rain, and you shouldn't regulate the math.

hinged on whether Bitcoin met the definition of "money" or a "security" under Federal law.

The Court ruled that Bitcoin is indeed a form of money or currency, noting that it can be used to purchase goods or services and to pay for individual living expenses. Because Bitcoin met this definition, the court concluded that the "investment of money" prong of the *Howey* test was satisfied, thus bringing the scheme under the jurisdiction of the SEC as an investment contract. This case, alongside *United States v. Faiella* (2014), helped establish the precedent that digital assets operate within the functional definition of currency in the eyes of the law.

From the perspective of digital realism, however, *Shavers* reveals the fundamental "Subjectivity Trap" of unbacked digital assets. While the court correctly identified Bitcoin as a medium of exchange, it failed to recognize that Bitcoin lacks the "Objectivist" underlay required for true Constitutional tender. Because Bitcoin is not backed by gold, silver, or any Real-World Asset (RWA), it possesses no inherent, objective value that the government can "regulate" under Article I, Section 8. It exists entirely on the plane of Psychological Solvency, where its price is determined by the collective "Whims of Men" rather than the crystalline certainty of a physical reserve.

This makes Bitcoin effectively the world's first and most successful Memecoin. Unlike the KIROS token, which is anchored to a fractal reserve of assets, Bitcoin's value is purely subjective. While it has a high market price, it is a "Hollow Man" in the context of the Section 10 mandate because it is not a "Thing" with a production-based floor. The government cannot regulate the "Value" of a subjective opinion; they can only regulate the conduct of those who trade in it. Therefore, while Bitcoin is a currency medium, it cannot be a "Legal Tender" of the Republic because it fails the forensic test of objective stability.

Ultimately, *SEC v. Shavers* serves as a bridge between the old world of fiat and the new world of the ledger, but it does so by ignoring the "Legal Tether" required for sound money. By labeling it a security in the context of a fraud, the court inadvertently highlighted the danger of unbacked assets: they are susceptible to "Gimmie" schemes because their value has no floor. In a digital republic, we must distinguish between "Subjective Memecoins" like Bitcoin and "Objective Species" like RWA-backed tokens. Supporting cases like *Wisconsin v. EPA* remind us that the government cannot expand its regulatory reach into the "subjective" without a clear mandate, further emphasizing that Bitcoin remains a laboratory of private contract rather than a pillar of public tender.[71]

---

[71] Cooper's Logic Check → The banksters love Bitcoin because it is the only thing That is more "Subjective" than their own fiat. Logic check: If you have a currency backed by nothing, and you compare it to a currency backed by "faith," you are just comparing two different flavors of clouds. Bitcoin is a brilliant piece of math, but as a "Tender," it is a memecoin with a fancy tie. In digital realism, we want the "Thing." If I can't touch the

SEC v. Ripple Labs (2023): The Programmatic Sales Distinction

In *SEC v. Ripple Labs* (2023), the Southern District of New York addressed whether the sale of XRP, the native token of the Ripple network, constituted the unregistered offer and sale of securities. The SEC alleged that Ripple had raised billions of dollars through the sale of XRP to fund its operations. Judge Analisa Torres issued a landmark summary judgment that bifurcated the nature of the sales based on the identity of the purchaser and the context of the transaction.

The court established the Programmatic Sales Distinction, ruling that while "Institutional Sales" (direct sales to hedge funds and institutional buyers) were securities because they involved an expectation of profit from Ripple's efforts, "Programmatic Sales" on public exchanges were not. The rule of law here rests on the idea that retail buyers purchasing from an exchange did not know they were buying from Ripple specifically, and therefore could not have a "reasonable expectation of profits" derived from Ripple's efforts. This distinction provided a temporary shield for the retail digital asset market, utilizing the logic of *United Housing Foundation, Inc. v. Forman* (1975) to limit the reach of the *Howey* test.

RWA behind it, then the value is just a feeling. Feelings are great for art; they are terrible for an 8,000-square-foot steel-framed house.

From the perspective of digital realism, however, the *Ripple* decision reveals a deep forensic problem regarding the definition of a "blockchain." While the court focused on the sales, a technical audit of the XRP Ledger (XRPL) shows that it is a Centralized Ledger **Coin** rather than a true cryptocurrency. Because the XRPL has historically lost 32,000 blocks of its early history and operates on a permissioned validator model with no mining incentive or Proof-of-Work/Stake competition, it fails the "Decentralization" test. It is not a sovereign Layer 1 protocol; it is a corporate-controlled database masquerading as a blockchain.

Consequently, XRP should not be afforded the protections typically found in cryptocurrency legislation designed for decentralized, permissionless protocols. As a centralized "Hollow Man" asset, it lacks the cryptographic immutability and anti-fragility that define a true digital species. Furthermore, the advertising methodologies used to promote XRP to retail investors—often framing it as the "standard" for banking rails despite its centralized nature—warrant intense regulatory scrutiny. Unlike the "Objectivist" clarity of a truly decentralized ledger, the XRPL relies on the "Subjective" marketing of a central entity, making it functionally distinct from the digital assets Part II of this book seeks to defend.

Ultimately, *SEC v. Ripple Labs* provides a useful judicial tool through its programmatic sales logic, but the asset at the center of the case is a forensic anomaly. We must distinguish between the "Programmatic" protection of the law and the "Centralized" reality of the protocol. Cases like *SEC v. LBRY, Inc.* (2022) remind us that the lack of decentralization often leads to the very "Common Enterprise" that digital realism seeks to avoid. For the digital republic to thrive, we must ensure that our legal protections are reserved for actual decentralized blockchains, not centralized corporate ledgers that have "hollowed out" their own history.[72]

Loper Bright Enterprises v. Raimondo (2024): The Death of Chevron and Regulatory Deference

In *Loper Bright Enterprises v. Raimondo* (2024), the Supreme Court addressed a challenge by Atlantic herring fishermen against a federal regulation that required them to pay the salaries of government monitors stationed on their vessels. The core legal question was not just about fishing, but about the validity of the "Chevron Deference"—a forty-year-old doctrine from *Chevron U.S.A., Inc. v. Natural Resources Defense Council, Inc.* (1984) that required

---

[72] Cooper's Logic Check → The banksters love Ripple because it is a "Bank-Friendly" version of the future—which is just another way of saying they still hold the keys. Logic check: If you lose 32,000 blocks of your "ledger," you don't have a blockchain; you have a paper shredder with a Wi-Fi connection. A real blockchain is a "Constant Ledger" that does not have "missing pieces" when it suits the issuer. They want to use the *Ripple* case as a shield, but the tech behind it is a sieve. In digital realism, we don't protect centralized corporate coins; we protect the Sovereignty of the Math.

courts to defer to a federal agency's "reasonable" interpretation of an ambiguous statute.

The Court's ruling effectively overturned *Chevron*, declaring that the Administrative Procedure Act (APA) requires courts to exercise their independent judgment in deciding whether an agency has acted within its statutory authority. The rule of law now dictates that judges, not "unqualified" bureaucratic gatekeepers, are the final arbiters of what a law means. This decision, bolstered by the logic in *Relentless, Inc. v. Department of Commerce*, signaled the end of the era where agencies could unilaterally expand their own jurisdiction through "Strategic Ambiguity."

For digital assets, the death of Chevron is a forensic earthquake that destabilizes the "Bureaucratic Hammer." For years, agencies like the SEC have relied on the ambiguity of the *Howey* test to "interpret" their way into regulating decentralized protocols, assuming that courts would simply defer to their supposed expertise. *Loper Bright* removes this "Subjectivist" shield, allowing innovators to challenge the SEC's jurisdictional land grabs on a level playing field where the "Rule of Math" and the actual text of the law—not agency whim—determine the outcome.

This shift means that the "You are what we say you are" paradigm of the administrative state is legally bankrupt. If a statute does not explicitly grant an agency power over a specific "Digital Species," the court is no longer obligated to believe the agency's self-serving definition. Supporting cases like *FDA v. Brown & Williamson Tobacco Corp.* (2000) remind us that agencies cannot "discover" transformative powers in old statutes; with *Chevron* dead, the digital republic finally has a judicial path to neutralize the "Wastrel" regulators who have used deference to protect the legacy banking cartel.

Ultimately, *Loper Bright Enterprises v. Raimondo* represents the restoration of the "Lodestone" of the Constitution. It re-establishes the Judiciary as a check on the Executive's "Gimmie" tendencies to over-regulate. In the trade wars of 2026, this decision provides the "Active Citizen" with the legal armor necessary to defend innovation from agencies that have historically favored "Hollow" legacy systems over transparent, decentralized protocols. The "Death of Chevron" is the birth of a new era of Regulatory Accountability, where the burden of proof is back on the government, where it belongs.[73]

---

[73] Cooper's Logic Check → The banksters are mourning *Chevron* because it was the "Invisibility Cloak" for their pet regulators. Logic check: If the law is so "ambiguous" that only a bureaucrat can understand it, then it is not a law—it is a secret handshake. They want "Deference" because they can't win on the "Math." Now that the courts have to actually *read* the statutes again, the SEC is finding out that "because we said so" is not a legal argument. In digital realism, we don't defer to "experts" who can't tell a smart contract from a citrus grove.

Coinbase, Inc. v. SEC: Challenging the Boundaries of Exchange Definition

In *Coinbase, Inc. v. SEC*, the legal battle centered on whether a digital asset exchange must register as a national securities exchange, broker, and clearing agency under the Securities Exchange Act of 1934. The SEC filed suit in June 2023, alleging that Coinbase facilitated the trading of "crypto asset securities" without proper registration. Coinbase responded with a motion for judgment on the pleadings, arguing that the tokens traded on its secondary market platform did not meet the definition of "investment contracts" because they lacked a formal, ongoing contractual obligation between the issuer and the purchaser.

The District Court initially allowed much of the case to proceed, reasoning that the SEC had plausibly alleged that certain transactions on Coinbase's platform could be investment contracts under the *Howey* test. However, the litigation took a significant turn in early 2025 and 2026 as the regulatory tide shifted. Following a series of appellate maneuvers—including a Third Circuit remand regarding the SEC's denial of Coinbase's rulemaking petition—the SEC ultimately moved toward a global resolution of several major crypto enforcement actions. By March 2026, the agency began dismissing cases with prejudice, signaling a move away from the "Regulation by Enforcement" era that characterized the previous administration.

From a forensic standpoint, *Coinbase v. SEC* highlights the absurdity of attempting to shoehorn a high-velocity digital marketplace into a centralized 1930s "Exchange" definition. Coinbase argued that when a token is purchased on its platform, it is an asset sale akin to a parcel of land or a collectible, not a participation in a common enterprise. This distinction is critical for digital realism; a true exchange matches buyers and sellers of "Things," whereas a securities exchange manages "Claims." By treating utility tokens as securities, the SEC was attempting to regulate the "Marketplace" itself as if it were a corporate issuer, ignoring the programmatic, autonomous nature of the transactions.

The "Coinbase Defense" relied heavily on the **Major Questions Doctrine**, asserting that the SEC could not unilaterally expand its jurisdiction to cover the entire digital asset economy without explicit Congressional authorization. The eventual retreat by the SEC in 2026 validates this "Objectivist" push for clarity. As we saw in the *Jarkesy* and *Loper Bright* decisions, the era of administrative agencies "discovering" new powers in old statutes is over. For Coinbase, the victory was not just about avoiding fines, but about forcing the government to acknowledge that the "Rules of the Road" for digital assets must be written by the legislature, not decreed by an enforcement division.

Ultimately, *Coinbase, Inc. v. SEC* represents the high-water mark of regulatory overreach and the subsequent judicial correction. It proves that the "Bureaucratic Hammer" can be neutralized when the "Active Citizen" and their corporate proxies stand on the crystalline logic of the Constitution. Supporting cases like *Ripple* and *Grayscale* provided the legal ammunition to show that the SEC's positions were "arbitrary and capricious." In the digital republic of 2026, Coinbase stands as a "Digital Gateway" that successfully defended the boundary between a "Security" and a "Sovereign Asset," ensuring that the trade wars of the future are fought on a fair and transparent playing field.[74]

Uniswap Labs vs. SEC: The Battle over Decentralized Protocol Liability

In the matter of *Uniswap Labs vs. SEC*, the conflict centered on the issuance of a Wells Notice by the SEC in April 2024, signaling an intent to recommend an enforcement action against the developer of the world's largest decentralized exchange (DEX). The SEC's theory posited that Uniswap Labs was operating as an unregistered securities exchange and broker-dealer, despite the fact that the Uniswap protocol itself is a suite of autonomous, immutable

---

[74] Cooper's Logic Check → The banksters loved the Coinbase lawsuit because it threatened to turn every digital wallet into a "Registered Broker-Dealer" nightmare. Logic check: If I sell you a digital sword for a game, I'm a merchant, not a "Clearing Agency." They tried to use the law to make the tech too expensive to use. But the courts finally noticed that the "Hollow Man" at the SEC didn't have a permit to build that particular wall. In digital realism, the "Exchange" is just the "Meeting Place" for the math. We don't need a 1934 registration to tell us that 1+1=2.

smart contracts. The agency sought to hold the developers liable for the secondary market trading of third-party tokens that the SEC "subjectively" classified as securities.

Uniswap Labs' defense rested on the technical reality of De-intermediation. They argued that the protocol is essentially open-source software—a "Thing" that exists independently of the company—and that the developer cannot be held liable for how third parties utilize a permissionless tool. The rule of law at play involves the distinction between a "software provider" and a "financial intermediary." Uniswap maintained that it never takes custody of user funds or exercises the "managerial control" required to meet the definition of a broker or exchange under the 1934 Act, echoing the logic found in *SEC v. Chenery Corp.* (1947) regarding the limits of administrative discretion.

Applying the "Hollow Man" standards of 20th-century regulation to a decentralized protocol like Uniswap is a forensic impossibility. In the *Uniswap* case, there is no "Centralized Counterparty" to serve a subpoena to for the halting of trades; the math executes autonomously on the blockchain. Forcing protocol liability onto software developers is a terminal overreach that threatens the 1st Amendment right to publish code, as established in *Bernstein v. Department of Justice* (1999). If a developer provides a "Standard of Math" for others to use, they are not an exchange; they are a publisher of logic.

This battle represents the front line of Protocol Personhood. The SEC's attempt to punish Uniswap Labs for the behavior of a decentralized ledger is a jurisdictional land grab that ignores the "Code Veil." By 2025 and 2026, as the "Major Questions Doctrine" was increasingly applied, the argument that an agency could unilaterally re-define "exchange" to include autonomous software became untenable. As seen in *Failla v. SEC* (2025), the judiciary began to recognize that "Liability" cannot exist without "Control," and since Uniswap Labs does not control the immutable contracts, the "Bureaucratic Hammer" has no legitimate target.

Ultimately, *Uniswap Labs vs. SEC* serves as the definitive test for decentralized liability in the digital republic. It highlights the desperate attempt of the legacy cartel to "Choke Point" the software that makes their 0% reserve intermediaries obsolete. The eventual dismissal of these aggressive theories in 2026 confirms that the "Supreme Law" acts as a shield for autonomous code. By protecting the right to build and deploy decentralized protocols, the courts have ensured that the "Active Citizen" can engage in commerce through "Pure Math," free from the predatory "Gimmies" of an unqualified gatekeeper.[75]

---

[75] Cooper's Logic Check → The banksters hate Uniswap because it is a bank that does not need them. Logic check: If I write a recipe for bread and someone else uses it to make a sandwich, I'm not a "Restaurant Manager." The SEC wanted to sue the guy who invented the "Recipe" for the "Sandwich" that someone else ate. In digital realism, the code is the "Natural

Custodia Bank v. Federal Reserve: The Right to Master Account Access

In *Custodia Bank v. Federal Reserve*, the central dispute focused on the Federal Reserve's refusal to grant a "Master Account" to a Wyoming-chartered Special Purpose Depository Institution (SPDI). Custodia Bank, designed to operate as an "Objectivist" institution with a 1:1 reserve model for digital assets, sought access to the Federal Reserve's payment rails to settle transactions directly in central bank money. The Federal Reserve Board and the Federal Reserve Bank of Kansas City denied the application, arguing that Custodia's business model presented "significant precautionary risks" to the financial system.

The legal battle turned on the interpretation of the Monetary Control Act of 1980, with Custodia arguing that the statute mandates that Federal Reserve services "shall be available to nonmember depository institutions." The rule of law at stake was whether the Federal Reserve possesses "absolute discretion" to pick and choose which chartered banks can access the national payment system. In early 2024, a District Court ruled in favor of the Fed's discretionary power, but the subsequent appeal and the shifting judicial landscape of 2025-2026 brought the "Right to

---

Law" of the network. You can't arrest the law of gravity because someone fell down, and you shouldn't sue a developer because a smart contract did exactly what it was programmed to do.

Access" back into the forensic spotlight as a core issue of equal protection.

From the perspective of digital realism, the *Custodia* case is a textbook example of "Economic Treason" by the legacy cartel. By denying a 100% reserve bank access to the rails while simultaneously providing "Master Accounts" to foreign banking subsidiaries and high-risk "Wastrel" institutions, the Federal Reserve is actively suppressing innovation to protect the 0% reserve status quo. The Fed's "risk" argument is forensically hollow; a bank that holds 1:1 reserves is mathematically safer than the "Hollow Man" institutions currently audited for systemic fraud in Chapter 4.

The denial of a Master Account acts as a "De Facto Ban" on the "Digital Species," as it forces innovators to rely on "Intermediary" legacy banks who can—and often do—cut off access at the whim of the regulator. Supporting cases like *Fourth Corner Credit Union v. Federal Reserve Bank of Kansas City* (2017) highlight this ongoing struggle for fair access. In the digital republic of 2026, the "Right to Master Account Access" is seen as a fundamental requirement for a competitive multi-currency framework. Without the ability to settle on the primary rails, the "Active Citizen" is permanently disadvantaged against the state-sponsored banking monopoly.

Ultimately, *Custodia Bank v. Federal Reserve* represents the "Choke Point" maneuver in its most transparent form. It exposes the Federal Reserve not as a neutral utility, but as a "Gatekeeper" for the legacy cartel. As the "Major Questions Doctrine" and the "Death of Chevron" continue to strip away the administrative state's "Subjective" discretion, the mandate for "Clear Notice" and "Non-Discriminatory Access" becomes a constitutional necessity. To restore the republic, we must ensure that the "Rails of Value" are open to any institution that meets the objective mathematical standards of solvency, regardless of whether they threaten the "Gimmies" of the old guard.[76]

West Virginia v. EPA (2022): The Major Questions Doctrine in Crypto

In *West Virginia v. EPA* (2022), the Supreme Court addressed whether the Environmental Protection Agency (EPA) possessed the authority to issue sweeping regulations that would shift the nation's energy generation away from coal-fired plants under Section 111(d) of the Clean Air Act. The EPA had attempted to utilize a "generation shifting" approach that would effectively restructure the entire power sector. The Court ruled that such a transformative

---

[76] Cooper's Logic Check → The banksters say that Custodia is "too risky" because it deals with digital assets. Logic check: Custodia wanted to hold 100% of its deposits in cash and high-quality liquid assets. The "safe" banks they like only hold about 0% to 10%. They are not worried about "risk"; they are worried about **Honesty**. If a bank that actually has the money starts competing with banks that don't, the game is over. In digital realism, the "Master Account" shouldn't be a "Members Only" club for the "Wastrels"—it should be a public utility for anyone who can prove their math.

expansion of regulatory power was beyond the agency's statutory mandate, as Congress had not explicitly granted the EPA the authority to oversee the nation's energy mix.

The Court utilized this case to formally codify the Major Questions Doctrine. This rule of law dictates that in "extraordinary cases" where an administrative agency claims the power to make decisions of vast "economic and political significance," it must point to clear and specific congressional authorization. The doctrine serves as a structural check on the administrative state, ensuring that agencies cannot "discover" new, far-reaching powers in old, vague statutes. This precedent, later reinforced in *Loper Bright* (2024), effectively ended the era of judicial deference to "unqualified" bureaucratic interpretations on matters of national importance.

For the digital republic, *West Virginia v. EPA* is the "Constitutional Kill-Switch" for the SEC's attempt to regulate the entire digital asset economy. The agency's claim that it has jurisdiction over nearly all digital tokens under the 1946 *Howey* test is a "major question" of immense economic significance, affecting trillions of dollars in market value and the future of American financial infrastructure. Applying the doctrine, the SEC lacks the "clear congressional authorization" to treat decentralized protocols as securities; as seen in the 2026 **SEC interpretation led by Paul Atkins**, the commission finally acknowledged that it cannot unilaterally "interpret" its way into the digital species without a mandate from the People's representatives.

The logic of this case law prevents the "Hollow Man" of the administrative state from performing a jurisdictional land grab. If the regulation of digital assets is to be the most significant shift in monetary policy since 1913, then the "Rules of the Road" must be written by Congress, not "decreed" by a committee of enforcers. Supporting cases like *Biden v. Nebraska* (2023) further establish that agencies cannot use "modest" statutory language to achieve "transformative" economic results. In the trade wars of 2026, the Major Questions Doctrine acts as a crystalline shield for the "Active Citizen," ensuring that innovation is not strangled by an agency that has wandered far outside its "traditional lane."

Ultimately, *West Virginia v. EPA* represents the triumph of the "Objectivist" legal tradition over the "Subjective" whims of the bureaucracy. It restores the separation of powers by requiring that the most impactful decisions of the republic be made in the light of legislative debate rather than the shadows of administrative rulemaking. In the jurisprudence of digital assets, this means the "Bureaucratic Hammer" is effectively neutralized. By early 2026, as the SEC dismissed its overreaching suits, the Major Questions Doctrine was proven to be the lodestone that guided the republic back to the original intent of the Constitution.[77]

The Liability of the DAO: Identifying the "Responsible Person"

In the developing jurisprudence of digital realism, the Decentralized Autonomous Organization (DAO) represents the most significant challenge to the traditional concept of "Corporate Personhood." A DAO is a functional entity governed by smart contracts, where decisions are made through the collective voting of token holders rather than a centralized board of directors. Historically, the legal system has struggled to categorize these entities, often defaulting to the "General Partnership" model, as seen in the *CFTC v. Ooki DAO* (2023) case. In that instance, the court ruled that a DAO could be served process as an "unincorporated association," effectively making every voting member potentially liable for the protocol's actions.

The "Responsible Person" standard is a forensic tool borrowed from tax and environmental law, intended to identify individuals who have the authority and duty to

[77] Cooper's Logic Check → The banksters loved the idea that a bureaucrat could just "decide" what money is. Logic check: If I give you a permit to build a dog house, you can't use it to rebuild the city's power grid. The EPA tried to use a "Dog House" permit to run the energy sector, and the Supreme Court finally said "No." The SEC tried to do the same thing with the "Citrus Grove" permit of 1946. In digital realism, the "Major Questions" are for the People to decide through their representatives, not for a "Wastrel" in a suit to decide over lunch.

ensure an entity's compliance with the law. In a centralized "Hollow Man" corporation, this is a simple task: the CEO, CFO, or Board are the responsible parties. However, in an autonomous protocol, the "duty" is distributed across a global ledger of "Active Citizens." The rule of law currently stands at a crossroads: either we must accept a new form of "Code Veil" that protects individual participants from the actions of an autonomous machine, or we risk a state of "Collective Liability" that would chill all innovation in the digital republic.

Applying the "Responsible Person" standard to a DAO reveals the terminal absurdity of legacy thinking. If a protocol executes a transaction that a regulator subjectively deems illegal, who is the responsible party? Is it the developer who wrote the open-source code years ago (protected by the 1st Amendment under *Bernstein*), the validators who processed the block (the "Rails"), or the thousands of token holders who may not have even voted on that specific execution? In a truly decentralized system, there is no "Single Point of Failure" and therefore no single "Responsible Person." To force such a label onto a DAO is to ignore the "Objectivist" reality that the software is acting as its own agent.

The "General Partnership" designation used in *Ooki DAO* is a "Subjective" trap that treats participation as a crime. If every user of a protocol is liable for the protocol's systemic errors, then no one will use the protocol, effectively allowing the "Wastrel" banking cartel to maintain its monopoly through fear. Supporting cases like *Serebryakov v. Golden* (2024) have begun to suggest that liability should be limited to those who exercise "actual control" over specific illegal acts, rather than general participation. In the digital realism of 2026, we argue for the recognition of the Autonomous Protocol as a distinct legal entity, where liability is assessed against the "Treasury" of the DAO itself rather than the private property of its decentralized members.

Ultimately, identifying the "Responsible Person" in a DAO requires a new legal taxonomy for autonomous entities. We must move away from the "Hollow Man" pursuit of individuals to blame for the actions of a machine. If a DAO is to be a part of the more perfect union, its "Personhood" must be defined by its code and its assets, not by the "Gimmie" desire of a regulator to find a neck to wring. By establishing a "Protocol Liability" standard that respects the "Code Veil," we protect the "Active Citizen" and ensure that the digital republic remains a laboratory of innovation rather than a minefield of collective debt.[78]

---

[78] Cooper's Logic Check → The banksters love the "General Partnership" ruling because it scares people away from the "Exit" door. Logic check: If you buy a share of a mutual fund and the fund breaks the law, the police don't come to your house to arrest you. But they want to tell you that if you vote on a DAO proposal, you are suddenly responsible for the whole machine. That is not "Law"; That is an **Intimidation Tactic**. In digital realism, the "Responsible Person" is the one who actually signed the transaction with their private key, not every person who

Conclusion: A New Legal Taxonomy for Autonomous Entities

The forensic synthesis of the case law analyzed in this chapter reveals a terminal misalignment between the legacy "Hollow Man" regulatory framework and the objective reality of the digital species. By dissecting the failure of the 1946 *Howey* citrus grove standard and the subsequent "Strategic Ambiguity" utilized by agencies to perform jurisdictional land grabs, we find that the American legal system has been attempting to regulate spaceships with horse-and-buggy statutes. The "Programmatic Sales" distinction in *Ripple* and the "Death of Chevron" in *Loper Bright* signify a judicial pivot back to the "Lodestone" of the Constitution, signaling that the era of administrative agencies "decreeing" decentralized code into existence as a security is over.

When we strip away the "Subjective" interpretations of the SEC and CFTC, we find that a decentralized digital asset is neither a share in a common enterprise (Security) nor a raw bulk good (Commodity). Instead, it is a **Currency Medium**—a "Thing" designed for the high-velocity transfer of value through an autonomous, constant ledger. As seen in the logic of *SEC v. Shavers*, the courts have already acknowledged the functional reality of these assets as money. Therefore, the proper "Objectivist" path for the Republic is to recognize these assets as a "Species of

---

happens to hold the token. It is time to stop the "Guilt by Association" and start following the **Logic of the Ledger**..

Tender" whose oversight naturally belongs to the Office of the Comptroller of the Currency (OCC), rather than an enforcement-focused commission.

Moving digital assets under the jurisdiction of the OCC aligns the tech with the Section 8 power to "regulate the Value" of the nation's medium of exchange. The Comptroller is designed to manage the safety and soundness of the "Rails," ensuring that the math of the vault is solvent rather than hunting for "Subjective Profits" in a decentralized cloud. This shift provides the "Clear Notice" required by Due Process and neutralizes the "Bureaucratic Hammer" by treating tokens as the financial infrastructure they are. Cases like *Custodia Bank* highlight the necessity of this move; for a more perfect union to exist, the "Active Citizen" must have non-discriminatory access to the primary rails of the republic through institutions that follow the logic of the ledger.

The logical conclusion of defining digital assets as currencies is the immediate cessation of their treatment as "Property" for capital gains purposes. Under a constitutional multi-currency framework, it is a "Repugnance to the Law" to tax the use of a medium of exchange as a capital event. In the trade wars of 2026, the United States cannot remain competitive if every transaction—from buying a coffee to settling a contract for an 8,000-square-foot steel home—is a taxable "sale" of an asset. To restore the "Velocity of Value," the tax code must recognize the 0% sales tax standard for the exchange of currency, allowing the digital species to flow through the economy without the "Entropy of Fiat" drag.

This new legal taxonomy for autonomous entities effectively creates a "Code Veil" that protects the producer while holding the "Responsible Person"—the signer of the transaction—accountable. By applying the Major Questions Doctrine, we assert that the "Hollow Man" regulators cannot unilaterally decide to tax the people's innovation out of existence without an explicit Congressional mandate. Supporting cases like *West Virginia v. EPA* provide the final shield, ensuring that the "Gimmies" of the administrative state are replaced by the "Objectivist" certainty of legislative clarity. The digital republic is not seeking a "new" law, but a return to the "Supreme Law" that protects the medium of exchange from debasement and overreach.

Ultimately, the jurisprudence of digital assets represents the "Hard Reset" of the American economic engine. We are moving from a world where the "Wastrel" banking cartel picks winners and losers through litigation to a world where the "Active Citizen" uses the math of the ledger to build a prosperous future. The "Supreme Law as a Shield" has been re-forged through this case law to protect the "Thing-ness" of the token and the sovereignty of the individual. As we close Chapter 7, the legal map is clear: digital assets are the modern species of the Republic, and it is time for the law to treat them with the same crystalline respect it accords to the math of the vault.[79]

[79] Cooper's Logic Check → The banksters love "Property Tax" on crypto because it makes the "Exit" too expensive to use. Logic check: If I change a twenty-dollar bill for two tens, I don't owe the government a "capital gains" tax on the ink. They want you trapped in a system where the currency devalues by 10% but you pay 20% to use a better one. That is not "Regulation"; That is a Ransom. In digital realism, the OCC manages the money, the IRS stays out of your "medium of exchange," and the math does the rest. It is time to stop taxing the "Truth" and start punishing the "Fraud.".

Chapter 8: Legislative Friction. Analyzing the gap between the CLARITY Act and bureaucratic survival instincts.

"One of the penalties for refusing to participate in politics is that you end up being governed by your inferiors."

Plato[80]

To be fair, some members of congress are trying to make the situation better. They are a vast minority in the current system. Until lobbying is more highly regulated (or banned), the United States will still be at the disposal of the political party system and the lobbyists. Clarity, along with its predecessor Genius, is designed to put the United States at a disadvantage in the global cryptocurrency market. Because many congresspeople are owned by the American Bankers Cartel, there is little hope that the law will be a fair law. The only hope is that the President vetos the law.

This is not to say that Clarity does not have any good points, it does. But they are very rare. The cryptocurrency community needs to be regulated by the Office of the Comptroller of Currencies. Cryptocurrency is a form of private currency, which precludes it from being a security or a commodity.

---

[80] Staff (2026). "Politics Quotes." Brainy Quote at https://www.brainyquote.com/search_results?x=0&y=0&q=Politics.

The attempts of the law to "shoehorn" the information into the "boxes" that it wants are destructive to both the law and the industry. We need a better law, preferably one based on the United Nations DCBAS model law which gives clarity to KYC, regulating bodies, and on the duties of exchanges and wallets.[81]

The CLARITY Act: A Blueprint for Algorithmic Certainty

The legislative struggle over the CLARITY Act (and its companion, the GENIUS Act) serves as a forensic case study in how the "Wastrels" of the legacy banking system utilize the political machine to stifle the velocity of value. While the Act is marketed as a "Safe Harbor" for digital assets, a deeper audit reveals a battlefield where algorithmic certainty is being sacrificed to preserve the "Hollow Man" dominance of the American Bankers Association (ABA). The friction we observe is not a byproduct of complexity, but a calculated effort to maintain the jurisdictional fog that allows the banking cartel to extract economic rent through outdated infrastructure.

---

[81] Cooper's Logic Check → The banksters love to say that "regulation takes time because it is complicated." Logic check: It is only "complicated" when you are trying to figure out how to make a 1:1 reserve protocol look like a "security" so you can ban it. They don't want "Clarity"; they want a **Fog Machine**. If the law were clear, you wouldn't need a million-dollar lobbyist to tell you how to vote. In digital realism, the law should be like the code: if the conditions are met, the transaction happens. It is time to stop the "Legislative Friction" and start building on the "Rails of Truth."

The Good: Fragments of Algorithmic Certainty

On its surface, the CLARITY Act offers the first legitimate legislative attempt to create a "Mature Blockchain Test," distinguishing decentralized protocols from the citrus-grove era of *Howey*. It acknowledges the "Thing-ness" of the digital species by establishing a 1:1 reserve requirement for payment stablecoins—mandating that every digital dollar be backed by high-quality liquid assets (HQLA) such as U.S. Treasuries or central bank deposits. This provision, if enacted without "Gimmie" amendments, would move the United States toward a system of Objective Solvency, where the risk of a "run" is neutralized by the math of the vault. Furthermore, the Act provides a pathway for federal charters, potentially allowing innovators to bypass the "Patchwork Policy" of state-by-state licensing.

The Bad: The Jurisdictional Hijack

The "Bad" within the CLARITY Act is the persistent attempt to keep digital assets under the thumb of agencies whose "Survival Instincts" are tied to the legacy cartel. By failing to explicitly move the oversight of private currencies to the Office of the Comptroller of the Currency (OCC), the Act leaves the door open for "Regulation by Enforcement." It continues to treat digital assets as "Claims" rather than "Mediums," forcing them into a disclosure framework designed for 1930s equity markets. This mismatch is destructive to the industry; it adds an "Administrative Tax" to innovation that ensures only the "bought and paid for" incumbents can afford to stay in the game.

The Ugly: Anti-Competitive Bribes and National Security

The "Ugly" reality of the CLARITY Act is the intense lobbying—or more accurately, the Anti-Competitive Bribes—deployed by the ABA regarding "Stablecoin Yield." The banking cartel has argued that allowing stablecoins to pay interest would cause "deposit flight" from community banks, undermining the financial system. However, forensic data from the White House Council of Economic Advisers (April 2026) shows that a total yield ban would only marginally increase bank lending while costing consumers nearly $800 million in lost rewards. The ABA's push to prohibit yield is not a safety measure; it is an attempt to legally mandate that the "Active Citizen" keep their money in low-interest "Wastrel" accounts.

This legislative friction is more than just a domestic trade war; it is a Threat to the National Security of the United States. By hampering the competitive marketplace for digital dollars, the ABA and its legislative proxies are driving innovation offshore to jurisdictions like the EU and Singapore, where the "Rules of the Road" are clearer. Every month that the CLARITY Act remains stalled by yield prohibitions is a month where the U.S. Dollar’s status as the global reserve medium is eroded. The "Lobbying Wall" has effectively become a barricade against the future, ensuring that the "Hollow Man" banks can survive one more cycle at the expense of American technological dominance.[82]

Bureaucratic Survivalism: Why Agencies Fight for Jurisdictional Turf

The administrative state operates on a primal directive of self-preservation that is often directly at odds with the "Objectivist" requirement for clear, limited governance. In the trade wars of 2026, we see this manifest as a desperate jurisdictional land grab by agencies like the SEC and CFTC, who view the rise of the "Digital Species" as either a threat to their relevance or an opportunity to expand their "Budget-Maximizing" footprint. This Bureaucratic Survivalism is not about the protection of the consumer; it is about the protection of the agency's "Turf." Under the logic of public choice theory, a bureaucrat's prestige and salary are tied to the size and complexity of their department. Therefore, a crystalline, self-executing model like the UN DCBAS law—which would simplify regulations and remove the need for massive

---

[82] Cooper's Logic Check→ The banksters say they want a "level playing field." Logic check: If you have a 0% reserve bank and I have a 100% reserve protocol, and the government forces me to pay 0% interest just like you, That is not a "level field"—That is a **subsidy for your failure**. They are terrified of a currency that actually works and pays the user instead of the "Gimmies." In digital realism, the yield is a reflection of the math, not a "gift" from a lobbyist. If we don't fix the CLARITY Act to protect the marketplace from these anti-competitive bribes, the only thing we'll be "clarifying" is the decline of the American economy.

enforcement divisions—is viewed by the administrative class as an existential threat.

The "Turf War" mentality created an era of "Regulation by Enforcement" where agencies intentionally maintained "Strategic Ambiguity" to justify their overlapping intervention. By early 2026, the failure of this model became so glaring that even the "Hollow Man" administrators were forced to pivot. The January 2026 announcement of Project Crypto—a joint initiative between SEC Chair Paul Atkins and CFTC Chair Michael Selig—marks a forensic admission that the previous "Enforcement-First" approach was a terminal failure. While this "Memorandum of Understanding" (MOU) signed in March 2026 signals a move toward harmonization, it remains a fragile peace. Without the "Safe Harbor" of statutory law like the CLARITY Act, this joint oversight is merely a temporary ceasefire between two "Wastrel" entities trying to avoid a total loss of authority in the wake of the "Death of Chevron."

Furthermore, this survivalist instinct drives a "Jurisdictional Hijack" where agencies compete to define digital assets in a way that maximizes their own power. If an asset is a "Security," the SEC maintains its hammer; if it is a "Commodity," the CFTC gains a new kingdom. Neither definition acknowledges the reality of a Currency Medium that should be under the OCC. This fragmentation ensures that the "Active Citizen" is caught in a regulatory crossfire, forced to navigate redundant compliance frameworks that serve no purpose other than to keep the bureaucrats employed. The "Lobbying Wall" supports this chaos, as legacy banks prefer a fragmented, inefficient regulator that can be "bought and paid for" over a streamlined, mathematical standard that operates with "Algorithmic Certainty."

Ultimately, bureaucratic survivalism is the "Entropy of Fiat" applied to the law. Agencies would rather have a "Patchwork Policy" that they control than a "Fair Law" that they do not. The resistance to moving digital asset oversight to the OCC is the final stand of the "Gimmies," who know that once the "Species of Tender" is treated as a currency, the era of arbitrary "Discretionary Power" is over. To neutralize this survivalist instinct, the Republic must insist on a "Rule of Math" where the law is a public utility, not a private fiefdom for the administrative state. Until the "Code Veil" is respected as a legal boundary, the "Bureaucratic Hammer" will continue to swing, not to build the future, but to keep the old walls from falling.[83]

---

[83] Cooper's Logic Check → The "experts" say they need "coordinated oversight" to protect you. Logic check: If you have two different bosses telling you two different ways to do your job, you are not being "protected"—you are being **extorted**. They finally signed an MOU because they realized if they didn't stop fighting each other, Congress might actually fire them both and give the job to the OCC. In digital realism, the "Turf" belongs to the people who build the protocols, not the "Wastrels" who want to tax the air around them. It is time we stopped feeding the survival instincts of a system That is already extinct.

The Lobbying Wall: Legacy Finance's Role in Stalling Digital Law

In a functional republic, laws are passed based on their "Objectivist" merit and their alignment with the Constitution. However, the legacy financial sector operates on the "Subjective" value of political contributions. When the American Bankers Association (ABA) or the "Big Four" banks deploy hundreds of millions of dollars into Congressional campaign funds, they are not merely "expressing an opinion." They are purchasing Regulatory Stagnation. This is a forensic bribe: the exchange of capital for a "Legislative Friction" that prevents the CLARITY Act or the GENIUS Act from providing the safe harbor the industry needs.

By stalling these laws, the cartel ensures that digital assets remain in a "Jurisdictional Fog." This fog serves as a protection racket; as long as the rules are unclear, the "Hollow Man" regulators can continue to use the "Bureaucratic Hammer" to suppress competitors. The bribery is evident in the "Specific Carve-outs" found in draft legislation—provisions that would allow legacy banks to provide digital custody while placing impossible capital requirements on decentralized startups. This is not "consumer protection"; it is the legal mandate of a monopoly.

The Yield Prohibition: Economic Treason as Policy

The most egregious example of this lobbying-as-bribery is the current fight over Stablecoin Yield. As audited in previous sections, the legacy banks have lobbied aggressively to prohibit stablecoin issuers from sharing interest with their users. Their argument is that such a move would cause "bank instability." Forensic reality tells a different story: they are bribing legislators to prevent the public from accessing a 1:1 reserve asset that pays more than their 0.01% "Wastrel" savings accounts.

This is a form of Economic Treason. By using their "Lobbying Wall" to prevent American citizens from benefiting from the "Velocity of Value," the cartel is hampering the security of the United States. They are effectively bribing the government to keep the marketplace inefficient so they can continue to profit from the spread. In the trade wars of 2026, this friction drives innovative capital offshore, weakening the dollar's global standing simply to protect the "Gimmies" of a domestic banking cartel that has already failed its audit.

The "Revolving Door" and the Capture of Intent

The "Lobbying Wall" is further reinforced by the "Revolving Door" between the administrative state and legacy finance. When an SEC or CFTC official knows that a multi-million dollar "Consulting" role at a major bank awaits them after they "successfully" delay a digital asset law, the bribe is deferred but no less real. This capture of intent ensures that even when a "Fair Law" is proposed, it is "Hollowed Out" during the markup process by staffers who are being coached by the very cartel the law is supposed to regulate.

Breaking the Wall

To restore the Republic, we must recognize that the "Lobbying Wall" is a terminal threat to the "Rule of Law." Until lobbying is either banned or so strictly regulated that it cannot function as a "Regulatory Purchase," the United States will remain at the disposal of the Bankers Cartel. We must demand a "Hard Reset" where the law is based on the UN DCBAS model—a crystalline standard that cannot be "negotiated" away in a smoke-filled room.

The "Active Citizen" must realize that the friction in D.C. is not a sign that the tech is "too complicated"; it is a sign that the bribe was large enough to buy another year of delay. In digital realism, we do not ask for permission to use the math, and we should not have to out-bribe a cartel to have "Clear Notice" of the law. It is time to treat the "Lobbying Wall" for what it is: a criminal obstruction of American innovation.[84]

---

[84] Cooper's Logic Check → The banksters say that "Lobbying is an essential part of the democratic process." Logic check: If I have to pay five million dollars to a "consultant" just to get a Congressman to read a bill that helps the country, That is not "democracy"—it is a **shakedown**. They want to keep the "Wall" high because they know they can't compete with a transparent ledger on a level playing field. In digital realism, the only "Lobby" we need is the **Code**. The code does not take lunch meetings, it does not have a "PAC," and it does not care about your re-election. It just works. It is time we made the law do the same.

Executive Orders vs. Legislative Intent: The Power Struggle

The tension between Executive Orders and Legislative Intent represents a fundamental fracture in the constitutional architecture of the Republic. Under Article I of the Constitution, the legislative branch is established as the primary authority of the government because it is the only branch directly accountable to the People through the power of the purse and the sole authority to "make all Laws." When the President utilizes executive orders to bypass the deliberate, albeit slow, process of Congress, the result is a move away from the Rule of Law and toward a "Rule of Decree." This power struggle is particularly visible in the digital asset sector, where the executive branch has frequently used administrative directives to "shoehorn" innovation into regulatory frameworks that Congress never authorized.

The primary danger of "Governance by Executive Order" is the instability it introduces into the marketplace. An executive order is as transient as the administration that signs it; what is permitted today can be criminalized by a stroke of a pen tomorrow. This creates a state of perpetual anxiety for the active citizen and the innovative capitalist, who cannot deploy long-term resources in an environment where the "Supreme Law" is subject to the political whims of the White House. While the executive branch is meant to "faithfully execute" the laws passed by

Congress, it has increasingly sought to "create" law through agency mandates, effectively performing a jurisdictional hijack that ignores the Tenth Amendment and the sovereignty of the States.

This struggle is a forensic symptom of a "Hollow Man" government that has lost its connection to its founding principles. When Congress fails to provide "Clear Notice" through legislation, a vacuum is created that the administrative state is all too happy to fill. However, as the Supreme Court reaffirmed in cases like *West Virginia v. EPA*, the executive cannot "discover" transformative powers in old statutes to regulate matters of vast economic and political significance. The digital species, being a foundational shift in the global medium of exchange, is a matter that belongs exclusively to the People's representatives. Using executive orders to "Choke Point" banking access or to force digital assets into the "Security" box is not an act of leadership; it is an act of bureaucratic survivalism.

To restore the balance of power, the Republic must return to a system where the legislative intent is the absolute lodestone of policy. The legislative branch was designed to be the "Main Branch" because its friction is a feature, not a bug—it ensures that any law affecting the life, liberty, or property of the citizen has been thoroughly debated and reconciled. When the President attempts to bypass this friction, they are not just fighting Congress; they are fighting the very "Objectivist" checks and balances that prevent the rise of a centralized monopoly. The path forward requires a "Hard Reset" where the executive branch returns to its role as a neutral administrator, leaving the definition of the digital republic to the branch that is closest to the math of the vault and the will of the people.[85]

Patchwork Policy: The Friction of State-by-State Digital Licensing

The current regulatory landscape for digital assets in the United States is a fragmented "Patchwork Policy" that functions as a systemic friction point for innovative capital. Rather than a unified national standard, the Republic is currently governed by fifty distinct sets of rules, forcing every "Active Citizen" and protocol developer to navigate a labyrinth of state-by-state licensing. This state of affairs is not a byproduct of healthy federalism; it is a "Jurisdictional Trap" that rewards legacy incumbents with the resources to manage fifty different compliance departments while effectively bankrupting the startup in a Pennsylvania garage.

---

[85] Cooper's Logic Check → The banksters love executive orders because they only have to lobby one person instead of five hundred and thirty-five. Logic check: If the "Rule of Law" can change every four years because someone moves into a new office, then there is no law—there's just a "Management Directive." They want to bypass Congress because the "Lobbying Wall" is easier to maintain in the shadows of an agency than in the light of a public hearing. In digital realism, the code is permanent, and the law should be too. It is time to stop the "Power Struggle" and start following the Constitution.

The Friction of the Patchwork

The most egregious examples of this friction are found in jurisdictions like New York and California. New York's "BitLicense" and California's recently enacted "Digital Financial Assets Law" represent the pinnacle of "Bureaucratic Survivalism." These states have created high-cost, high-friction gatekeeping systems that require companies to undergo exhaustive, overlapping audits just to offer basic digital species services. This "Regulatory Entropy" ensures that capital remains stationary rather than fluid. When a company must spend millions on legal fees just to determine if they can serve a customer in Los Angeles vs. one in Miami, the "Velocity of Value" is intentionally throttled to protect the "Wastrel" banking cartel.

This patchwork is a "Hollow Man" version of oversight. It does not provide more security; it only provides more complexity. Each state's "Money Transmitter License" (MTL) was designed for a 19th-century world of physical wires and paper checks, not for the 2026 reality of high-frequency, autonomous protocols. Forcing a global, borderless technology into these localized "boxes" is a category error that ignores the "Thing-ness" of the digital medium.

Fluidity via the UN DCBAS Model and the OCC

To restore the "Lodestone" of American innovation, we must move toward a single, federal license based on the United Nations DCBAS Model Law. This framework provides a crystalline blueprint for KYC, wallet security, and exchange duties that is both technologically neutral and forensically sound. By adopting this model and placing its oversight under the Office of the Comptroller of the Currency (OCC), we replace fifty localized frictions with one "Safe Harbor" of algorithmic certainty.

A single OCC license would allow for a "Passporting" system where a compliant institution could operate across the entire Republic without seeking further permission from state-level gatekeepers. This creates "Greater Fluidity" by allowing capital to move at the speed of the code. The OCC is uniquely qualified for this role because its mandate is the safety and soundness of the "Currency Medium," which is exactly what a digital species represents. Under this model, the "Rule of Math" becomes the standard, and the "Permission Slip" of the state bureaucrat becomes obsolete.

The Sovereignty Doctrine: Rendering State Overreach Moot

The adoption of a federal standard under the OCC would trigger the Sovereignty Doctrine (and the Supremacy Clause of Article VI), effectively making the restrictive laws of California and New York moot. Under the doctrine of "Federal Preemption," when the Federal government occupies a field—especially one as critical as the national medium of exchange—state laws that conflict with or add "undue burden" to that federal standard are legally neutralized.

If a digital asset is recognized as a currency medium by the Comptroller, the "BitLicense" becomes a historical relic of "Regulatory Treason." New York and California cannot constitutionally "tax" or "license" the use of a federal species of tender any more than they could require a separate license to spend a U.S. Dollar. By reclaiming federal sovereignty over the "Rails of Value," we remove the "Gimmie" tolls established by state-level bureaucrats and restore a unified, high-velocity marketplace. This is not just a legal convenience; it is a requirement for the "Active Citizen" to engage in the trade wars of 2026 without being shackled by 19th-century state lines.

Harmonizing the Republic

The "Patchwork Policy" is a terminal failure that only serves the interest of the "Lobbying Wall." It is the "Strategic Ambiguity" of the administrative state applied at the state level. By harmonizing our law with the UN DCBAS model and centering it in the OCC, we are choosing "Objectivist" clarity over "Subjective" chaos. We are ensuring that the digital republic is a unified engine of production, where the only boundary is the math of the ledger, and the sovereignty of the federal tender is respected from sea to shining sea.[86]

---

[86] Cooper's Logic Check → The "experts" in New York say their license is the "gold standard" for safety. Logic check: If it is so safe, why did it take ten years for them to realize it just drove all the good companies to Singapore? They are not "protecting" you; they are **taxing** your right to use a better system. In digital realism, the "Rails" don't care about state borders, and neither should the law. A single OCC license is the "Hard Reset" that

Global Arbitrage: How Legislative Stagnation Drives Innovation Offshore

The phenomenon of Global Arbitrage is the natural economic consequence of the "Legislative Friction" currently paralyzing the United States. In the digital realism of 2026, capital is no longer tethered to geography; it is a high-velocity asset that flows toward "Crystalline Certainty." When the American "Wastrels" use the "Lobbying Wall" to stall the CLARITY Act, they are not stopping innovation—they are simply exporting it. This legislative stagnation acts as a de facto subsidy for foreign jurisdictions, driving the "Active Citizen" and their productive energy offshore to environments that respect the "Rule of Math."

The Mechanics of the "Brain Drain"

Innovation does not wait for a "Permission Slip" from an unqualified gatekeeper. When an American developer faces the threat of "Regulation by Enforcement" at home but finds a clear, statutory "Safe Harbor" in Dubai, Singapore, or the European Union's MiCA framework, the choice is forensically simple. This is Regulatory Arbitrage: the process of moving operations to a jurisdiction where the "Legal Tether" is attached to reality rather than the "Subjective" whims of a bureaucrat.

The United States is currently suffering from a terminal "Brain Drain." The most brilliant minds in

---

puts the power back in the hands of the people and tells the state-level "Gimmies" that their time is up.

decentralized architecture—the "Objectivists" of the 21st century—are fleeing the "Jurisdictional Fog" of the SEC. By the time the American Bankers Cartel finishes its "Gimmie" maneuvers to stall domestic law, the primary infrastructure of the global digital economy will have already been built on foreign soil. This is a "Managed Decline" orchestrated by legacy institutions that would rather rule over a decaying monoculture than compete in a thriving, transparent marketplace.

The Erosion of the Dollar's Digital Sovereignty

Legislative stagnation is not merely a domestic inconvenience; it is a direct threat to the National Security of the Republic. The global trade wars of 2026 are being fought on the "Rails of Value." By refusing to adopt a unified federal standard under the OCC or the UN DCBAS model, the United States is voluntarily surrendering its role as the world's financial lodestone. While Congress bickers over "Anti-Competitive Bribes" regarding stablecoin yield, other nations are busy codifying the rules for the next century of trade.

Every project that moves offshore represents a loss of "Sovereign Control." When the "Species of Tender" is developed in a jurisdiction that does not share the Republic's commitment to the Constitution, the "Active Citizen" loses the protection of the "Supreme Law." The stagnation of the CLARITY Act has created a vacuum that is being filled by foreign banking subsidiaries, ensuring that the "Velocity of Value" benefits everyone *except* the American taxpayer. This is the ultimate "Hollow Man" outcome: a government so focused on protecting its "Wastrel" sponsors that it destroys its own competitive advantage.

The Failure of the "Wait and See" Strategy

The "Lobbying Wall" often argues for a "Wait and See" approach to regulation, claiming that the tech is "too new" for definitive law. Logic check: The first block was mined in 2009. We are nearly two decades into this evolution. The "Wait and See" strategy is actually a "Stall and Copy" strategy. The legacy cartel wants to keep the innovators in a state of "Legislative Friction" until the big banks can build their own "Black Box" versions of the technology.

This delay is a forensic fraud against the public. By the time the "Wastrels" are ready to "allow" a law to pass, they will have engineered it to include "Barriers to Entry" that make it impossible for anyone but them to participate. This ensures that the "Digital Republic" is never truly born, replaced instead by a "Digital Feudalism" where the legacy banks own the rails and the people pay the tolls. The only way to break this cycle of arbitrage is to bypass the "Gimmies" and pass a "Fair Law" that provides immediate, non-discriminatory access to the global market.

Reclaiming the Frontier

To stop the flight of innovative capital, the Republic must provide a "Reason to Stay." This requires more than just "less regulation"; it requires Better

Regulation. A single license under the OCC, grounded in the UN DCBAS model, would immediately neutralize the "Global Arbitrage" incentive. It would transform the United States from a "Regulatory Minefield" back into a "Global Frontier."

We must recognize that the "Legislative Friction" in D.C. is a choice, not a necessity. It is the result of "Subjective" politics overriding "Objective" economics. In the digital realism of 2026, we do not have the luxury of another decade of stagnation. The "Lodestone" must be re-set, and the "Bureaucratic Hammer" must be laid down in favor of a "Crystalline Standard" that allows the American spirit of production to compete—and win—on the global stage.[87]

Conclusion: Harmonizing Law with Technological Reality

The harmonization of law with technological reality requires a definitive rejection of the "Legislative Friction" that has defined the last decade of American financial policy. As we have forensically audited, the current stagnation is not a result of technical

---

[87] Cooper's Logic Check → The banksters say they are "protecting the American system" by taking their time with the law. Logic check: If you are protecting a house by locking the doors while it is on fire, you are not a guard—you are an **arsonist**. They want to keep the tech offshore so you can't see how much better it works than their 0% reserve "Hollow Man" system. In digital realism, the "Rails" are global. If we don't build them here, we'll end up paying rent to the people who did. It is time to stop the "Stagnation" and start the "Hard Reset."

complexity, but a calculated maneuver by the "Wastrel" banking cartel to maintain a "Jurisdictional Fog." By utilizing "Anti-Competitive Bribes" and "Strategic Ambiguity," the legacy cartel has successfully stalled the transition to a 1:1 reserve standard, effectively choosing "Managed Decline" over the transparent competition of the digital republic. To neutralize the "Bureaucratic Hammer," we must move beyond the "Gimmie" economics of the lobbyist and return to a jurisprudence that recognizes the "Code Veil" as a sacred boundary of innovation.

Harmonizing the law means recognizing that the "Patchwork Policy" of state-by-state licensing is a terminal failure that serves only the interest of the "Hollow Man" incumbents. The path to "Algorithmic Certainty" lies in a single federal license under the Office of the Comptroller of the Currency (OCC), grounded in the crystalline standards of the UN DCBAS model law. This shift would trigger the "Sovereignty Doctrine," rendering the restrictive gatekeeping of jurisdictions like New York and California moot and restoring the "Velocity of Value" across the entire Republic. Until the medium of exchange is treated as a currency rather than a "Subjective" security, the "Lobbying Wall" will continue to act as a barrier to the future.

The "Global Arbitrage" currently draining the Republic of its most productive "Objectivist" minds is the direct price of our refusal to provide "Clear Notice." Every month that the CLARITY Act remains a hostage to legacy banking interests, another layer of American financial sovereignty is exported to "Species-friendly" jurisdictions. We cannot win the trade wars of 2026 by clinging to the "Bureaucratic Survivalism" of agencies that prioritize their own "Turf" over the national interest. The "Hard Reset" requires a legislative branch that acts as the "Main Branch"—reclaiming its constitutional duty to "regulate the Value" of money from an executive branch that has relied too long on the "Rule of Decree."

Ultimately, the conclusion of this chapter serves as a call to action for the "Active Citizen." We must stop asking for "Permission Slips" from unqualified gatekeepers and start demanding a "Fair Law" that reflects the mathematical reality of the ledger. The digital species is not a threat to be managed, but a frontier to be explored; it is the "lodestone" that will guide the Republic toward a more perfect, 1:1 reserve union. By aligning our statutes with the "Logic of the Ledger," we ensure that the United States remains the global capital of digital realism, where the "Supreme Law" acts as a shield for the producer and the math of the vault remains the ultimate arbiter of truth.[88]

---

[88] Cooper's Logic Check → The banksters say that the "law of the land" should move slowly to avoid mistakes. Logic check: They don't mind the law moving fast when it is time for a "Bailout" or a new "Fee." They only want "Slow Law" when it is someone else's innovation on the line. In digital realism, the "Mistake" is not moving too fast—the mistake is staying tethered to a "Hollow" system while the rest of the world moves into the

future. It is time to stop the "Friction" and let the math lead the way.

Conclusion

“The darkest places in hell are reserved for those who maintain their neutrality in times of moral crisis.”

Dante Alighieri[89]

The forensic audit of Part II reveals a terminal collision between the Objectivist reality of decentralized protocols and the Subjective decay of the administrative state. Over the preceding chapters, we have documented the transition from the "Hollow Man" economy of 0% reserve banking to the "Crystalline Certainty" of the digital species. Chapters 5 through 8 have mapped the battlefield where the "Active Citizen" confronts a "Bureaucratic Hammer" fueled by "Strategic Ambiguity" and "Anti-Competitive Bribes." This section has served as a "Hard Reset" for the legal and structural understanding of value, proving that the "Velocity of Value" cannot be contained by 19th-century "Patchwork Policies" or 1946 citrus-grove precedents.

We have exposed the "Lobbying Wall" not as a forum for debate, but as a mechanism for institutionalized bribery designed to protect the "Wastrel" banking cartel. By stalling the CLARITY Act and weaponizing "Regulation by Enforcement," the legacy cartel has attempted to force the "Digital Species" into "boxes" where it does not belong. This "Jurisdictional Hijack"

---

[89] Staff (2026). “American Quotes.” Brainy Quote at https://www.brainyquote.com/search_results?x=0&y=0&q=Politics.

is a form of "Economic Treason" that intentionally drives innovation offshore through "Global Arbitrage." However, the "Death of Chevron" and the rise of the "Major Questions Doctrine" have provided the "Legal Tether" necessary to neutralize these survivalist instincts, ensuring that the "Rule of Math" begins to supersede the "Rule of Whim."

The synthesis of our jurisprudential analysis proves that cryptocurrencies are neither securities nor commodities, but a sovereign Currency Medium. The attempts to "shoehorn" these autonomous protocols into legacy definitions are "Repugnant to the Constitution" because they violate the "Right to Clear Notice" and "Due Process." By moving the oversight of these assets to the Office of the Comptroller of the Currency (OCC) and adopting a 1:1 reserve standard, the Republic can harmonize its law with technological reality. This transition is the only path to ending the "Managed Decline" orchestrated by institutions that have already failed their forensic audits.

Furthermore, we have defined the "Code Veil" as a sacred boundary of "Protocol Personhood." In the digital realism of 2026, the "Responsible Person" is no longer a centralized board of directors but the individual "Active Citizen" who signs a transaction with their private key. The "Liability of the DAO" must be understood through the lens of decentralized autonomy, protecting the "Objectivist" tradition of production from the "Gimmie" desire for collective punishment. To treat a decentralized ledger as a

"General Partnership" is a category error that ignores the "Thing-ness" of the protocol and the sovereignty of the individual participant.

The "Bureaucratic Hammer" is losing its grip because it cannot compete with the Logic of the Ledger. As we have seen in the "Project Crypto" taxonomy and the dismissal of overreaching SEC enforcement actions, the administrative state is being forced to retreat to the "Lodestone" of the law. The struggle between "Executive Orders" and "Legislative Intent" has highlighted the necessity of a "Main Branch" that is accountable to the People. The "Hollow Man" era of "Rule by Decree" is reaching its terminal velocity, replaced by a requirement for crystalline standards and non-discriminatory access to the "Rails of Value."

The "Patchwork Policy" of state-level gatekeeping, exemplified by the "BitLicense" and similar "Jurisdictional Traps," has been forensically identified as a tool of "Regulatory Entropy." Under the "Sovereignty Doctrine," these localized frictions must be rendered moot by a unified federal standard grounded in the UN DCBAS model law. Greater fluidity in the marketplace is not a luxury; it is a national security requirement in the trade wars of 2026. By removing the "Gimmie" tolls of state-level bureaucrats, the Republic can finally reclaim its position as the global capital of digital realism.

We must also recognize that the "Taxation of Truth"—the treatment of currency exchange as a capital event—is a terminal drag on the American economy.

A 0% sales tax on the use of digital species as a medium of exchange is the only logical conclusion of our forensic audit. To tax the velocity of value is to fund the "Wastrel" state at the expense of the producer's energy. The "Hard Reset" of Part II demands a system where the "Standard of Value" is protected from debasement and the "Active Citizen" is free to contract and settle debts using the most efficient "Species of Tender" available.

As we conclude this section, the "Legal Map" of the digital republic is complete. We have identified the rot in the old system and provided the "Blueprint for Algorithmic Certainty." Part II has demonstrated that the "Supreme Law" is the ultimate shield for the "Active Citizen" against the "Hollow Man" cartel. We now stand at the threshold of the final transformation: moving from the theory of law to the reality of the assets themselves. The "Lodestone" has been re-set, the "Hammer" has been neutralized, and the math of the future is ready to be mapped in the chapters to come.[90]

---

[90] Cooper's Logic Check → The banksters want you to think this section was "complicated" so you'll stop reading and go back to their "safe" 0% reserve accounts. Logic check: It is only "complicated" when you are trying to hide a lie. The truth of Part II is simple: **Math is the law of the ledger, and the Constitution is the law of the land.** They tried to use the "Fog Machine" to keep you from seeing the exit, but we just forensically dismantled the machine. In digital realism, the only "Permission Slip" you need is a valid private key. It is time to stop studying the "Friction" and start enjoying the "Fluidity."

Part III: Detracting Factors in the Classic System

"I weep for the liberty of my country when I see at this early days of its successful experiment that corruption has been imputed to many members of the House of Representatives, and that the rights of the people have been bartered for promises of office."

Andrew Jackson [91]

The grand vision of a republic was built on the dream of a meritocracy of peers. The initial founding was, of course, flawed with women and those of different races being denied the equality of being peers; however, slowly but surely we have corrected, or started down the path of correction for those sins of the past. One of the greatest sins which we have allowed to influence our nation was not a failure of the Constitution, but a failure of the men who came afterwards- allowing for lobbying to become such a major part of the political system.

Lobbying is bribery with a license. It is wholly offensive to the underlying principles of the democracy. If you would be outraged if the wealthy paid someone to vote so they did not have to go to the voting booth, why then are not you not up in arms that people can pay others to go and lobby for

---

[91] Staff (2026) "Corruption Quotes." Brainy Quote at https://www.brainyquote.com/topics/corruption-quotes.

changes in the law because they themselves do not have time to do this. What makes matters even worse is that lobbyists are not bound by congressional districting, a California activist can pay a lobbying firm in Florida and a Texas oilman can pay a lobbying firm in Seattle; completely undermining the concept that representatives are directed to represent the people in their district. This has been a problem with the House of Representatives since Jackson's time; and has been corrupting the senate since 1913.

This negative environment for freedom has caused some major problems for the United States. Chapter 9 looks at the middleman economy which has sprung from "lazy citizenship."[92] This chapter walks you through the parasitic layer that has formed around the different businesses in the United States. First it comes in as helping people with a task they do not want to do, then the "help" becomes the main cost factor in the industry. This has moved very quickly into banking and undermined the stability of the system.

Chapter 10 moves directly to the discussion of monetary debasement as theft. Each time that the Federal Reserve prints more money, they take their share and charge interest. Each time this happens your dollar becomes worth less and less utility. Because a dollar is always worth a dollar, at least at current times, the dichotomy of value becomes less

---

[92] This roots back to civics and home economics not being taught regularly in schools.

and less visible. Instead of the “dollar going down” the “cost of gas is going up,” or “the cost of hamburger is rising. There is a moral hazard for the laziness which brings this to the table, who is getting paid and who is getting screwed.

Chapter 11 looks at one of the greatest cost vectors in the world, time. Each time there is a transaction, there is an amount of time that it takes. Domestically, it generally takes three days for a check to clear- even electronic ones. This is because the bank credits the value to the bank, holds it for three days, collects interest, then gives you your money. With international transactions it can take even longer. The danger lies in the fact that the value of money is changing (rarely for the good) during this time, which costs billions yearly for regular people and trillions for businesses!

The key weapon that is being used against us is the topic of Chapter 12, information asymmetry. How many of you reading this check out the Federal Reserve or FDIC website daily? Weekly? Monthly? Yearly? I would wage that most people have never looked at their information update page, relying on a bought an paid for media reporting on what the bought and paid for representatives tell you about the current money or interest rate. While the information on the websites is valid, it is often old. This oversight apathy has created a negative relationship with the people of the United States and the economy. Laziness is our own fault.

To engage with the economy, we must know the economy. This means that we need to do our due diligence, at least in election years. A citizenry that knows where its money is going is an empowered citizenry. However, 90% of people do not even know how many subscriptions come out of their checking account each money- as long as there is money there when they need it they do not care what happens. We need to teach children that this is not a good method for commerce (we can suggest or demand that banks in their apps have a "automatic withdrawal" dashboard so we can see it. Beyond our personal finances, the government should also have a "continuing resolution" dashboard so everyone can see where we are sending money each year AND if there is a lobbying group pushing for it. If people knew where their money was going, they would still be lazy but at least they may vote once a year.

Chapter 9: The Intermediary Tax. Quantifying the billions lost to the "middleman" economy

"The essence of money is in that it is absolutely worthless."

Norman O. Brown[93]

As a global economy, we have allowed the development of a parasitic layer within all of our financial transactions. There is always a "middleman" who takes their share and "smooths" the process. Why? The systems are digital systems, the processes occur automatically. So why do we see the need to pay someone for something for which we are already paying? Because that is how the system is designed.

To make matters worse, there is an "automatic defense" for these hidden transactions. "Someone has to pay for the software and servers…" is the most common reply that you will hear. This is true, we call them banks and they should be doing this as part of the normal course of business. When we allow the system to have this pre-defined inefficiency, we have allowed a "leak" in the monetary system.

We need to move away from the correspondent banking model. The development of cascading fees is like the subscription system in society, it has the sole

---

[93] Staff (2026). "Money Changers Quotes." Brainy Quote at https://www.brainyquote.com/search_results?x=0&y=0&q=money+changers.

purpose of separating us from our money counting on our laxness. We already pay administrative fees to the banks, if they are not doing the transaction but are still collecting these fees- what are the fees for? This requires digital disintermediation, the process of mathematically removing the middleman. This allows us to increase GDP growth by eliminating the inefficiencies within the system. The only people who do not want this are the banks who are making more money off of every transaction.[94]

The Parasitic Layer: Identifying the Hidden Tolls in Every Transaction

The identification of the Parasitic Layer begins with the recognition that modern financial infrastructure is designed for extraction rather than transit. In the digital realism of 2026, we find ourselves operating within a "Middleman Economy" where every pulse of capital is intercepted by a series of invisible toll booths. While the process of moving value from point A to point B is now mathematically instantaneous, the legacy cartel has engineered a "Managed Delay" to justify the extraction of fees. Forensic data from early 2026 indicates that global payments revenue is

---

[94] Cooper's Logic Check → The banksters say the "Middleman" is there to provide "liquidity and security." Logic check: If I send you ten dollars digitally and it takes three days to arrive and costs two dollars in fees, where is the "liquidity"? They are not "smoothing" the process; they are speed-bumping it so they can charge you for the suspension repair. In digital realism, the math *is* the security. You don't need a "trusted third party" when you have a "verifiable ledger." It is time to stop paying a cover charge just to enter the marketplace.

projected to exceed $3.1 trillion by 2028, a staggering figure that represents the "Intermediary Tax" levied against the global producer. This is the parasitic reality: a system where the cost of moving money has become untethered from the actual cost of the technology performing the move.

This layer thrives on the Hollow Man excuse of "operational overhead." We are told that high fees are necessary to maintain servers, ensure compliance, and mitigate risk, yet these very processes have been offloaded to automated, AI-driven systems. In reality, the parasitic layer is a "Leak" in the monetary system that drains the "Active Citizen" of their productive energy. For example, embedded finance—the practice of hiding financial services within non-financial platforms—is expected to surge to $7 trillion in transaction value by the end of 2026. This is not innovation; it is the "Fragmentation of Extraction," where a new set of "Gimmie" enablers takes a secondary cut of a transaction that should have been peer-to-peer.

The tolls are not only found in the explicit fees but in the "Waterbed Effect" of regulatory compliance. When the Credit Card Competition Act of 2026 attempted to cap "swipe fees," the banking cartel responded by raising checking account fees and slashing consumer rewards, effectively ensuring that their "Gross Intake" remained constant. This reveals the parasitic layer's true nature: it is a resilient, self-adjusting organism that protects its "Rent-Seeking" status at all costs.

The administrative burden of this layer acts as a "Secondary Tax," where the cost of "identifying" a transaction via legacy correspondent banking—which still averages 6% to 7% for cross-border moves—exceeds the marginal cost of the transaction itself by a factor of thousands.

Identifying these hidden tolls is the first step toward the "Hard Reset" of digital disintermediation. We must see the "Middleman" not as a helper, but as a "Strategic Friction" point that exists solely to slow the "Velocity of Value" for profit. In an economy where AI agents are increasingly negotiating B2B contracts and executing retail purchases, the 9-to-5, Monday-to-Friday schedule of the legacy clearinghouse is forensically absurd. The parasitic layer is the ghost of a paper-based world haunting a digital republic; it is a "Repugnance to Logic" that we continue to pay for "smoothing" in a system where the math is already perfect. By quantifying this leakage, we provide the "Objectivist" evidence that the only way to grow the GDP is to starve the parasite and restore the 1:1 reserve sovereignty of the producer.[95]

---

[95] Cooper's Logic Check → The "Money Changers" say they need their cut because "moving money is risky business." Logic check: If I send an email, it is free and instant. If I send "Digital Money" through their system, it takes three days and costs a lunch. They are not "managing risk"; they are **managing a monopoly**. They love the "Parasitic Layer" because it is the only place they can hide their "Gimmies" from a public That is finally starting to count the change. In digital realism, the math does not have a "service charge," and neither should your sovereignty.

Quantifying the Leakage: The Multibillion-Dollar Cost of Global Clearing

Quantifying the Multibillion-Dollar Leakage within the global clearing and settlement infrastructure reveals the true scale of the "Intermediary Tax." In the digital realism of 2026, the traditional financial system continues to rely on a fragmented network of central counterparties (CCPs), clearinghouses, and correspondent banks that process staggering volumes of value. Forensic data from early 2026 indicates that global cross-border payments have surpassed $200 trillion annually, with B2B transactions alone accounting for over $30 trillion. Yet, this massive flow of capital is currently shackled by a clearing process that extracts an estimated $150 billion to $200 billion in direct fees every year. This is not just a cost of doing business; it is a systematic "bleed" that siphons the productive energy of the global "Active Citizen."

The inefficiency of this leakage is most visible in the "Settlement Gap." While a digital instruction to move funds happens in milliseconds, the actual "finality" of that settlement often takes two to five days as it moves through the correspondent banking chain. This delay creates a "Liquidity Trap," where billions of dollars are held in Nostro/Vostro accounts as collateral to manage the risk of these pending transactions. By April 2026, BIS international banking statistics showed banks' global cross-border claims reached a record $45 trillion, much of which is essentially "dead capital" frozen in the pipes of the legacy clearing system. If this capital were released through instantaneous, tokenized settlement, it could fuel an unprecedented wave of "Objectivist" investment and production.

Furthermore, the "Administrative Leakage" of compliance and reconciliation adds a secondary layer of extraction. Legacy clearing systems are not designed for "Algorithmic Certainty"; they are built on a "Hollow Man" model of manual audits and batch processing. When a transaction fails or requires an "Exception Check"—which occurs in roughly 5% to 10% of cross-border moves—the cost of the transaction can skyrocket as multiple intermediaries charge "Correction Fees." This "Strategic Friction" ensures that the "Gimmie" class of clearing agents remains profitable, even as their technology becomes increasingly obsolete. By contrast, real-time on-chain data from decentralized protocols can replace these legacy audit trails at a fraction of the cost, providing a "Hard Reset" for the global ledger.

The economic impact of this leakage extends beyond simple fees; it is a direct drag on Global GDP. In the trade wars of 2026, where global growth is projected to slow to a modest 3.1%, the elimination of clearing friction represents the most significant "unlocked" productivity gain available to the Republic. The "Intermediary Tax" is effectively a global sales tax on innovation. By removing the middleman and transitioning to a 1:1 reserve, tokenized settlement model, we could redirect an estimated $250 billion annually from the pockets of "Wastrel" clearinghouses back into the hands of the producers. This is the math of the digital republic: every basis point saved from the "leak" is a basis point added to the "Sovereignty" of the American innovator.[96]

Correspondent Banking and the Inefficiency of Cascading Fees

The correspondent banking model is the "Hollow Man" of global financial infrastructure—a legacy system that remains the primary conduit for international value transfer despite being forensically obsolete. In the digital realism of 2026, we see that most international payments are rarely subject to a single fee; instead, they are burdened by a "Correspondent Banking Problem" where a transaction must pass through one or more intermediary institutions before reaching its final destination. Each handoff in this chain introduces a new layer of friction, including visible transfer fees, foreign exchange (FX) margins, and the predatory practice of intermediary deductions. This structure

---

[96] Cooper's Logic Check → The clearinghouses say their fees are the "insurance" you pay for a stable market. Logic check: If you are paying for insurance and the house still takes three days to put out the fire, you are not insured—you are being **robbed**. They love the "Settlement Gap" because they get to play with your money while you are waiting for it to arrive. In digital realism, the "Clearance" is the "Math." If the transaction is signed, it is finished. There is no "Gap" to fill with fees. It is time we stopped paying for the "Smoothing" of a system That is designed to be bumpy.

ensures that by the time a payment reaches the recipient, its original value has been diluted by the "Entropy of Intermediation."

Forensic audits of the major U.S. banks in 2026 reveal a staggering lack of transparency in the correspondent network. While a sender may pay an upfront "Wire Fee" of $25 to $50, this is merely the visible tip of the iceberg. The real "leak" occurs mid-transit. Because many banks lack direct bilateral relationships, they rely on a chain of "Nostro" and "Vostro" accounts. Each intermediary bank along this path typically deducts a "Handling Fee" ranging from $15 to $50, often without prior notification to the sender or recipient. This results in the "Double Fee" phenomenon, where both the sender and the receiver are charged for the same movement of value, while the principal amount is systematically "hollowed out" by the intermediaries.

Cascading Fees: The Multi-Layered Extraction

The Cascading Fee structure is a mathematical absurdity designed to protect the "Gimmie" class of clearing agents. Beyond the flat handling fees, the most significant extraction occurs through the FX Markup. Banks typically add a spread of 3% to 5% over the mid-market exchange rate, pocketing the difference as a "hidden" profit. For a mid-sized manufacturer wiring $500,000 to an overseas supplier, a mere 1.5% retail B2B rate translates into a $7,500 loss. On a global scale, these percentages add up to $120 billion to $150 billion in annual transaction fees for B2B payments alone. This is capital that has been effectively stolen from the "Active Citizen" to fund the "Administrative Burden" of a system that refuses to innovate.

The inefficiency is further compounded by the Liquidity Trap inherent in the correspondent model. To ensure settlement, banks must maintain approximately $27 trillion in pre-funded Nostro/Vostro accounts globally. This is "Dead Capital" that sits idle, incurring an opportunity cost of 3% to 5% annually in lost yield. In a high-interest environment like early 2026, parking $1 billion in a Nostro account costs a bank roughly $50 million per year. These costs are not absorbed by the "Wastrel" banks; they are passed directly to the consumer through higher spreads and cascading fees, creating a "Secondary Tax" on the velocity of global trade.

The Sovereign Solution: Digital Disintermediation

The only forensic solution to this cascading failure is Digital Disintermediation. By transitioning to decentralized protocols and RWA stablecoins, the Republic can bypass the correspondent chain entirely. Stablecoins replace the multi-bank "shuffles" with direct, peer-to-peer blockchain settlement that occurs in seconds rather than the three-to-five-day window typical of the legacy system. Moving to an "Objectivist" model of settlement eliminates the need for Nostro accounts and mid-transit deductions, reducing the total cost of cross-border payments by more than 90%.

Ultimately, the correspondent banking model persists only because the "American Bankers Cartel" utilizes its "Lobbying Wall" to prevent the adoption of more efficient "Rails of Value." Cases like *Custodia Bank* highlight the desperation of the legacy system to maintain its gatekeeping role. However, as the global average cost of remittances continues to hover around 6.49%—well above the G20's 3% target—the "Repugnance to Logic" of the old system becomes impossible to ignore. In the digital republic of 2026, we must decouple our commerce from this rent-seeking class and restore the 1:1 sovereignty of the global ledger.[97]

The Administrative Burden: Compliance Costs as a Secondary Tax

The administrative burden of modern finance has evolved into a "Secondary Tax"—a pervasive, non-legislated extraction that drains the "Active Citizen" of both time and capital. While the legacy cartel justifies these costs under the banner of "Safety and Soundness," a forensic audit reveals that the majority of this expenditure is directed toward maintaining a

---

[97] Cooper's Logic Check → The "Money Changers" love to talk about the "complexity" of international banking. Logic check: If I can send a 4K video across the planet for free in a second, why does it take five days and fifty dollars to send a line of text that says "I owe you ten bucks"? The "complexity" is just a **fog machine** they use to hide the fact that they are reaching into your pocket three different times for the same transaction. In digital realism, the "Cascading Fee" is just a fancy word for "Institutionalized Shakedown." It is time to stop paying for the "plumbing" and start using the "Math."

"Hollow" compliance theater designed to protect the "Wastrel" banking system from the transparency of the ledger. By 2026, global spending on financial compliance is estimated to exceed $100 billion, with large systemic banks reportedly spending up to $1 billion annually just to maintain regulatory status quo. These costs are not absorbed by the institutions; they are passed directly to the consumer, acting as a regressive tax on every participant in the global economy.

The inefficiency of the current compliance model is rooted in its reliance on manual intervention and "Strategic Ambiguity." Despite the digital nature of 2026 commerce, many institutions still rely on human-heavy "Exception Checks" and legacy batch processing for AML/KYC protocols. Forensic data shows that digital businesses lose approximately 4.3% of total revenue to compliance liabilities and penalties, a figure that distorts economic reality by hollowing out the margins of productive innovators. This "Administrative Leak" is further exacerbated by the operational toll on finance teams, who spend an average of 30 hours per month on manual sales tax and regulatory filings—wasting thousands of dollars in salary on tasks that should be handled by autonomous code.

Lower Thresholds and Expanded "Gimmies"

By April 2026, the administrative burden intensified as Federal AML amendments lowered reporting thresholds, effectively expanding the "Bureaucratic

Hammer" to capture smaller, rapid transactions. This shift from reactive compliance to "Continuous Oversight" has forced even smaller firms to redesign their workflows, integrating automated alerts with human escalation protocols. The "Secondary Tax" is most visible here: smaller banks face a disproportionate strain as fixed compliance costs rise relative to their asset size, forcing them into the arms of the "American Bankers Cartel" for survival. This is not about stopping crime; it is about "Industrializing Compliance" to ensure that the "Rails of Value" remain under the control of those who can afford the entry fee.

Tax Reporting as an Innovation Barrier

The 2026 cost-basis reporting requirements for digital assets represent the final "Patchwork Policy" intended to stall the digital republic. By requiring brokers to report gross proceeds and cost-basis for every transaction, the IRS has effectively added a "Complexity Tax" to the use of digital species as a medium of exchange. This introduces hidden risks, such as backup withholding, where brokers may be forced to liquidate a portion of an investor's assets (at a 24% rate) to satisfy a "Subjective" tax obligation. This is a terminal drag on the "Velocity of Value," forcing the "Active Citizen" to navigate a minefield of corrected 1099 forms and inconsistent data gaps that serve only to discourage the move away from fiat.

Ultimately, the administrative burden is the "Strategic Friction" used to keep the "Hollow Man" economy alive. If the system were truly designed for efficiency, it would adopt the UN DCBAS model—where the math of the ledger provides an immutable audit trail, rendering the $100 billion compliance industry largely obsolete. Instead, we are forced to pay for a "smoothing" process that is intentionally designed to be bumpy. In the digital realism of 2026, we must recognize that every dollar spent on a "BSA Officer" is a dollar stolen from the "Producer." The only "Objectivist" solution is the Hard Reset of digital disintermediation, replacing the "Wastrel" compliance tax with the crystalline certainty of autonomous protocols.[98]

Digital Disintermediation: The Math of Removing the Middleman

Digital disintermediation is the forensic process of stripping away the "Parasitic Layer" and replacing the "Hollow Man" intermediary with the crystalline certainty of the ledger. In the digital realism of 2026, the "Middleman" is no longer a technical requirement; they are a strategic friction point maintained by the

---

[98] Cooper's Logic Check → The "Money Changers" say they need more "Compliance Officers" to catch the bad guys. Logic check: If you have more "Officers" than "Transactions," you are not catching criminals—you are hiring a private army to guard your monopoly. They love "Compliance" because it is a tax you have to pay them just to exist. In digital realism, the "Compliance" is in the Smart Contract. If the math does not check out, the transaction does not happen. You don't need a billion-dollar department to tell you what the code already knows. It is time to stop paying for their "Paperwork" and start trusting the "Protocol."

"American Bankers Cartel" to extract economic rent. The math of removing the middleman is a zero-sum recovery for the producer. Every transaction that moves through a traditional correspondent banking chain is subject to a (total cost) that is the sum of $f_1, f_2 \ldots f_n$(cascading fees) plus the o_c(opportunity cost) of the settlement delay. By utilizing decentralized protocols, we reduce this equation to a single, minimal gas fee or protocol incentive, effectively recapturing billions in "Dead Capital" that previously sat idle in Nostro/Vostro accounts.

The "Hard Reset" of disintermediation relies on the shift from Subjective Trust (believing a bank will settle) to Objective Verification (knowing the code has settled). When we eliminate the clearinghouse, we eliminate the 3-to-5-day "Settlement Gap" that the legacy system uses to hide its "Gimmies." Forensic audits of on-chain transactions in early 2026 show that peer-to-peer settlement via RWA assets reduces the total transaction cost by an average of 98.2% compared to the legacy SWIFT network. This is the math of the digital republic: if a transaction costs $0.01 to execute on-chain but $50.00 through a correspondent bank, the bank is not providing "service"; they are performing a shakedown. The administrative burden of "reconciling" these transactions—a process that costs banks over $100 billion annually—is rendered moot when the transaction and the settlement are the same event.

Removing the middleman also neutralizes the "Secondary Tax" of compliance theater. In the legacy model, "Risk Management" is a manual, high-cost hurdle used to justify bureaucratic survivalism. In the disintermediated model, compliance is "Baked into the Math." Using the UN DCBAS model, KYC and AML protocols are integrated directly into the smart contract layer, providing an immutable audit trail that removes the need for a billion-dollar "Compliance Army." This allows the "Active Citizen" to bypass the "Lobbying Wall" of the big banks and engage in global trade with the same fluidity as a local cash transaction. The only people who fear this math are the "Wastrels" who realize that in a world of transparent, automated settlement, their "smoothing" services are forensically worthless. By decoupling our commerce from the rent-seeking class, we ensure that the "Velocity of Value" is limited only by the speed of the code, not the greed of the gatekeeper.

Redirecting Lost Capital: Theoretical GDP Growth in a Frictionless Economy

The theoretical redirection of lost capital in a frictionless economy represents the most significant "Objectivist" opportunity for global prosperity in the 2026 trade wars. For decades, the global financial system has been burdened by a "managed inefficiency" that siphons billions into the pockets of the rent-seeking class. By performing a forensic "Hard Reset" of our payment rails—replacing the fragmented correspondent banking model with instantaneous, 1:1 reserve tokenized settlement—we do not just "save on fees"; we unlock an estimated $27 trillion to $45 trillion in "Dead Capital" currently trapped in Nostro/Vostro accounts. This is the math of the digital republic: liquidity that was once frozen as collateral for slow-moving "Wastrel" transactions can now be redirected into the "Real Economy" of production and innovation.

Quantifying the impact of this transition reveals a profound shift in global GDP trajectory. According to 2026 growth projections, the shift to real-time, disintermediated payments is estimated to support over $164 billion in formal GDP across major emerging economies and upwards of $173 billion in the G5 nations alone. When capital moves at the speed of code, the "Velocity of Money" increases exponentially. In a traditional economy, a dollar might take five days to settle a debt before it can be re-deployed by the recipient. In a frictionless digital economy, that same dollar can settle ten different debts in the same timeframe. This "Efficiency Multiplier" effectively expands the money supply without the "Entropy of Inflation," because it is based on the increased velocity of existing value rather than the "Hollow" printing of new fiat.

Starving the Parasite, Feeding the Producer

The redirection of the $150 billion to $200 billion currently lost to global clearing fees acts as a direct, non-legislated stimulus package for the producer. In the trade wars of 2026, where profit margins are under siege by geopolitical instability and "Strategic Friction," a 2% to 3% recovery of total transaction value can be the difference between a project's solvency and its failure. By starving the "Parasitic Layer" of its unearned "Gimmies," we provide the "Active Citizen" with the capital necessary to fund 8,000-square-foot ambitions and multi-volume intellectual pursuits. This is not "theoretical" growth; it is the forensic recovery of stolen energy.

The Frictionless Frontier: A GDP Revolution

Ultimately, a frictionless economy is the only path to achieving the 3.3% to 5% global GDP growth targets required to stabilize the post-fiat world. The "Lobbying Wall" of legacy finance fights this transition because they know that a frictionless system is a transparent system. They prefer the "Settlement Gap" because it is the only place where their "Subjective" value can still hide. However, as more nations adopt the UN DCBAS model and bypass the correspondent chain, the "Global Arbitrage" will force the hand of the remaining "Wastrels." Harmonizing our law with the reality of instant settlement is not just about efficiency—it is about the "Sovereignty" of a republic that refuses to pay a "Middleman Tax" for the privilege of using its own math.[99]

---

[99] The banksters say that "frozen capital" is a necessary part of a "stable" system. Logic check: If I have a million dollars and I have to let it sit in a "Nostro" account for five days just so I can send it to you, that million dollars is not "stable"—it is **unemployed**. They want to keep the "Dead Capital" in their vaults so they can look at it while you are waiting to build your

Conclusion: Decoupling Commerce from the Rent-Seeking Class

The quantification of the **Intermediary Tax** reveals a systemic "Monetary Leak" that is as deliberate as it is destructive. As we have forensically audited throughout this chapter, the "Parasitic Layer" of legacy finance exists not to provide security, but to extract rent from a "Hollow Man" infrastructure that has long since been surpassed by the math of the ledger. By maintaining the "Strategic Friction" of the correspondent banking model and the "Settlement Gap" of global clearinghouses, the "Wastrel" banking cartel has successfully siphoned hundreds of billions of dollars from the productive energy of the "Active Citizen." This extraction is a "Repugnance to Logic" in a digital republic where autonomous code and 1:1 reserve assets provide a "Hard Reset" for the velocity of value.

Decoupling commerce from the rent-seeking class is the only viable path to realizing the "Efficiency Multiplier" required for modern GDP growth. The redirection of "Dead Capital" from pre-funded Nostro/Vostro accounts into the real economy represents a structural recovery of sovereignty that far outweighs any "Subjective" stimulus package the state could offer. Digital disintermediation is not merely a technological upgrade; it is an "Objectivist"

---

factory. In digital realism, the only "Stability" we need is the **Math of Finality**. If the capital is not moving, it is not working. It is time to fire the "Wastrels" and put the money back to work.

reclaiming of the "Rails of Value" from the "Money Changers." By stripping away the "Secondary Tax" of manual compliance theater and cascading fees, we ensure that the "Standard of Value" remains untainted by the "Gimmies" of the gatekeeper, allowing the "Active Citizen" to trade at the speed of the code.

Ultimately, the conclusion of Chapter 9 serves as a forensic mandate for the adoption of a frictionless, 1:1 reserve economy. We must move beyond the "Hollow" excuse that the "Middleman" is a necessary evil and recognize them as a historical relic whose "Smoothing" services are now a terminal drag on global innovation. As we move toward the final sections of this work, the choice is crystalline: we can either continue to fund the "Entropy of Intermediation," or we can embrace the "Algorithmic Certainty" of the protocol. The "Lodestone" has been set, and the math proves that a world without middlemen is not just possible—it is a requirement for a more perfect, productive union.[100]

---

[100] Cooper's Logic Check → The banksters want you to be afraid of a world without "Intermediaries" because they are afraid of a world where they have to get a real job. Logic check: If the "Middleman" is the only thing keeping the system from falling apart, then the system is already broken. They are not the "Glue" of the economy; they are the **Grease** that only works if you keep paying for it. In digital realism, the math does not need to be "smoothed" because it was never meant to be bumpy. It is time to stop paying the "Intermediary Tax" and start keeping the "Change.".

Chapter 10: Monetary Debasement as Theft. The legal and moral failure of targeted inflation.

“The first panacea for a mismanaged nation is inflation of the currency; the second is war. Both bring temporary prosperity; both bring permanent ruing. Both are the refuge of political and economic opportunists.”

Ernest Hemingway[101]

How do you make money without actually doing any work? If you live in Rome or the Middle East around the time of Christ, you would do something called “coin shaving.” This was a process where a person would sand a fraction of the edge off of a coin, then melt the silver, copper, or gold down and sell it at the commodity rate. This debasement of the currency was devastating to economies because there was the same amount of currency but a greatly reduced amount of value in the system.

In modern times, shaving the coins is too much work for those looking to steal from the citizenry. Further, the pittance that they would get shaving the coins and selling the commodity pales in comparison to the billions which they steal every year. Now the world uses a process called “quantitative easing,” or in

---

101 Staff (2026). “Currency Quotes.” Brainy Quote at https://www.brainyquote.com/search_results?x=0&y=0&q=Currency+.

layman's terms- printing more money. Since the value of currency is based off of "the full faith and credit" of the United States (or another country), they are printing money that is worth nothing, devaluing other currency that is worth nothing, on the promise that the citizen tax payer will pay back the system with money that is worth nothing. This is why we have to elect morons like Eric Swallwell, Matt Gaetz and Maxine Waters to congress, if we had competent people who were not bought by the banks they would see through this problem.

One of the reasons that a move to a digital system, like KIROS, is so important for liquidity is the maintaining of a fractal reserve. This gives people property rights in their currency, rather than just "monetary policy" telling them what it is worth. Now, this is where the gold people jump in saying that "money should be gold backed." This is a red herring from people who want the government to buy the gold that they foolishly bought back at the prices Devane and Kiyosaki told them it would be worth. The truth is gold was selected as a model for currency because it was heavy, shiny and easy to mold. This made gold worthless for weapons in ancient time but still strong enough to be coins rattling around in your purse. The same goes for silver. Now, gold and silver have a commodity value. This is the value of their use in industrial (mainly technology) projects. The part that scares people the most is that the commodity value of gold and silver is not even a quarter of the "spot" value which hucksters on TV have ran up. Gold and silver are not a pyramid scheme that people hope you are dumb enough to buy into.

We also have a moral hazard when we are looking at monetary debasement. When money is worth less, who gets the money needed to cover costs. So, first of all, let us rule out the regular people who are paying the taxes, the government and the banks do not care about that. Most likely, the first one to cash out is Israel, then the banks, then the government. If the politicians are lucky, some of them will get a windfall too. Then comes the fighting over taxing the people to pay off the rest. This is a violation of the social contract which the people authorized the government to manage, replacing this with a smart contract removes the “human” error of the government.

The result of this system, or rather continuing on the current path, is that we are seeing the systematic impoverishment of the citizenry as the K shaped economy becomes more pronounced. This also forces the Sovereign debt trap, where the government keeps the currency losing value so the common people are constantly running on an uphill treadmill. Governments were never meant to run the currency, because a failing currency is the in the government’s best interest. To fix this problem we need to move to a private currency with oversight by the government and the people (not just the paid for government). The digital world gives us that pathway.[102]

The Stealth Confiscation: Inflation as an Unvoted Tax

The concept of inflation as a "Stealth Confiscation" is the ultimate forensic evidence of the social contract's breach. In a functional Republic, the power to tax is the most guarded prerogative of the people, requiring legislative debate, public accountability, and an explicit vote. However, through the "Hollow Man" mechanism of targeted inflation, the administrative state has bypassed the Constitution entirely. Inflation functions as an unvoted tax because it achieves the exact same result as a direct levy: it transfers purchasing power from the "Active Citizen" to the government and the "American Bankers Cartel" without a single ballot being cast. It is a "Gimmie" of such scale that it renders the legislative process for traditional taxation almost performative.

---

[102] Cooper's Logic Check → The "Money Changers" say that 2% inflation is "good for the economy." Logic check: If I broke into your house every year and stole 2% of everything you owned, you wouldn't call it "economic growth"—you'd call the police. They want "Inflation" because it is the only way they can pay for their "Gimmies" without having to ask you for a vote. In digital realism, the value of your money should be a reflection of your work, not a reflection of how many trillions a "Wastrel" decided to print for their friends. It is time to stop the "Stealth Confiscation" and start trusting the Math.

The Forensic Mechanics of the Drain

When the government engages in "Quantitative Easing" or maintains a deficit funded by the central bank, it is essentially performing a digital version of "coin shaving." By increasing the supply of currency backed by nothing but "faith," they dilute the value of every existing dollar in the system. If you have $10,000 in a savings account and the government prints enough money to cause 10% inflation, you still have ten thousand pieces of paper, but you have lost $1,000 of actual energy. That thousand dollars did not simply vanish into the "Subjective" void; it was forensically transferred to the first spenders of the new money—the government and the banks—before the prices in the market could adjust. This is the "Stealth" element: the theft occurs at the point of issuance, not at the point of sale.

This process is a "Repugnance to Logic" because it punishes the very behavior that a healthy society requires: thrift, long-term planning, and savings. The "Wastrel" class thrives on inflation because their debts are "hollowed out" over time, while the "Active Citizen" who works for a fixed wage or lives on a fixed pension sees their "Standard of Value" eroded. In the trade wars of 2026, where the cost of living has outpaced wage growth for decades, this unvoted tax is the primary driver of the "K-shaped" economy. It forces the citizenry onto an "uphill treadmill" where they must work more hours just to maintain the same level of survival, while the "Gimmie" class at the top of the Cantillon pyramid watches their asset values inflate.

The Legal Fraud of the "Full Faith" Mandate

From an "Objectivist" legal perspective, inflation is a violation of property rights. If a currency is a "Medium of Exchange" authorized by the government, the government has a fiduciary duty to maintain its value as a constant ledger. When the state intentionally targets a 2% or 3% loss in value, it is essentially admitting to a planned theft of the citizenry's property. This creates a "Strategic Friction" in the law: the government defines currency as property for the purposes of taxation, but treats it as a "Subjective Utility" for the purposes of debasement. They want it both ways—to tax your gains but to "shave" your principal through the printing press.

Ultimately, the "Stealth Confiscation" is the foundation of the "Sovereign Debt Trap." The government cannot afford to pay back its trillions in debt with "Honest Money," so it must ensure the money is "Hollow." This is why a move to a private digital currency like KIROS is the only "Hard Reset" available. By using a Fractal Reserve and a smart contract that cannot be "shaved" by a political opportunist, we return the power of the "Standard of Value" to the individual. We must reclassify targeted inflation for what it forensically is: a criminal breach of the public trust and an unconstitutional tax on the labor of the Republic. Until we stop the printing press, we are not governed by laws, but by the "Strategic Theft" of a system that has run out of ideas.[103]

Legal Precedent for Property Rights vs. Monetary Policy

The conflict between Property Rights and Monetary Policy is a forensic battleground where the "Objectivist" principles of the Constitution have been systematically hollowed out by the "Subjective" needs of a debt-laden state. Under the Fifth Amendment, the "Takings Clause" provides a crystalline mandate: private property shall not be taken for public use without just compensation. In the digital realism of 2026, we must ask: if the government intentionally devalues the currency—the very medium used to measure property—is that not a "Regulatory Taking" of the citizenry's labor and savings? Historically, the courts have avoided this question through the "Hollow Man" logic of necessity, yet the legal precedents reveal a long-standing tension between individual sovereignty and administrative "Gimmies."

---

[103] Cooper's Logic Check → The "experts" say that inflation is necessary to "encourage spending." Logic check: If I told you that your car would lose its wheels if you didn't drive it today, you wouldn't be "encouraged"—you'd be threatened. They want you to spend your money because they are afraid of what happens if you actually save enough to stop needing their "Gimmies." In digital realism, the "Velocity of Value" should come from a thriving marketplace, not from a government fire under your seat. It is time to stop the "Stealth Confiscation" and start holding the "Money Changers" accountable for the missing 98% of our dollar's value.

The Legal Tender Cases: Reversing the Species Standard

The first major fracture occurred with *Knox v. Lee* (1871), which overruled the earlier *Hepburn v. Griswold* (1870). The Supreme Court initially held that forcing creditors to accept paper "Greenbacks" for debts incurred in gold or silver was an unconstitutional violation of the contracts clause. However, in a swift reversal driven by political survivalism, the *Knox* court ruled that Congress possessed the "auxiliary power" to print paper money during wartime. This established the dangerous precedent that "Monetary Policy" could override "Property Rights" in times of perceived emergency, shifting the definition of currency from an objective species to a subjective government mandate.

The Gold Clause Cases: The Death of Contractual Certainty

The most terminal blow to monetary property rights came in 1935 with the Gold Clause Cases (notably *Norman v. Baltimore & Ohio Railroad Co.*). During the Great Depression, Congress passed a Joint Resolution declaring that contracts requiring payment in gold were null and void, allowing debtors to pay in devalued currency instead. The Supreme Court, in a narrow 5-4 decision, ruled that the government's power to "regulate the value of money" superseded private contracts. Justice James C. McReynolds, in a stinging dissent, famously declared that "The Constitution is gone," identifying the abrogation of these clauses as a forensic seizure of property. This ruling effectively turned every private agreement into a "Subjective" document that the state could "shave" at its discretion.

The Modern Frontier: Inflation as a Regulatory Taking

In the digital republic of 2026, the argument for property rights has been re-invigorated by cases like *Horne v. Department of Agriculture* (2015), which affirmed that the Fifth Amendment protects personal property (not just real estate) from government seizure. If the government can be sued for taking raisins, it should forensically be liable for taking the value of the currency through "Quantitative Easing." While the courts currently utilize the "Rational Basis" test to shield economic policy, the "Major Questions Doctrine" established in *West Virginia v. EPA* suggests that agencies cannot unilaterally devalue the nation's "Standard of Value" without explicit Congressional authorization.

Ultimately, the "Legal Precedent" for monetary policy has been a history of "Strategic Friction" intended to protect the state's ability to inflate its way out of debt. However, the "Hard Reset" of the digital world—where tokens like KIROS provide a Fractal Reserve and a crystalline audit trail—re-establishes the "Active Citizen's" property rights. We must argue that currency is not a "Public Utility" to be managed, but private property to be protected. By re-coupling the "Rule of Math" with the "Rule of Law," we can finally close the loophole that allowed the "Wastrels" to use the printing press as a weapon against the prosperity of the Republic.[104]

The Moral Hazard of the Cantillon Effect: Who Gets the Money First?

The Cantillon Effect is the forensic cornerstone of modern economic inequality—a "Hollow Man" mechanism that explains why the "Wastrel" class thrives during inflation while the "Active Citizen" is systematically impoverished. Named after Richard Cantillon, an 18th-century economist, the theory posits that money is not "neutral." When the government or a central bank prints new currency, that money does not enter the economy simultaneously for everyone. Instead, it enters at a specific point—typically through the "American Bankers Cartel" and government contractors—and trickles down to the rest of the population only after it has already begun to drive up prices.

The Mechanics of the "Gimmie" Headstart

In the digital realism of 2026, the Cantillon Effect operates with predatory precision. When the Federal Reserve engages in "Quantitative Easing" or the

[104] Cooper's Logic Check→ The "Money Changers" say that the government has the right to "manage the economy." Logic check: If I managed your bank account by taking 5% every year for my own "emergencies," you'd call it a **Crime**. They used the *Gold Clause Cases* to tell you that a promise is not a promise if the government changes its mind. In digital realism, a contract is **Code**. It does not care about "emergencies," and it does notcare about "Rational Basis." It just executes. It is time to move our property out of their "Policy" and back into our "Sovereignty."

government initiates a new round of "Social Infrastructure" spending, the new dollars are first distributed to the "Early Receivers." These entities—large banks, defense contractors, and geopolitical beneficiaries—get to spend the "Hollow" money while its purchasing power is still at 100%. By the time that money reaches the small business owner in Pennsylvania or the retiree in Florida, it has passed through dozens of hands, driving up the cost of fuel, food, and housing along the way. By the time the "Active Citizen" receives their share, the dollar is only worth 90% or 80% of its original value.

The Moral Hazard

The moral hazard of this system is that it rewards "Proximity to the Printing Press" rather than "Productive Energy." In a healthy Republic, wealth should be the result of creating value; under the Cantillon Effect, wealth is the result of being first in line for the "Gimmie." This creates a terminal incentive for the banking cartel to maintain a state of permanent "Monetary Debasement." Because they are the primary dealers of the new currency, they are the permanent winners of the inflation game. They use this "First-Mover Advantage" to buy up real-world assets—real estate, commodities, and technology—before the "Active Citizen" even realizes their savings have been shaved.

This process is a "Repugnance to Logic" that fuels the "K-shaped" economy. While the stock market and luxury real estate (assets held by the early receivers) inflate to record highs, the "Standard of Value" for the common worker deflates. The "Moral Hazard" extends to the government itself; because they can "print" their way out of a deficit, they have no incentive to balance a budget or respect the social contract. They simply "shave" the value of the Republic's labor to fund their geopolitical ambitions, leaving the taxpayer to foot the bill through a "Stealth Confiscation" that they never voted for.

Who Gets the Money First? The Forensic Hierarchy

If we perform a forensic audit of the 2025-2026 fiscal cycle, the hierarchy of the Cantillon Effect becomes crystalline. The money flows in a pre-defined sequence that ensures the "Active Citizen" is always the last to eat:

1. **The Central Bank & Primary Dealers:** The "Big Four" banks receive the liquidity first, using it to shore up their own fractal reserves and engage in low-risk arbitrage.
2. **Government Contractors & Geopolitical Interests:** As noted in our intro, entities like Israel or large-scale defense firms receive the next windfall through "Emergency Appropriations."
3. **The "Wastrel" Administrative State:** Government agencies expand their "Bureaucratic Hammer" using the new funds before the public cost of living adjustment (COLA) can even be calculated.

4. **The Asset Class:** Large-scale institutional investors (the "Black Rocks" of the world) use cheap credit to buy up fixed assets, pricing the "Active Citizen" out of the housing market.

5. **The Active Citizen:** Finally, months or years later, the money reaches the worker in the form of "wage growth"—which is almost always lower than the rate of price inflation they have already endured.

The "Hard Reset" Solution

The only way to neutralize the Moral Hazard of the Cantillon Effect is to move to a Private, Decentralized Currency like KIROS. By utilizing a smart contract to manage issuance and a Fractal Reserve that is transparent and immutable, we eliminate the "Early Receiver" advantage. In a digital republic, money should enter the system based on "Proof of Value" or "Mathematical Consensus," not based on who has the best lobbyist in D.C. Replacing the "Human Error" of the Federal Reserve with the "Objectivist" certainty of the ledger ensures that the "Standard of Value" is the same for the CEO as it is for the student.

Ultimately, the Cantillon Effect is the "Strategic Friction" that allows a failing system to survive by cannibalizing its own citizens. It is the economic version of "Coin Shaving," performed on a global, digital scale. By reclassifying this effect as a forensic fraud, we can begin the process of "Decoupling" from the "Hollow Man" economy. The trade wars of 2026 will be won by the nation that stops rewarding the

"Gimmie" class and starts protecting the sovereignty of the producer.[105]

Contractual Erosion: How Debasement Voids the Long-Term Agreement

The concept of Contractual Erosion is the forensic evidence of a system that has abandoned the "Objectivist" sanctity of the agreement in favor of "Subjective" administrative survival. In a healthy Republic, a contract is a fixed point—a meeting of minds where value and time are locked into a crystalline obligation. However, through the twin forces of monetary debasement and aggressive lobbying by the American Bankers Association (ABA), the very "Right to Contract" is being systematically hollowed out. When the currency used to fulfill a contract is intentionally devalued, the long-term agreement is not being "managed"; it is being forensically voided.

The ABA and the Institutionalized Breach

The American Bankers Association operates as the primary architect of the "Lobbying Wall" that prevents

---

[105] Cooper's Logic Check → The "Money Changers" say that the Cantillon Effect is just "how money flows." Logic check: If I'm at a buffet and I eat all the steak before you are even allowed in the room, and then I charge you ten dollars for the leftover salad, Which is not "flow"—That is a **shakedown**. They love being at the top of the pyramid because they get to spend "New Money" while it still buys "Old Prices." In digital realism, the money should be "Instant and Equal." If the code says a token is worth X, it should be worth X for everyone at the same time. It is time to flip the pyramid and put the math back in charge.

the Republic from moving toward a 1:1 reserve reality. In their 2026 Blueprint for Growth, the ABA has explicitly identified the "Curbing of Interest/Earnings/Rewards on Payment Stablecoins" as a primary policy priority. This is a direct assault on the right to contract. By lobbying Congress to prohibit the payment of yield on digital species, the ABA is attempting to use the "Bureaucratic Hammer" to prevent private citizens from entering into high-velocity, interest-bearing agreements that compete with their "Wastrel" 0.01% savings accounts.

This is a forensic shakedown: the ABA is not arguing that these contracts are fraudulent; they are arguing that they are too efficient. Their claim that stablecoin rewards would "undermine community bank lending" is a "Hollow Man" argument designed to protect a monopoly. By restricting the types of digital contracts citizens can enter into, the ABA is effectively demanding that the government grant them a "Right to the Citizen's Deposits." This is a violation of the "Sovereignty of the Producer," as it forces the "Active Citizen" into a low-yield "Jurisdictional Trap" where their capital is used to fund the very "Gimmie" system that impoverishes them.

Monetary Debasement as a "Force Majeure" Fraud

Contractual erosion is further accelerated by the "Stealth Confiscation" of inflation. When two parties sign a twenty-year mortgage or a long-term service agreement, they are contracting for a specific amount of "Energy." If the government and the "Bankers

Cartel" then "shave" the value of the dollar by **10%** through quantitative easing, they have effectively rewritten the terms of every private contract in the Republic. This is a "Regulatory Taking" of the future. The borrower pays back "Hollow" dollars, and the lender (if they are not part of the Cantillon "Early Receiver" class) receives a fraction of the value they originally provided.

In digital realism, we recognize that a contract that can be altered by the printing press is not a contract; it is a "Subjective Hope." The ABA's resistance to the GENIUS Act's interest provisions is an attempt to keep the "Active Citizen" tethered to this eroding system. They fear the "Hard Reset" of the smart contract, where the "Standard of Value" is locked into the code and cannot be "shaved" by a political opportunist. By undermining the legal recognition of yield-bearing digital assets, the ABA is ensuring that the "Social Contract" remains a one-sided agreement that only benefits the "Rent-Seeking" class.

The Sovereign Solution: Reclaiming the Right to Contract

To stop the erosion, the Republic must recognize that the "Right to Contract" is an extension of the right to property. If a citizen chooses to hold their value in a 1:1 reserve KIROS token that pays a market-driven yield, no "Wastrel" bank or "Administrative Proxy" should have the power to void that agreement. The transition to the OCC as the primary regulator for digital species would provide the "Sovereignty

Doctrine" necessary to protect these contracts from state-level interference and ABA-driven prohibitions.

Ultimately, the "American Bankers Association" is not protecting the financial system; they are protecting the "Friction" that allows them to extract "Cascading Fees." Their opposition to digital disintermediation is a forensic admission that they cannot compete in a world of "Algorithmic Certainty." We must re-establish the "Objectivist" principle that a contract is the "Supreme Law" between parties, and that any "Monetary Policy" or "Lobbying Maneuver" that seeks to devalue or prohibit that agreement is a terminal breach of the Republic's foundation. In the digital republic of 2026, the only "Permission Slip" we need is the math of the ledger and the will of the participants.[106]

Systematic Impoverishment: The Impact of Devaluation on Fixed-Asset Holders

The systematic impoverishment of the citizenry through currency devaluation is the "Hollow Man" strategy applied to the very foundation of the middle class: the fixed asset. In the digital realism of 2026,

---

[106] Cooper's Logic Check → The ABA says they want to "protect local lending." Logic check: If you have to pass a law to **stop** people from moving their money to a better contract, then your "local lending" model is already dead. They are not "protecting" the community; they are **kidnapping** the community's capital so they can lend it back at a 20% markup. In digital realism, a contract should be a "Safe Harbor," not a "Gimmie" for a bank That is too lazy to innovate. It is time to stop the "Erosion" and start trusting the **Code**.

we see that the "Active Citizen" who followed the "Objectivist" tradition of saving, investing in property, and building a pension is precisely the person targeted by the administrative state's "Stealth Confiscation." When the "Standard of Value" is intentionally hollowed out by the "American Bankers Cartel" and the printing press, the nominal value of a house or a retirement account may remain stagnant or even appear to rise, but its forensic "Energy Value" is in terminal decline. This creates a "K-shaped" economy where those who own the "Early Receiver" assets of the Cantillon Effect thrive, while the fixed-asset holder is forced onto an "uphill treadmill" just to maintain a deteriorating status quo.

For the retiree or the worker on a fixed income, devaluation is a "Regulatory Taking" without the dignity of a court date. Their "Long-Term Agreement" with the state—the promise that their labor today would provide for their survival tomorrow—is being forensically voided. This is the "Sovereign Debt Trap" in action: the government requires the currency to fail so it can pay off the debts of the "Wastrels" with money that is worth nothing. By the time, the "Active Citizen" realizes that their $500,000 nest egg now buys only half the "Goods and Services" it did a decade ago, the theft is already complete. This systematic impoverishment is not a side effect of the system; it is the "Gimmie" that funds the survival of a bureaucracy that has run out of honest ways to tax the people.

Furthermore, the impact on fixed-asset holders creates a "Jurisdictional Trap" that prevents social mobility. As the "Standard of Value" erodes, the cost of maintaining, insuring, and taxing a fixed asset like a home increases, even as the owner's relative wealth decreases. This forces the "Active Citizen" into a state of "Asset Poverty," where they are rich on a "Subjective" paper ledger but poor in "Objective" liquid reality. To fix this "Repugnance to Logic," we must move toward a private digital system like KIROS, where the Fractal Reserve ensures that property rights are inherent in the currency itself. Only by decoupling our assets from the state's mismanagement can we stop the systematic impoverishment of the Republic and restore the sovereignty of the producer.[107]

The Sovereign Debt Trap: Why Governments Require Currency Failure

The Sovereign Debt Trap is the forensic realization that the administrative state has reached a point of no return, where the survival of the government necessitates the systematic destruction of the

---

[107] Cooper's Logic Check → The "Money Changers" tell you that your house doubling in price is "wealth creation." Logic check: If your house doubled in price but it also costs double to buy bread, gas, and a new house, you are not "richer"—you are just **standing in the same place while the ground sinks**. They want you to feel "rich" on paper, so you don't notice they are "shaving" your actual life savings through the printing press. In digital realism, wealth is measured by what you can *do*, not by how many zeros a "Wastrel" adds to a devalued dollar. It is time to stop the "Impoverishment" and start trusting the **Math**.

currency. In the digital realism of 2026, the United States finds itself shackled by a national debt that has surged past $39 trillion, with annual deficits projected at $1.9 trillion. At this stage, the "Wastrel" state is no longer borrowing to invest; it is borrowing to pay the interest on what it has already spent. This creates a terminal incentive for the government to ensure the currency fails—because the only way to "liquidate" such a massive debt load without a formal default is to pay it back with "Hollow" dollars that possess only a fraction of their original purchasing power.

The Arithmetic of Mandatory Debasement

The mechanics of the trap are driven by the "Debt-to-GDP" ratio, which in early 2026 is estimated to be hovering around 120%. Historically, once a nation's debt exceeds its total economic output, the "Standard of Value" becomes a secondary concern to the "Subjective" survival of the bureaucracy. To manage this burden, the government utilizes Financial Repression: a strategy where interest rates are kept artificially lower than the rate of inflation. This ensures that the "Real Value" of the debt shrinks over time, effectively transferring the cost of the government's mismanagement to the "Active Citizen" who holds the currency. This is why the government "requires" currency failure; a stable or strengthening dollar would make the debt mathematically impossible to service, leading to an immediate sovereign default.

War and Inflation: The Twin Pillars of Ruin

As Hemingway forensically noted, when a nation is mismanaged, it turns first to inflation and then to war. In 2026, we see this playing out as the "American Bankers Cartel" and the government coordinate to fund geopolitical ambitions through the printing press. By the time, the "Active Citizen" realizes that 17% of total federal spending is now dedicated solely to "maintaining the debt," the "Stealth Confiscation" is already complete. The "Sovereign Debt Trap" forces the state to become a predator of its own people's labor, using the "Bureaucratic Hammer" to enforce a tax-and-spend cycle that produces nothing but "Hollow" growth.

Digital Disintermediation as the Exit Strategy

The only "Objectivist" escape from this trap is to decouple the "Standard of Value" from the state's failure. The move to a private digital currency like KIROS—backed by a Fractal Reserve and governed by the "Rule of Math"—removes the government's ability to "shave" the value of the Republic's savings. While the "Wastrels" in Congress continue to play with "Hollow" fiat, the innovative producer must move their capital into the "Sovereign Ledger" of the digital world. By 2026, the "Global Arbitrage" is already shifting toward jurisdictions that respect property rights over monetary policy. The choice is crystalline: stay tethered to the sinking ship of a failing sovereign currency, or embrace the "Algorithmic Certainty" of a system that cannot be devalued by a political opportunist.[108]

Conclusion: Reclassifying Inflation as a Human Rights Violation

108 Cooper's Logic Check → The "experts" say that the national debt "does notmatter because we owe it to ourselves." Logic check: If I steal twenty dollars from your wallet and tell you it "does notmatter" because we live in the same house, you are still **missing twenty dollars**. They want you to believe the debt is a "Subjective" number, so you don't notice the "Objective" hole in your grocery budget. In digital realism, the only thing that matters are the **Math of the Vault**. If they can't pay it back without printing it, they havealready defaulted—they are just waiting for you to realize it. It is time to move the "Furniture" of your life into a ledger they can't burn.

Chapter 11: The T+Settlement Anchor. How delayed settlement cycles create artificial risk and suppress capital growth.

"If you spend too much time thinking about a thing, then you will never get it done."

Bruce Lee[109]

What if I told you that the longer something takes, the more money I make off of it? This would sound like you are paying someone hourly and you would keep a watchful eye over me to ensure that I was working at full speed. However, what if an additional constraint was that I decided how long I was going to take to do something, and you had no recourse to challenge that? This is a corrupt system, the systems unions use to debase industry and banks use to create long term transaction fees.

The good news is that this model is dying. Digital transactions are much more efficiency, most settling in under a second and eliminating the need for interbank transfers which take multiple days to settle, SWIFT which can take over a day to settle and even web2 crypto-clones like XRP which can take up to hours in the case of high network latency or block

---

[109] Staff (2026) "Time Quotes." Brainy Quote at https://www.brainyquote.com/search_results?x=0&y=0&q=Time.

loss.[110] Instantaneous agreements would save the country billions of dollars each year and this would be augmented by the new liquidity layer which would may payment method and currencies (whether digital or fiat) seamless.[111]

The Physics of Delay: Why "T-Plus" is an Obsolete Constraint

The "Physics of Delay" in the modern financial system is a forensic artifact of a bygone era—a "Hollow Man" constraint that exists only because the administrative state and the "American Bankers Cartel" have yet to be forced into a "Hard Reset." In a world of digital realism, where information moves at the speed of light, the persistence of "T-Plus" settlement cycles (the time between a trade execution and the actual transfer of ownership) is a "Repugnance to Logic." This delay is not a technical necessity; it is a strategic friction point designed to maintain the "Jurisdictional Fog" that allows intermediaries to extract "Gimmies" from the "Active Citizen."

---

110 Most XRP transactions take approximately 5 seconds to settle.

111 Cooper's Logic Check → The banksters say that "T+1" is a massive achievement for "market efficiency." Logic check: If I can send you a message on my phone instantly, why does it take a "massive achievement" to send the money to pay for it one day later? They want you to think a 24-hour delay is "fast" so you don't realize that **T+0** has been possible for a decade. In digital realism, the "T" stands for "Truth," and the truth does notneed 24 hours to "settle." It is time to stop thinking about the "Thing" and just get it done.

The Chronological Friction of the Legacy System

To understand why "T-Plus" is obsolete, we must audit its origin. The settlement cycle was originally designed to accommodate the physical movement of paper certificates and the manual reconciliation of ledgers by rooms full of "Wastrel" clerks. When the market moved to "T+3," and later "T+2" and "T+1," the banking cartel marketed these shifts as "innovations." However, in the context of 2026 technology, "T+1" is still an eternity. A 24-hour delay in a high-frequency trading environment is equivalent to a century of missed opportunity. This is the "Physics of Delay" at work: by artificially slowing the "Velocity of Value," the legacy system creates a "Settlement Anchor" that prevents capital from being truly fluid.

This chronological inefficiency serves as a "hidden tax" on the producer. While your capital is "in flight"—meaning you have sold an asset but the cash has not "settled"—that value is effectively dead. It cannot be reinvested, it cannot be used to settle debts, and it cannot be used to fund the next 8,000-square-foot project. During this window, the clearinghouse and the "Hollow Man" banks are the ones who benefit, often using the aggregate "float" of unsettled trades to shore up their own liquidity or engage in low-risk overnight arbitrage. They are making money on the "Physics of your Delay."

The Atomic Alternative: T-Zero as the New Standard

In the digital republic, the "Thing-ness" of an asset is tied to its cryptographic signature. There is no logical reason for the trade and the settlement to be two separate events. Atomic Settlement (T-Zero) collapses these two steps into a single pulse of the ledger. When a KIROS token or a tokenized RWA is traded, the change in ownership and the transfer of value happen simultaneously. This removes the "Intermediate State" entirely, neutralizing the "Counterparty Risk" that the "Wastrels" use to justify their billion-dollar clearing fees.

The "Physics of Delay" is also a primary driver of market contagion. As we will explore in the next section, the "T-Plus" window is a breeding ground for "Artificial Risk." When a market shock occurs, the 24-hour settlement gap creates a "Liquidity Lockdown," as institutions scramble to meet margin calls with capital that is technically "on the books" but forensically "not there." By breaking the chains of chronological inefficiency, we do not just speed up the market; we stabilize it. Moving to a "Sovereign Ledger" where is the ultimate "Hard Reset" for a republic that has spent too much time thinking about the "thing" and not enough time getting it done.[112]

---

[112] Cooper's Logic Check → The banksters love to say that "T+1" is the "speed of trust." Logic check: If I trust the math of a blockchain to settle in seconds, why do I need to "trust" a bank to do it in twenty-four hours? They want the "Delay" because if the money moves too fast, you might realize you don't need them to hold your hand. In digital realism, "Trust" is just code that hasn't

Artificial Risk: The Danger of the Unsettled Intermediate State

The Unsettled Intermediate State is the forensic "No Man's Land" of modern finance—a 24-hour window where an asset has been sold but the value has not yet arrived. In the digital realism of 2026, this gap is the primary source of Artificial Risk. This is not a risk inherent to the asset itself, but a risk manufactured by the "Physics of Delay." When we operate under a T+1 or T+2 settlement cycle, we are forced to exist in a "Subjective" reality where ownership is a legal fiction waiting for a "Wastrel" bureaucrat to hit a button. During this state, the "Active Citizen" is exposed to counterparty failure, market volatility, and "Liquidity Lockdown," all because the "American Bankers Cartel" refuses to embrace the "Hard Reset" of atomic settlement.

The danger of this intermediate state is most visible during a "Market Contagion." If a major institution fails during the settlement window, every transaction linked to that entity is suddenly cast into a "Jurisdictional Fog." Because the trade has executed but not settled, the capital is "trapped" in the pipes of the clearinghouse. This creates a domino effect: Party A cannot pay Party B because their funds from a trade with the failing Party C are stuck in "stasis." This is "Artificial Risk" in its purest form—a systemic

---

failed yet. We don't need "T-Plus"; we need **T-Now**. It is time to stop letting the "Wastrels" tell us that the sun needs an extra day to rise on our own money.

seizure caused entirely by chronological inefficiency. If the settlement were **Atomic**, the failure of a counterparty would have zero impact on the rest of the market, as every trade would be finalized the moment it was made.

Furthermore, the "Hollow Man" regulators use this intermediate state to justify the existence of massive, multibillion-dollar "Guaranty Funds" and clearinghouse requirements. They claim these funds are necessary to "protect" the market from settlement failure. Logic check: If you eliminate the settlement delay, you eliminate the possibility of settlement failure. By maintaining the "Unsettled State," the banking cartel ensures a permanent demand for their "smoothing" services and "Gimmie" fees. They have built a billion-dollar industry around managing a risk that should not exist in a digital republic.

Ultimately, the intermediate state is a violation of the **Sovereignty of the Producer**. It forces the citizen to extend an involuntary, interest-free loan to the financial system for 24 to 48 hours every time they move their wealth. In an era where AI-driven "Trade Wars" occur in milliseconds, a one-day delay is a terminal vulnerability. To restore the "Standard of Value," we must demand a system where "T" always equals "Zero." We must bridge the "Settlement Gap" with the crystalline certainty of the ledger, ensuring that the "Intermediate State" becomes a historical relic of a mismanaged nation.[113]

Capital Opportunity Cost: Calculating the Wealth Lost in Stasis

The concept of Capital Opportunity Cost in the context of settlement delay is the forensic measurement of "Economic Stagnation" by design. In the digital realism of 2026, we must recognize that money has a "Time Value" that is being systematically drained by the "Physics of Delay." When capital is held in the "Unsettled Intermediate State"—even for a single day—it is effectively removed from the productive cycle of the Republic. This "Stasis" is not merely a technical pause; it is a multibillion-dollar "Hollow Man" tax on the global economy. By calculating the wealth lost in this chronological vacuum, we expose the true price of the "Settlement Anchor" maintained by the legacy banking cartel.

The Math of the "Day of the Dead"

To quantify the leakage, we must look at the Daily Settlement Volume of the global markets. In early

---

113 Cooper's Logic Check → The banksters say the "Intermediate State" is a "safety buffer" to catch errors. Logic check: If you are driving toward a cliff, do you want a "buffer" that takes 24 hours to work, or do you want **Brakes** that work the second you hit them? They call it "Safety"; I call it a Hostage Situation. They want your money in "stasis" so they can use it as collateral while you are waiting for the green light. In digital realism, the only "Safety" is Finality. If the trade is done, the money should be there. It is time to stop paying for the "Buffer" and start trusting the Math.

2026, the Depository Trust & Clearing Corporation (DTCC) and similar global entities process approximately $10 trillion to $15 trillion in securities transactions every single day. Under a T+1 settlement cycle, that $15 trillion is "locked" for 24 hours. If we apply a conservative "Risk-Free Rate" of 5% (the current yield on 1:1 reserve assets or short-term treasuries), the daily opportunity cost of that stasis is roughly $2 billion per day.

Over a standard 252-day trading year, the "Active Citizens" of the world are losing over $500 billion in potential yield and reinvestment energy simply because the system refuses to move to Atomic Settlement. This is capital that could have been used to fund R&D, infrastructure, or decentralized liquidity pools. Instead, it sits as "Dead Capital" on the books of the clearinghouses, providing a "Subjective" buffer for a system that is too "Wastrel" to innovate. In the trade wars of 2026, this half-trillion-dollar drag is a terminal disadvantage for the American innovator.

Compounding Inefficiency: The Velocity of Stasis

The opportunity cost is not just a linear loss; it is a compounding failure of the "Velocity of Value." In a frictionless, T-Zero economy, a single dollar can be traded, settled, and reinvested multiple times in a single day. In the legacy T+1 environment, that dollar's "Work Cycle" is limited to once every 24 to 48 hours. This difference creates an "Innovation Gap" between the "Digital Republic" and the "Legacy Cartel." By forcing capital into stasis, the "Hollow

Man" regulators are effectively capping the GDP growth of the nation to protect the "Gimmie" fees of the middleman.

For the small-to-mid-sized producer, this stasis is particularly destructive. While a "Big Four" bank can manage its liquidity through the Cantillon "Early Receiver" advantage, the individual producer often operates on tight margins where one day of "Liquidity Lockdown" can lead to a missed opportunity or a forced high-interest bridge loan. This is the "Strategic Friction" of the banking cartel: they make the plumbing so slow that you have to pay them for a "fast pass" or a "liquidity line" just to keep your own business running. It is a forensic fraud that treats your capital as their collateral.

Recovering the Stolen Time

The only "Objectivist" solution to the wealth lost in stasis is the Hard Reset of the "Sovereign Ledger." By moving to 1:1 reserve digital species that settle at T-Zero, we reclaim the half-trillion dollars in annual opportunity cost. We replace the "Physics of Delay" with the "Logic of the Ledger," ensuring that capital is always "Active" and never in "Stasis."

We must stop viewing the settlement window as a "safety feature" and start viewing it as a "theft of time." In digital realism, the value of an asset includes its immediacy. A dollar that takes a day to arrive is worth less than a dollar that arrives now. By calculating the wealth lost in stasis, we provide the "Active Citizen" with the evidence needed to demand a 1:1 reserve union. It is time to stop paying the "Chronological Tax" and start putting our capital back to work at the speed of light.

Liquidity Lockdown: How Slow Settlement Suppresses Market Agility

The "Day of the Dead" is not merely a chronological void; it is the catalyst for Liquidity Lockdown—a systemic paralysis where capital is present on a ledger but absent from the marketplace. In the digital realism of 2026, market agility is the primary determinant of success in the global trade wars. However, the legacy "T-Plus" settlement cycle acts as a "Bureaucratic Anchor," forcing institutions and individuals into a state of involuntary illiquidity. When capital is locked in the unsettled intermediate state, the "Active Citizen" is prevented from responding to real-time market shifts, creating a "Hollow Man" economy where the speed of opportunity is throttled by the sloth of the intermediary.

The Collateral Trap: Financing the Friction

The primary mechanism of Liquidity Lockdown is the Mandatory Margin Requirement. Because the "American Bankers Cartel" operates on a T+1 delay, clearinghouses (CCPs) must require massive amounts of "Initial Margin" and "Variation Margin" to cover the risk that a trade might fail during that 24-hour window. Forensic data from early 2026 indicates that global margin requirements for unsettled trades have surged past $1.2 trillion. This is not productive capital; it is "ransom money" held by the system to mitigate a risk that only exists because the system is too "Wastrel" to settle at T-Zero.

This "Collateral Trap" suppresses market agility by draining the liquidity pools that would otherwise be available for high-velocity trading or decentralized lending. For a mid-sized firm, having millions of dollars tied up in a clearinghouse "Safety Buffer" means they cannot pivot into a new asset class or hedge against a sudden geopolitical shock. The "Gimmie" class of banks thrives on this lockdown because they provide the high-interest "Liquidity Lines" that firms are forced to use when their own capital is "Dead." They have created a system where they profit from the very paralysis they mandate.

The Agility Deficit: Missing the "Objectivist" Pulse

Market agility is defined by the ability to move from "Cash to Asset" and "Asset to Cash" with zero friction. In a frictionless, atomic economy, the "Standard of Value" is always ready for deployment. Under the "Day of the Dead" model, the agility deficit creates a "Latency Risk" that is terminal for the producer. If a market-moving event occurs—such as a sudden change in "Digital Economic Theory" or a forensic audit of a major competitor—the T+1 investor is a day late to the "Hard Reset." They are forced to watch the opportunity pass while their capital sits in the "Jurisdictional Fog" of the clearinghouse.

This lockdown is particularly destructive for Real-World Asset (RWA) Tokenization. The "Cerberus" methodology and the "KIROS" ecosystem are designed for 24/7, instantaneous liquidity. However, when these high-velocity assets are forced to interact with legacy T+1 "On-Ramps," the efficiency of the blockchain is negated by the inefficiency of the bank. This "Strategic Friction" is intended to protect the legacy brokers who cannot survive in a world of "Algorithmic Certainty." They use Liquidity Lockdown to ensure that the "Active Citizen" cannot leave the "Wastrel" system without enduring a 24-hour "cooling off" period that often results in lost profits.

Breaking the Lockdown

Breaking the Liquidity Lockdown requires more than just "faster computers"; it requires the total Digital Disintermediation of the settlement process. By moving to a 1:1 reserve, atomic settlement model, we release the $1.2 trillion in trapped collateral back into the hands of the producers. We replace the "Hollow" safety of the clearinghouse with the "Objective" safety of the ledger, ensuring that capital is always "Active" and never "Dead."

In the trade wars of 2026, the nation with the most agile capital will be the nation that leads the global economy. We must reject the "Physics of Delay" and the "Day of the Dead" as obsolete constraints. The "Standard of Value" must be as fluid as the code that defines it. It is time to unlock the marketplace and restore the sovereignty of the producer by demanding a T-Zero reality where the only "Lockdown" is the one we place on the "Money Changers" who have been living off our delay.[114]

The Instantaneous Alternative: Atomic Settlement in Digital Assets

The move to Atomic Settlement is the "Hard Reset" that finally kills the "Day of the Dead." In the digital realism of 2026, we no longer need to wait for a "Hollow Man" clearinghouse to reconcile the books. Atomic settlement—facilitated by 1:1 reserve digital species like KIROS—collapses the entire lifecycle of a trade into a single, crystalline event. The trade execution, the transfer of ownership, and the movement of value occur simultaneously. If the "Active Citizen" initiates a trade, the ledger updates in milliseconds. There is no "intermediate state," no "strategic friction," and no room for the "Gimmie" class to extract a fee for "smoothing" the delay.

Atomic settlement operates on the principle of Conditional Finality. In a traditional "T-Plus" environment, the trade and the settlement are decoupled, creating a gap where risk can fester. In a

---

114 Cooper's Logic Check → The "experts" say that "Liquidity Lockdown" is a necessary "cooling-off period" for market stability. Logic check: If your house is on fire, do you want a "cooling-off period" before the fire department can turn on the water? They call it "Stability"; I call it a Gag Order on your money. They want your capital locked up so you can't move it when they make a mistake. In digital realism, the only "Stability" that matters is Real-Time Finality. If you can't move your money when you need to, it is not really your money—it is just a "Subjective" IOU. It is time to pick the lock and get back to work.

digital republic, the transaction is governed by a smart contract that acts as an "Objectivist" judge. The contract ensures that the asset is delivered if and only if the payment is received. This "Delivery versus Payment" (DvP) occurs on-chain, removing the need for a central counterparty to hold collateral. The math of the ledger becomes the "Standard of Value," ensuring that the "Velocity of Money" is limited only by the speed of the network, not the "Chronological Inefficiency" of a bank's back office.

Ending the "Collateral Shakedown"

By moving to the instantaneous alternative, the Republic recovers the trillions of dollars currently trapped in "Liquidity Lockdown." When settlement is atomic, there is no "Day of the Dead" to insure, meaning the $1.2 trillion in mandatory margin requirements can be released back to the producers. This is the ultimate "Efficiency Multiplier." Instead of capital sitting as "Dead Capital" in a "Wastrel" clearinghouse, it is immediately available for the next trade or investment. For the innovator building the "Dysart-Detroit-Dallas" corridor, this means their capital is always "Active," working 24/7 in a market that never sleeps and never "locks down."

The Sovereign Advantage of T-Zero

Atomic settlement is the "Sovereignty Doctrine" in practice. It removes the "American Bankers Cartel" from their role as the gatekeepers of time. When you can settle a cross-border transaction in under a second—bypassing the "Correspondent Banking" shakedown—you have effectively decoupled your commerce from the rent-seeking class. This is the "Hard Reset" that the "Wastrels" fear most: a world where the math is so perfect that their "smoothing" services are forensically worthless. In the trade wars of 2026, the instantaneous alternative is not just a technical choice; it is the only way to protect the "Active Citizen" from the "Strategic Friction" of a dying system.[115]

Stress Testing the System: Why Latency Causes Market Contagion

The "Day of the Dead" is not just a drain on capital; it is a fracture point in global stability. In the digital realism of 2026, we have witnessed a shift where "Market Contagion" is no longer solely a result of bad assets, but a result of Settlement Latency. When the system is put under stress—whether by geopolitical friction, AI-driven leveraged unwinds, or sudden energy price spikes—the 24-hour settlement gap in the "T+1" model acts as a conductor for systemic failure. Latency transforms a localized liquidity squeeze into a global epidemic, as the "Artificial Risk"

[115] Cooper's Logic Check → The "Money Changers" say that atomic settlement is "too fast" and does notallow for "error correction." Logic check: If you send an email and realize you made a typo, you don't ask the post office to hold it for three days "just in case." You fix the error in the next email. They want the "Delay" because That is where they hide their "Gimmies." In digital realism, "Fast" is just another word for "Honest." If the code is right, the trade is done. It is time to stop paying for the "Slow" and start embracing the Now.

of unsettled trades cascades through the "Hollow Man" clearinghouses.

The Domino Effect of the "Unsettled" Intermediate State

The primary driver of contagion in 2026 is the Interdependence of Delayed Finality. In a T+1 environment, financial institutions operate in a chain: Bank A depends on Bank B to settle, and Bank B depends on Bank C. If a sudden shock—like the leveraged position unwinds we saw in January 2026—causes Bank C to delay its delivery of funds, the latency immediately propagates. Because Bank B is waiting on "Dead Capital" from the intermediate state, it cannot fulfill its obligations to Bank A. In an atomic, T-Zero system, this chain never forms; either the trade settles instantly or it does not happen. Under T+1, the delay allows the "infection" of non-payment to spread across the entire network before the first 24-hour cycle is even complete.

In early 2026, the widespread adoption of similar AI decision models has created a "Correlated Behavior" risk. When market conditions shift, these AI agents respond to shocks in near-simultaneous ways, intensifying short-term price movements. However, while the *trading* happens at the speed of light, the *settlement* is still stuck in the "Wastrel" T+1 schedule. This mismatch creates a terminal pressure point. As AI-driven redemptions intensify, the volume of "unsettled" claims grows exponentially, straining the liquidity of the clearinghouses and forcing "Strategic

Friction" in the form of higher margin calls. This is the "Stress Test" the system is currently failing: the math of the trade is moving faster than the plumbing of the settlement, and the resulting friction is the heat of a market fire.

Operational Fragility and the "Gimmie" Defense

Stress testing also reveals the "Operational Fragility" of the legacy infrastructure. The January 2026 payments settlement outage, caused by a simple failure in "intermediate certificate lifecycle management," demonstrated that the "American Bankers Cartel" is often one technical error away from a total "Liquidity Lockdown." During such outages, "Artificial Risk" becomes the only reality. The "Gimmie" class of banks responds to this fragility by increasing settlement delays for their smaller trading partners to "manage" their own overdraft risk—a move that forensically transfers the pain to the "Active Citizen." This strategic delay is not a safety measure; it is a "Hollow Man" defense that ensures the core banks survive at the expense of the periphery.

Ending the Contagion with Atomic Certainty

The only forensic cure for latency-driven contagion is the Hard Reset of Atomic Settlement. By collapsing the "Day of the Dead" into an instantaneous event, we remove the "Intermediate State" where contagion breeds. We replace the "Subjective" hope of T+1 with the "Objectivist" certainty of the ledger. In the trade wars of 2026, a resilient system is one where "Finality" is not a 24-hour promise, but a millisecond reality. To protect the Republic from the next market contagion, we must decouple our settlement from the "Chronological Inefficiency" of the past and embrace a T-Zero standard that moves at the speed of thought.[116]

Conclusion: Breaking the Chains of Chronological Inefficiency

The productive energy of the Republic is sacrificed at the altar of "T-Plus" inefficiency. As we have documented, the "Settlement Anchor" is not a technical necessity of the digital era, but a strategic friction point maintained by the "American Bankers Cartel" to extract economic rent from the "Unsettled Intermediate State." This artificial delay creates a "Liquidity Lockdown" that traps trillions in "Dead Capital," forcing the "Active Citizen" to pay for "Gimmie" liquidity lines while their own wealth sits in the "Jurisdictional Fog" of a clearinghouse.

Breaking the chains of chronological inefficiency requires a "Hard Reset" to the "Sovereign Ledger" of atomic settlement. By collapsing the trade, clearing,

---

[116] Cooper's Logic Check → The banksters say that "speed kills" and we need the T+1 delay to "catch our breath" during a crisis. Logic check: If you are in a crowded theater and someone smells smoke, do you want the exit doors to stay locked for 24 hours so everyone can "calm down"? They want the doors locked because they are the only ones with the keys to the back exit. In digital realism, the "Latency" is the Smoke. If you can't settle now, you are already in trouble. It is time to unlock the "Atomic" exit and stop paying the "Wastrels" to hold the door shut while the room gets hot.

and settlement phases into a single, instantaneous pulse of the ledger, we eliminate the "Artificial Risk" that fuels market contagion. In the digital realism of 2026, the only "Standard of Value" that can survive the velocity of AI-driven trade is one that settles at T-Zero. This transition is not just about "faster computers"; it is about the "Objectivist" reclaiming of time as a property right, ensuring that the "Velocity of Value" is no longer throttled by the rent-seeking class.

The move toward instantaneous finality provides the "Efficiency Multiplier" necessary to win the 2026 trade wars. By releasing the billions of dollars currently held in "stasis" back into the hands of the producers, we enable a level of market agility that the "Wastrel" legacy system cannot possibly match. This is the ultimate "Sovereignty Doctrine": a system where the producer and the receiver interact directly, with the math of the ledger serving as the only judge. When the "Settlement Gap" is closed, the "Money Changers" lose their primary tool for extraction, and the "Active Citizen" finally regains control over the pulse of their own capital.

Ultimately, we must reject the "Hollow" excuses of the legacy system that claim delay equals safety. In a world of "Algorithmic Certainty," delay is only a hiding place for risk and extraction. As we move forward, the Republic must adopt the "Atomic Standard" as a foundational requirement for economic growth. By ending the "Day of the Dead," we do more than just save time; we restore the moral and economic integrity of the marketplace. The chains of the "T-Plus" anchor have been forensically identified; now, it is time for the "Active Citizen" to cut them and embrace a future where value moves at the speed of thought.[117]

---

[117] Cooper's Logic Check → The banksters say that "speeding up the system" is risky because it does notgive them time to "fix mistakes." Logic check: If I give you a haircut and mess it up, you don't wait twenty-four hours to scream—you do it now. They want the "Delay" because they are the ones making the mistakes with *your* money, and they need the time to hide the evidence. In digital realism, the "Mistake" is the "Delay" itself. If the math is right, the trade is done. It is time to stop paying the "Slow-Motion Tax" and start living in the Now.

Chapter 12: Information Asymmetry. Why the legacy market is rigged through gated access to data.

"People feel like the system is rigged against them, and here is the painful part, they are right. The system is rigged."

Elizabeth Warren[118]

Very rarely do I agree with Senator Elizabeth Warren, however on this matter she is correct. When you allow monopolies, there is asymmetrical warfare going on against the people. To balance this out, we must break down the monopolies. As we know, those in power (including Warren) will likely fight against these changes because they are the funding mechanism which keeps the political machine running.

Therein lies the problem, the political machine. Whereas the government is necessary for the protection of the people, it is not necessary to control our daily lives. As such, we need to break down the propaganda machine of the legacy media and break down that monopoly as well. The government should not control any information except the names of spies and military secrets and technology. The fact that there is a slush fund for sexual assault claims within

[118] Staff (2026). "Rigged Quotes." Brainy Quote at https://www.brainyquote.com/search_results?x=0&y=0&q=rigged .

congress tells you all you need to know about the system.

We also need to renew the call for experts, real experts. I took the time to get 9 degrees, work in the field for 20 years, and maintain relationships with several professional associations. I still understand that there are experts in the field with more of a pedigree than myself. However, most of what we are seeing on the news is graduate students, activist and politicians acting as if they are experts. We need to redefined the title to ensure that “experts” in the field, especially those testifying before congress for change, are real experts. Athletes and celebrities (with the exception of Dolf Lungrin) should never be testifying on anything other than entertainment.[119]

Gated Access: The High Cost of the Institutional Data Monopoly

The "Gated Access" of the legacy financial system is the forensic architecture of a rigged game. In the digital realism of 2026, we are told that the marketplace is a meritocracy where the best ideas

---

[119] Cooper's Logic Check → The "experts" on TV say that the market is "too complicated" for regular people to understand without their help. Logic check: If a system is so "complicated" that you need a priest to translate it for you, it is not a "Market"—it is a Religion. They want "Gated Access" because they know that if you saw the actual numbers, you'd realize their "Smoothing" is just a fancy word for "Taking a Cut." In digital realism, the only "Expert" you need is the Math. If it does notadd up on the ledger, it is a lie. It is time to close the "Slush Funds" and open the Books.

win; however, a forensic audit of the Institutional Data Monopoly reveals that the winners are actually those who can afford the entry fee. By maintaining a paywall around the "Rails of Information," the legacy system ensures that the "Active Citizen" remains in a state of "Subjective" uncertainty, while the "American Bankers Cartel" operates with "Objectivist" clarity. This is the first and most effective layer of the "Lobbying Wall": making the truth so expensive that only the "Wastrels" at the top can afford to see it.

The $30,000 Barrier to Entry

The cornerstone of this monopoly is the institutional data terminal. As of 2026, the cost of a single professional terminal subscription—essential for real-time order flow, depth-of-market data, and global macro-economic alerts—hovers between $25,000 and $32,000 per year. For an independent producer or a small-scale innovator in Dysart or Detroit, this is not a business expense; it is a "Strategic Friction" point designed to keep them on the periphery. This creates a "Hollow Man" marketplace where retail traders and independent firms are forced to rely on "Delayed Data" (often 15 to 20 minutes behind) while institutional high-frequency traders (HFTs) front-run their decisions in milliseconds.

This pricing is not a reflection of the cost of the technology; it is a "Monopoly Tax" on intelligence. The data itself—the pulse of the market—should be a public good in a functioning Republic. Instead, the "Gimmie" class of data providers has transformed the

"Velocity of Information" into a gated community. By the time the "Active Citizen" sees a price shift on a free web2 platform, the institutional "Money Changers" have already executed their trades, harvested the spread, and moved on. This is "Asymmetrical Warfare" disguised as a service contract.

The Consolidation of the "Gimmies"

The 2025-2026 fiscal cycle saw a massive consolidation in the financial data industry, with three major players now controlling over 80% of the terminal market. This "Information Cartel" works in tandem with the "American Bankers Association" to ensure that the "Standard of Value" for data remains artificially high. They utilize "Restrictive Licensing" to prevent the redistribution of data, effectively criminalizing the democratized sharing of market insights. This ensures that the "Propaganda Machine" of the legacy media remains the only "free" source of information for the public—a source that is intentionally designed to be "Hollow" and lagging.

This gated access extends to the regulatory level as well. The "Slush Fund" mentality of the administrative state means that many of the most critical economic indicators and internal audit reports are shielded from FOIA requests or buried behind paywalls and "Subscriber Only" portals. When the government hides the names of the "Wastrels" receiving the Cantillon windfalls, they are participating in the same "Gated" strategy. They want the "Active Citizen" to remain blind so that the "Rigged System" can continue to operate without the "Repugnance to Logic" being exposed.

The Digital Reset: Breaking the Paywall

The only forensic solution to "Gated Access" is the Democratization of Data through the 1:1 reserve ledger. In a digital system like KIROS, the "Standard of Value" for information is zero—it is public, transparent, and atomic. By moving market activity onto an immutable ledger, we remove the need for a $30,000 terminal. The "Active Citizen" in their home library has the exact same access to the "Pulse of the Republic" as the CEO on Wall Street. This is the ultimate "Hard Reset": a world where the "Physics of Information" are equal for all, and the "Expert" title is earned through the analysis of open data rather than the possession of an institutional subscription.[120]

The Propaganda Machine: Manufacturing Consent for Inefficient Systems

The "Propaganda Machine" is the psychological infrastructure of the legacy financial complex, a system designed to ensure the "Active Citizen"

---

[120] Cooper's Logic Check → The "experts" say that the $30,000 terminal fee is necessary to "ensure data quality." Logic check: If the data is coming from a public marketplace, why do you have to pay a bank's salary just to look at the scoreboard? They don't want "Data Quality"; they want a Head Start. They want to be the only ones who can see the cards before the betting starts. In digital realism, the "Scoreboard" is the Ledger, and it is free for everyone who can read the code. It is time to stop paying for the "Gate" and start using the "Math."

remains a voluntary participant in their own economic hollowing. In the digital realism of 2026, we see that the "American Bankers Cartel" and the administrative state do not rely on overt force; instead, they utilize the "Propaganda Model" to manufacture consent for systems that are forensically inefficient. By filtering information through the five lenses of ownership, advertising, sourcing, flak, and ideology, the media-industrial complex ensures that any critique of the "Wastrel" status quo is dismissed as fringe or "unrealistic." This is the primary function of the legacy news cycle: to convince the producer that the "Strategic Friction" of the current system is not only necessary but also moral.

The mechanism of "Manufacturing Consent" relies on the selective presentation of "Worthy" and "Unworthy" economic outcomes. When the printing press is used to fund a trillion-dollar "slush fund" for geopolitical interests or failing banks, the propaganda machine frames it as a "Systemic Stabilization"—a worthy sacrifice for the greater good. However, when the "Active Citizen" seeks the sovereignty of a 1:1 reserve digital system, they are met with "Flak" from the legacy media, which brands alternative financial rails as "dangerous" or "speculative." This is "Asymmetrical Warfare" on the psyche: the "Propaganda Machine" primes the public to associate legacy banking with "safety" and innovation with "risk," even as the actual data shows that the legacy system is the primary driver of the "Sovereign Debt Trap."

Furthermore, the machine operates through the "Expert Fallacy," where "Hollow Man" authorities—often activists masquerading as economists—are used to validate the state's narratives. These "sources" are chosen specifically because they reinforce the "Gimme" culture, providing a "Subjective" layer of academic jargon that masks the objective truth of monetary debasement. In 2026, the media's reliance on these gated sources ensures that the "Rails of Information" remain under the control of the political machine. To achieve a "Hard Reset," we must recognize that the "Propaganda Machine" is the primary barrier to the democratization of truth. Only by bypassing the legacy filters and moving toward an immutable ledger can the "Active Citizen" decouple their reality from the manufactured consent of a dying system.[121]

Psychological Priming: How Government Narratives Enforce Financial Compliance

Psychological priming is the "Invisible Hand" of the administrative state—a behavioral mechanism used to enforce financial compliance without the need for a

---

121 Cooper's Logic Check → The "experts" on the 6 o'clock news tell you that "Inflation is a sign of a strong economy." Logic check: If I keep cutting your paycheck every year, am I "strengthening" your budget? They call it "Consent"; I call it Gaslighting. They want you to believe the "Wastrel" system is the only thing standing between you and chaos, while they are the ones lighting the match. In digital realism, the "Truth" is not what a teleprompter says—it is what the Ledger proves. It is time to stop letting the "Machine" think for you and start trusting the Math.

"Bureaucratic Hammer." In the digital realism of 2026, the government has moved beyond mere legislation to the realm of Choice Architecture. By utilizing subtle linguistic cues, framing effects, and social-norm signaling, the "Wastrel" state primes the "Active Citizen" to accept monetary debasement and systemic extraction as both "natural" and "moral." This is the psychological foundation of the "Hollow Man" economy: a system that survives not because it is efficient, but because the citizenry has been primed to ignore its failures.

The Architecture of the "Nudge"

The primary tool of this priming is the "Nudge"—a concept popularized by behavioral economists and institutionalized into "Nudge Units" within federal agencies. These units specialize in Message Framing, where compliance-related information is delivered through a specific cultural or emotional lens to trigger a predictable response. For example, forensic data from 2026 reveals that tax compliance messages framed with a "relational" or "collectivist" focus—emphasizing the "public good" and "social duty"—yield significantly higher compliance rates than those focused on individual penalties. This is "Psychological Priming" in its purest form: bypassing the rational, "Objectivist" mind and activating a "Subjective" sense of guilt or social obligation to ensure the flow of capital to the state.

Social Norming and the "Nine-out-of-Ten" Trap

One of the most effective government narratives is the use of Social Proof to enforce financial compliance. By informing citizens that "Nine out of ten people in your area pay their taxes on time," the state creates a "Descriptive Norm" that makes non-compliance feel like social deviance. In reality, this narrative is a "Propaganda" mask used to obscure the "Repugnance to Logic" of the tax code itself. The "Active Citizen" is primed to fear being an outlier, leading them to voluntarily participate in a system of "Stealth Confiscation" rather than questioning the "Wastrel" spending that necessitates it. This "Psychological Priming" ensures that the "Status Quo Bias" remains the dominant economic force, preventing the "Hard Reset" that a 1:1 reserve digital system would provide.

Fear-Based Priming and the "Security" Narrative

The government also utilizes Negative Priming to enforce compliance during times of crisis. By associating alternative financial rails—such as private digital assets or decentralized protocols—with imagery of "crime," "instability," and "threats to national security," the state primes the public to associate safety with the legacy "American Bankers Cartel." This "Security Narrative" is a "Hollow Man" defense intended to maintain the "Jurisdictional Trap" of the fiat system. When the citizen is primed to fear the "New," they will tolerate the "Broken" out of a manufactured sense of self-preservation. In the trade wars of 2026, this fear-based priming is the primary weapon used to stall the adoption of the "Sovereign Ledger" and keep the producer tethered to the state's mismanagement.

Breaking the Prime: Toward "Algorithmic Sovereignty"

The only way to neutralize psychological priming is through the Democratization of Truth. When we move to a 1:1 reserve system like KIROS, the "Choice Architecture" is no longer controlled by a "Wastrel" bureaucrat; it is controlled by the "Rule of Math." On an immutable ledger, there is no room for "Framing" or "Social Norming" to hide the reality of the transaction. We must recognize that every government narrative is a form of "Strategic Friction" intended to manipulate behavior for the benefit of the rent-seeking class. By reclaiming our "Objectivist" awareness and decoupling our commerce from the state's "Propaganda Machine," we restore the moral and economic sovereignty of the Republic.[122]

---

[122] Cooper's Logic Check → The "experts" say that "Nudges" are just a way to help you make "better decisions." Logic check: If I have to trick you into making a "better decision," who is it actually "better" for? They call it "Libertarian Paternalism"; I call it Soft-Core Authoritarianism. They want to prime you to love your chains so they don't have to pay for the locks. In digital realism, a "Decision" should be based on Data, not "Feelings" manufactured by a government focus group. It is time to stop being "Nudged" and start being **Sovereign**.

The "Expert" Fallacy: Using Complexity as a Barrier to Public Understanding

The "Expert" Fallacy is the forensic use of perceived authority to silence dissent and obscure the "Repugnance to Logic" inherent in the legacy financial system. In the digital realism of 2026, we find ourselves governed by a "Technocratic Elite"—a collection of "Hollow Man" authorities who utilize specialized jargon and complex models to create an "Information Moat" around the administrative state. By framing economic policy as a subject too complex for the "Active Citizen" to grasp, the "Wastrel" class ensures that the "Standard of Value" remains a "Subjective" tool of the state rather than an "Objectivist" right of the producer.

This barrier to entry is not a side effect of advanced science; it is a "Strategic Friction" point designed to protect the "Gimmie" culture of the "American Bankers Cartel." When a true expert—someone who has spent decades in the field, earning the necessary "Objectivist" pedigree—attempts to point out the simple fraud of monetary debasement, they are met with a wall of "Academic Flak." The system prefers "Experts" who are actually activists or politicians in disguise, because these individuals will validate the "Propaganda Machine" in exchange for a seat at the table of power.

The Jargon Shield: Manufacturing Confusion

The primary mechanism of the Expert Fallacy is the use of "Jargon" as a defensive shield. Terms like "Quantitative Easing," "Transitory Macro-Fluctuations," and "Macroprudential Oversight" are used to describe what is, forensically, the printing of money and the hollowing out of the social contract. By wrapping simple concepts in layers of linguistic complexity, the "Wastrel" experts ensure that the average taxpayer feels unqualified to challenge the "Sovereign Debt Trap." This is a form of "Intellectual Gaslighting," intended to make the producer feel like a "Hollow Man" in the face of institutional complexity.

In the digital realism of 2026, we see this most clearly in the "Lobbying Wall" built around digital asset legislation. "Experts" testifying before Congress use technical "Strategic Ambiguity" to argue that the 1:1 reserve model is "untested" or "systemically risky," despite the mathematical certainty of the ledger. They rely on the fact that most lawmakers—who are often the "Morons" we were forced to elect—will defer to the "Expert" rather than doing the forensic work themselves. This ensures that the "Rules of the Game" remain written in a language that only the "Money Changers" and their paid consultants can speak.

The Institutional Gatekeeper: Pedigree vs. Performance

The "Expert" Fallacy also thrives on the prioritization of "Pedigree" over "Performance." The legacy system recognizes "Expertise" only if it comes from a sanctioned "Hollow Man" institution, regardless of that institution's track record of failure. We are told to trust the "experts" who failed to see the inflation of 2021 or the banking contagions of 2024, simply because they hold a degree from the "right" university or a title in the "right" agency. This is a "Repugnance to Logic" that values the "Subjective" credential over the "Objective" reality of the ledger.

To achieve a "Hard Reset," we must demand a new standard for expertise. A true expert in the digital republic must be an athlete of the intellect—someone whose work is transparent, auditable, and grounded in the "Physics of Value." We must reject the celebrity "Experts" and the political activists who use their platform to enforce financial compliance. In the trade wars of 2026, the only "Expert" we should trust is the one who can explain the system in a way that empowers the "Active Citizen" rather than silencing them. Expertise should be a bridge to understanding, not a "Bureaucratic Hammer" used to maintain the status quo.

Complexity as a Weapon: The Illusion of Necessity

Complexity is often the last refuge of the "Wastrel" who has run out of honest arguments. By making a system unnecessarily complex, the state creates an "Illusion of Necessity," convincing the public that the "Middleman" and the "Intermediary" are the only ones capable of managing the chaos. This is the "Gimmies" hidden in the plumbing: if the pipes are so complicated that only a "Master Plumber" (the Bank) can understand them, then the bank can charge whatever "Cascading Fees" it wants for "maintenance."

The "Objectivist" solution is the radical simplicity of the Immutable Ledger. A system like KIROS removes the need for the "Expert" translator because the "Truth" is baked into the code. When the "Standard of Value" is 1:1 and transparent, the "Information Asymmetry" vanishes. The "Expert" Fallacy falls apart when the "Active Citizen" can audit the "Physics of the Transaction" themselves. We must move away from a system that requires "High Priests" of finance and move toward a republic where the math is the only authority.[123]

Algorithmic Transparency vs. State-Sponsored Obfuscation

The conflict between Algorithmic Transparency and State-Sponsored Obfuscation is the defining "Objectivist" struggle of the digital republic. In the digital realism of 2026, the administrative state relies

---

[123] Cooper's Logic Check → The "experts" on the news love to use big words to explain why you are getting poorer. Logic check: If I have to use a dictionary and a PhD to explain why I took five dollars out of your pocket, I'm not "explaining"—I'm distracting you. They love "Complexity" because it is the only way they can hide the "shaving" of the coins in 2026. In digital realism, "Expertise" means you can make the complicated simple, not the simple complicated. If they can't explain it to you in plain English, it is because they are trying to sell you a "Gimmie" you don't need. It is time to stop listening to the "Hollow Men" and start trusting the Math.

on "Strategic Ambiguity"—a form of obfuscation where the "Rules of the Game" are hidden behind the "Bureaucratic Hammer" of shifting interpretations and "Hollow Man" guidance. By contrast, algorithmic transparency represents a "Hard Reset" to a system of "Crystalline Certainty," where the math of the ledger replaces the "Subjective" whim of the regulator. This is the move from a "Trust Me" system to a "Verify Me" system, stripping the "Wastrel" class of their ability to hide the "Gimmies" in the fog of administrative law.

Obfuscation as a Weapon of Control

State-sponsored obfuscation is not an accident of a complex world; it is a deliberate "Strategic Friction." By refusing to provide "Bright-Line" rules for digital assets and tokenization, the "American Bankers Cartel" and their regulatory proxies ensure that the "Active Citizen" is always in a state of legal jeopardy. This "Jurisdictional Trap" allows the government to choose when and how to enforce its rules, targeting innovators who threaten the "Status Quo" while protecting the "Wastrels" who fund the political machine. This is a "Repugnance to Logic" that treats the law not as a "Standard of Value," but as a weapon of selective extraction.

Furthermore, the state utilizes "Slush Fund" accounting to hide the true destination of the "Stealth Confiscation" known as inflation. When the government refuses to provide a real-time, auditable trail of where the "New Money" flows—citing "National

Security" or "Administrative Privilege"—they are practicing obfuscation. This is the "Hollow Man" at work: a system that demands total transparency from the producer while maintaining total opacity for the tax-eater. In the trade wars of 2026, this lack of transparency is the primary driver of the "Sovereign Debt Trap," as the public is kept blind to the terminal mismanagement of the Republic's ledger.

The Algorithmic Standard: Code as the Supreme Law

The "Hard Reset" of algorithmic transparency is found in the Sovereign Ledger. When we move commerce to a 1:1 reserve system like KIROS, the "Standard of Value" is no longer a government promise; it is a mathematical proof. Algorithmic transparency means that the "Rules" are baked into the code—they are open-source, immutable, and equal for all participants. There is no "Strategic Ambiguity" in a smart contract; it either executes based on the pre-defined parameters or it does not. This "Algorithmic Certainty" removes the need for the "Expert" translator and the "Gimme" consultant, returning the "Right to Contract" to the individual.

This transparency is the ultimate deterrent to the "Cantillon Effect." When the issuance of currency is governed by a transparent algorithm rather than a "Subjective" committee, the "Early Receiver" advantage vanishes. The "Active Citizen" can audit the ledger in real-time, ensuring that no "shaving" of the coins is occurring in the dark. In 2026, the nation that embraces the "Glass Box" of algorithmic transparency will be the one that attracts the most capital and innovation. It is the only forensic way to rebuild the "Social Contract" on a foundation of truth rather than "State-Sponsored Obfuscation."

Piercing the Veil of the "Hollow Man"

Ultimately, the choice between transparency and obfuscation is a choice between a "Digital Republic" and a "Technocratic Dictatorship." We must reject the "Hollow" claim that the state needs "flexibility" to manage the economy. "Flexibility" is just a "Wastrel" word for "Theft by Interpretation." By demanding algorithmic transparency, we pierce the veil of the administrative state and restore the "Objectivist" clarity of the marketplace. The "Standard of Value" must be a light that exposes the "Gimmies," not a fog that hides them. It is time to stop playing the "Rigged Game" of the obfuscators and start building on the "Rails of Math."[124]

Weaponized Media: Discrediting Alternatives to Maintain the Status Quo

The "Weaponized Media" is the primary enforcement arm of the legacy financial complex, functioning as a

---

[124] Cooper's Logic Check → The "experts" say that "Regulatory Ambiguity" is necessary for a "Dynamic Market." Logic check: If I'm playing a game of poker and the dealer says he'll "decide the rules as he goes," That is not "Dynamic"—it is a Rigged Game. They want the "Obfuscation" because they are the only ones who know where the "Slush Fund" money is hidden. In digital realism, the "Algorithm" is the Dealer, and the rules are printed on the table for everyone to see. It is time to stop trusting the "Hollow Men" and start trusting the Code.

"Propaganda Machine" that protects the "American Bankers Cartel" by preemptively discrediting any forensic alternative. In the digital realism of 2026, the media does not merely report on the economy; it actively shapes the "Subjective" reality of the "Active Citizen" to ensure they remain tethered to "Wastrel" systems. By utilizing a strategy of "Strategic Discreditation," the media-industrial complex labels innovation as "danger" and transparency as "risk," effectively building a "Psychological Moat" around the failing structures of the administrative state.

This weaponization operates through the "Manufacturing of Consent," where any "Objectivist" move toward 1:1 reserve digital species or decentralized protocols is met with a coordinated "Flak" campaign. When a system like KIROS offers a "Hard Reset" to the "Sovereign Debt Trap," the legacy media responds by highlighting the "Unworthy" outliers of the crypto-world—the scammers and the hucksters—to paint the entire technology with the same brush. This is "Asymmetrical Information Warfare" intended to prevent the producer from recognizing that the real "Systemic Risk" is not the new ledger, but the "Hollow Man" bank they have been primed to trust.

The Economic Undermining: Throttling the Efficiency Multiplier

The weaponization of media directly undermines the economy by suppressing the adoption of the "Efficiency Multiplier." When the media spends its

"Velocity of Information" scaring the public away from digital disintermediation, they are effectively advocating for the continued extraction of the "Intermediary Tax." Every day the public is discouraged from moving to a T-Zero, frictionless economy is a "Day of the Dead" for capital growth. This "Strategic Friction" ensures that trillions of dollars remain trapped in "Liquidity Lockdown," serving the interests of the "Gimmie" class while the "Active Citizen" struggles under the weight of "Cascading Fees."

By maintaining the "Status Quo Bias," the media ensures that the "Velocity of Value" remains throttled. They frame the "Hard Reset" as an "Economic Threat" rather than an "Economic Opportunity," ignoring the forensic data that shows a move to 1:1 reserve assets would increase global GDP by trillions. This is a terminal drag on innovation; when the "Propaganda Machine" convinces the next generation of innovators that the "Sovereign Ledger" is a "Jurisdictional Trap," it diverts their productive energy back into the "Hollow" rails of the legacy system. The media is not just reporting on the slow economy—it is one of the primary reasons the economy is slow.

The Threat to the Republic: Hollowing the Social Contract

The most dangerous aspect of weaponized media is its assault on the Republic itself. A functioning Republic requires a "Democratization of Truth," where the "Active Citizen" has access to the "Standard of

Value" for both currency and information. When the media functions as a "Lobbying Wall" for the administrative state, it voids the "Social Contract." By discrediting alternatives to "Monetary Debasement," the media becomes an accomplice in the "Stealth Confiscation" of the citizenry's labor. They provide the "Subjective" cover for the "Wastrels" in Congress to continue their "Slush Fund" spending, ensuring that the public remains focused on "Culture Wars" while their "Objectivist" property rights are being shaved.

This weaponization undermines the "Rule of Law" by replacing it with the "Rule of Narrative." In 2026, we see the "Expert Fallacy" being used to silence those who point out the "Repugnance to Logic" in the current system. The media labels forensic critics as "extremists" or "threats to stability," effectively using the "Bureaucratic Hammer" of public shaming to enforce financial compliance. This creates a "Hollow" Republic where the appearance of choice exists, but the "Physics of Information" are rigged to ensure the "Money Changers" always win. The only way to save the Republic is to decouple the "Standard of Value" from the media's "Propaganda Machine" and return to the crystalline certainty of the immutable ledger.

Dismantling the Gatekeepers of "Truth"

Ultimately, the "Weaponized Media" is the last line of defense for a system that has run out of honest arguments. As the "Sovereign Debt Trap" tightens and the "Cantillon Effect" becomes impossible to ignore, the media's "Discreditation Campaigns" will only grow more desperate. We must recognize that the "Gimmies" of the legacy system are funded by the "Friction" that the media protects. By moving our commerce to the "Sovereign Ledger," we bypass the gatekeepers and restore the "Objectivist" reality of the marketplace.

The "Hard Reset" begins when the "Active Citizen" stops seeking "Consent" from the propaganda machine and starts seeking "Finality" from the math. In the trade wars of 2026, the victory will go to those who have the "Guts" to ignore the media's "Psychological Priming" and build on the "Rails of Truth." We must dismantle the monopolies of information just as we dismantle the monopolies of money, ensuring that the "Standard of Value" is owned by the people, not the "Wastrels" who benefit from its erosion. It is time to turn off the "Machine" and turn on the Ledger.[125]

Conclusion: The Democratization of Truth through the Immutable Ledger

The conclusion of Chapter 12 serves as a forensic autopsy of the "Information Asymmetry" that defines

---

[125] Cooper's Logic Check → The "experts" on the news tell you that "Alternative Systems" are a threat to your security. Logic check: If I'm standing in a burning building (the 2026 economy) and I tell you that the "Fire Exit" (KIROS/1:1 Reserves) is "dangerous" because it is new, I'm not "protecting" you—I'm trapping you. They want the "Media" to be the "Lock" on the door. In digital realism, the "Truth" is the only exit. They call it "Stability"; I call it a Hollow Promise. It is time to stop listening to the "Wastrels" and start checking the Math.

the 2026 economic landscape—a "Hollow Man" theater where the "Active Citizen" is forced to operate in a "Subjective" fog while the "American Bankers Cartel" enjoys the "Objectivist" clarity of the "Gated" market. As we have documented, the "Propaganda Machine" and the "Expert Fallacy" are not merely social nuisances; they are the "Strategic Friction" points of a rigged system. By monopolizing the "Velocity of Information" through $30,000 data terminals and weaponized media narratives, the administrative state ensures that the "Sovereign Debt Trap" remains hidden behind a veil of manufactured complexity and state-sponsored obfuscation.

The "Hard Reset" to this asymmetry is the Democratization of Truth through the immutable ledger. By moving the "Standard of Value" for both currency and data to a 1:1 reserve digital system like KIROS, we bypass the "Lobbying Wall" and the "Gated Access" of the legacy institutions. On a blockchain, the "Physics of Information" are equal for all; the "Active Citizen" in Dysart has the same real-time access to the "Pulse of the Republic" as the CEO of a "Big Four" bank. This is the ultimate threat to the political machine: a system where "Algorithmic Transparency" replaces the "Subjective" whim of the regulator, and where the "Code Veil" protects the producer from the "Bureaucratic Hammer."

To save the Republic, we must recognize that the "Weaponized Media" is the last line of defense for a "Wastrel" class that has run out of honest arguments.

Their "Strategic Discreditation" of alternatives is a terminal move to maintain a "Jurisdictional Trap" that benefits the rent-seekers at the expense of the producers. We must reject the "Hollow" expertise of the celebrity and the activist, demanding instead a "Standard of Truth" grounded in the "Rule of Math." When the "Information Moat" is drained, the "Money Changers" lose their primary tool for "Stealth Confiscation," and the "Active Citizen" finally regains the sovereignty of their own mind and capital.

Ultimately, the choice is between the "Rigged System" of the obfuscators and the "Digital Republic" of the innovators. We cannot fix a system that requires a "Slush Fund" for its misconduct and a "Propaganda Machine" for its survival. We must build on the "Rails of Truth," ensuring that the "Social Contract" is no longer a one-sided agreement written in a language only the "Experts" can translate. As we close this chapter, the forensic evidence is crystalline: the era of "Managed Deception" is ending, and the era of "Algorithmic Sovereignty" is beginning. It is time to turn off the "Propaganda" and turn on the Ledger.[126]

---

[126] Cooper's Logic Check → The "experts" say that "Total Transparency" would be "dangerous for market stability." Logic check: If your "Stability" depends on me not knowing what you are doing with my money, then you are not a "Banker"—you are a Con Artist. They want the "Obfuscation" because they can't survive the "Light." In digital realism, the only "Stability" that matters is The Truth. If the math works, the system is stable. If it doesn't, it is a "Hollow Man." It is time to stop paying for the "Fog" and start trusting the Math.

Information Asymmetry

Conclusion

"If repression has indeed been the fundamental link between power, knowledge and sexuality since the classical age, it stands to reason that we will not be able to free ourselves from it except at a measurable cost."

Michel Foucault[127]

Throughout Chapters 9 through 12, we have documented the "Strategic Friction" used by the "American Bankers Cartel" and their regulatory proxies to maintain a terminal grip on the "Active Citizen." From the "Cantillon Effect," which rewards proximity to the printing press, to the "T-Plus" settlement anchor that creates a "Day of the Dead" for capital, the system is designed to favor the "Wastrel" at the expense of the producer. This is not merely a collection of technical inefficiencies; it is a coordinated "Asymmetrical Warfare" campaign intended to ensure the "Gimmie" class survives while the "Standard of Value" is systematically shaved.

The "Moral Hazard" of this captured system is nowhere more evident than in the "Sovereign Debt Trap," where the government's survival necessitates the failure of its own currency. By reclassifying inflation as a "Human Rights Violation," we expose the "Stealth Confiscation" of the citizenry's life-energy

---

[127] Staff (2026). "Classical Economics Quotes." Brainy Quote at https://www.brainyquote.com/search_results?x=0&y=0&q=Classical+Economics.

as a terminal breach of the Social Contract. The administrative state requires a "Jurisdictional Trap" where the "Active Citizen" is forced to hold devaluing fiat, while the "Early Receivers" of the new money buy up the "Fixed Assets" of the Republic. This "Systematic Impoverishment" is the forensic proof that the legacy system has abandoned the "Objectivist" principles of property and contract in favor of a "Subjective" survival-at-all-costs mandate.

The "Physics of Delay" documented in Chapter 11 provides the plumbing for this extraction, creating an "Unsettled Intermediate State" that traps trillions in "Liquidity Lockdown." By maintaining obsolete settlement cycles, the "Money Changers" manufacture "Artificial Risk" to justify "Cascading Fees" and "Guaranty Funds" that serve as their own fractal reserves. The "Day of the Dead" is a chronological shakedown, a theft of time that throttles the "Velocity of Value" and prevents the "Efficiency Multiplier" of the digital republic from being realized. Only through "Atomic Settlement" can we collapse this "No Man's Land" and return the "Right to Contract" to its crystalline, instantaneous origin.

Furthermore, the "Information Asymmetry" explored in Chapter 12 reveals the "Lobbying Wall" of data that protects the status quo. The "Propaganda Machine" and the "Expert Fallacy" are used to manufacture consent for these inefficient systems, using complexity as a "Bureaucratic Hammer" to silence those who point out the "Repugnance to Logic" in the current plumbing. When the "Active Citizen" is barred from "Gated Access" to real-time data, they are forced to make decisions in a "Subjective" fog while the "Institutional Cartel" operates with the "Objectivist" clarity of a $30,000 terminal. This is the "Rigged Game" that Senator Warren identified, but which only a "Hard Reset" to the "Sovereign Ledger" can truly fix.

To achieve this reset, we must recognize that the "Administrative State" and the "American Bankers Association" are not protecting the economy—they are protecting the "Friction" from which they feed. The transition to a 1:1 reserve, digital species architecture is the only way to bypass the "Slush Fund" accounting of the "Wastrels." By moving our commerce to the "Rails of Truth," we reclaim the "Standard of Value" from the obfuscators and return it to the "Rule of Math." This is the "Democratization of Truth" that defines the future: a world where the "Code Veil" protects the individual and where "Algorithmic Transparency" ensures that no one can "shave" the coins in the dark.

As we move toward the final sections of this work, the forensic evidence of Part III remains crystalline: the legacy system is in a state of "Terminal Decay." It cannot be "reformed" by the very "Experts" who built the "Jurisdictional Trap" and the "Sovereign Debt Trap." It must be out-competed. The "Active Citizen" must embrace the "Atomic" reality of the ledger and decouple their productive energy from the "Hollow" promises of the administrative state. The trade wars of 2026 will not be won by those with the best lobbyists, but by those with the most agile capital and the most transparent data. We are no longer asking for permission to innovate; we are declaring our monetary independence.

Ultimately, Part III is a call to end the era of "Managed Deception." We refuse to be "Hollow Men" in a "Wastrel" economy, and we reject the "Psychological Priming" that tells us we are too small to challenge the "Cartel." The "Hard Reset" is here, and it is built on the "Objectivist" certainty that the truth—like the ledger—is immutable. It is time to stop paying for the "Delay," stop listening to the "Propaganda," and start building the "Digital Republic" on a foundation of 1:1 reserves and total transparency. The "Physics of Value" demand it, the "Sovereignty of the Producer" requires it, and the "Math" ensures it. It is time to turn off the "Machine" and move into the Light.[128]

---

[128] Cooper's Logic Check → The "experts" say that Part III is "too critical" of the current financial stability. Logic check: If your "Stability" is a house of cards built on debt, delay, and devalued dollars, then Gravity is "too critical" of your architecture. They want you to stay in the "Hollow" system because they are the ones charging you "Rent" to breathe. In digital realism, the only "Stability" that matters is the Truth of the transaction. If the system can't survive the "Light" of an audit, it shouldn't survive at all. It is time to stop worrying about the "Wastrels" and start protecting the Active Citizen.

Part IV: Economic Realism in the Digital Economy

"History shows that where ethics and economics come into conflict, victory is always with economics. Vested interests have never been known to have willingly divest themselves unless there was sufficient force to compel them."

B.R. Ambedkar[129]

Power is interesting. Everyone wants it, until they have it- then it is a burden, but people do not want to give it up. Ambedkar is correct in that those in power only give it up if forced to, which means that it is the role of government to ensure that no one gets too much power lest there be a situation where the government does not have the ability to restore normalcy. Economics seems to have a methodology which brings everything back to the lowest common denominator if things get to bad, that is capitalism.[130] The challenge is that we need to allow elements to come back to their resting state and mitigate the corruption that we see in the system.

In the first three parts of the book, we covered the past. This is why we are here revealing the concept.

---

[129] Staff (2026). "Economic Realism Quotes." Brainy Quote at https://www.brainyquote.com/search_results?x=0&y=0&q=Economics+REalism.

[130] Smithmyer, Christopher W. (2022). "Quadralectics" Nova Southeastern Dissertation.

Now we have to look at "where we are." As we can understand that there is a problem, more correctly problems, we are in a state now where we are looking for solutions. Fortunately, the solution is there, the question simply lies in whether we take the solution or continue in our failures.

Chapter 13 looks at the KIROS architecture for better digital economics. I am biased to this as I am the designer of the system; however, it was designed to fix the problems which we have in society. Linking liquidity, rather than wealth, to functional utility of goods and services opens the door to a more stable economy. It introduces an independent variable to the system, allowing the system to heal. Building strong rules and laws, such as the UN Model Law on Digital Assets and Exchanges, provides us a strong foundation for moving into a verifiable economy.

Next, we address one of the deadliest problems of classical currency- the one size fits all approach. Whereas retail transactions are generally private, institutional, and commercial transactions need to be audited for compliance. Fiat as designed in the US dollar failed in both of these matters. Personal transactions were tracked while corporate and institutional systems used double books and cooked books to keep things off of the radar. Blockchain offers the ability to fix this by allowing currency to be customized to the needs of the users in given situations.

Chapter 15 moves on to the august nation state model. Sovereign wealth cannot be at the expense of the people. Unfortunately, in many case this is the case. Blockchain allows us to put companies, individuals, and nations on equal footing and make them equally accountable when it comes to currency matters. Static currency creation, without the ability to do "quantitative easing" allows for the systems to be much more reliable and gives the world the ability to forecast. The era of the "Black Budget" is over, the world has come a realization that these corrupt practices are not part of civilization but of a pasts of which we are best rid.

Chapter 16 brings this section to a close with a discussion of hybrid economics. While the transition to digital money is already underway, fiat will stick around for decades to come. No one wants to use a digital transaction for something as small as a candy bar, so the brightly colored pieces of paper will not go away. Nostalgia will be another factor which keeps us in the past. Perhaps the most damning element, however, will be the propaganda put out by the failing banking system. Even now they accuse the digital world of the crimes they are committing:

1. Myth- "crypto makes it easier for criminals": False, since every transaction is registered on the blockchain, it is easier for law enforcement to follow transactions. Every wallet should be registered and KYC'ed to ensure compliance with current international treaty laws and

domestic wire transfer laws. Bank notes, however, are the most common way to move wealth for drug runners, sex traffickers, and other ne'er-do-wells.

2. Myth- "The system is unstable, you do not have access to your money all the time.": False, digital asset systems have, on average, a 99.99% uptime (only 52 minutes of downtime per year).[131] Compare this to banks, which are "down" 16 to 17 hours a day on week days, 21 hours on Saturdays and 24 hours on bank holidays and Sundays (which amounts to a 78% downtime).
3. Myth- "There is no way to catch crypto scammers." False: the government is exceptionally good at catching crypto scammers, they just do not press charges. Thousands of cases are referred to state and local authorities, with the blockchain records which are verifiable proof of the actions of the criminals; however, most jurisdictions have a "minimum" amount that they will press charges for on a case by case basis (to protect district attorneys records), scammers know this and do just under the amount with each person. Meanwhile, major bank scandals only became known after whistleblowers risked their lives (prior to the whistleblower protection acts), and

[131] Uptime analysis report at https://datacenter.uptimeinstitute.com/rs/711-RIA-145/images/2024.Resiliency.Survey.ExecSum.pdf.

> banks get away with a reprimand when they break major rules.

It is time to face the new economic reality that digital assets are simply better for the economy, moving away from debt-based finance to asset-based finance. While this will represent a major change in the system- it is a needed change. People should not be forced into debt so they can "show their worth" to society with a credit score, maybe we should score people on what they produce rather than what they siphon away from society into the coffers of an archaic banking system.

Chapter 13: The KIROS Architecture. Transitioning from speculative tokens to tokenized securities and RWA (Real World Assets).

"I would say do not take advice from people like me who have gotten incredibly lucky. We are very biased. You know, like Taylor Swift telling you to follow your dreams is like a lottery winner telling you 'liquidize your assets; buy Powerball tickets- it works!"

Bo Burnham[132]

Normally, I would not be overly specific on the methodology used to solve a problem. It is generally better to allow for individual markets of innovation to ensure that the best solution is put into place. However, when it comes to global liquidity, this can be a problem. This attempt was already made by the Federal Reserve/Central Banks, and has been an abject failure. As a result, we have seen years of problematic policy around the world. As such, in this chapter, we look at the necessity for a specific system rather than a general attempt at research. That is the KIROS model.

The goal of this system is to eliminate speculation within liquidity. This is a two fold effort, first we are looking to develop a backed liquidity system, rather

[132] Staff (2026). "Asset Quotes." Brainy Quote at https://www.brainyquote.com/search_results?x=0&y=0&q=Assets.

than the fiat system we have today. Next, we are looking to remove the liquidity layer from the retail market to ensure that the system if functional at all levels. This allows for a multi-level currency system which promotes for a more effective system. With tangible underlying assets, coupled with smart contract trusteeship, we have a system that can comply with regulations by its nature rather than by the actions of the holders. This creates the utmost scalability in the international market with the minimal drag for the citizens who use the system.[133]

Beyond the Speculative Bubble: Defining the Utility of Real-World Assets (RWA)

The transition from the "Speculative Bubble" to the Real-World Asset (RWA) standard is the forensic "Hard Reset" required to salvage the digital economy from its own "Hollow" excesses. In the digital realism of 2026, we must acknowledge that the first wave of cryptocurrency was largely a "Wastrel" exercise in "Subjective" value—tokens backed by nothing but the hope that a "Greater Fool" would buy in at a higher price. This speculative model is a "Repugnance to Logic" that mirrors the very fiat system it claimed to

---

[133] Cooper's Logic Check → The "Money Changers" say that you can't "back" a digital currency because the world is too fast for physical assets. Logic check: If I give you a piece of paper that says I owe you a steak, and another guy gives you a piece of paper that says he owes you "nothing but hope," which one are you taking to dinner? They want "Fiat" because they can't print "Land." In digital realism, the only "Standard" is the Asset. If it is not "Backed," it is "Hollow." It is time to stop buying "Powerball Tickets" and start building on the Bedrock.

replace. To move forward, the "Active Citizen" must embrace a "Standard of Value" that is anchored in the "Physics of Production."

The Failure of Purely Digital Scarcity

Defining the utility of RWA begins with identifying the terminal flaw of speculative tokens: their lack of "Tangible Underlays." While Bitcoin and its "Web2 Crypto-Clones" introduced the concept of digital scarcity, that scarcity is often divorced from economic utility. If a token does not represent a claim on land, energy, or industrial capacity, its price is merely a reflection of "Market Sentiment"—the most volatile and "Hollow" metric in existence. In a high-inflation, high-friction environment like 2026, the "Active Citizen" cannot afford to hold assets that evaporate during a "Liquidity Lockdown."

Real-World Assets provide the "Hard Reset" by tethering the digital ledger to the physical Republic. When we tokenize a 75-acre forest thinning project or a steel-frame residential facility, we are not creating a "lottery ticket"; we are digitizing Productive Energy. The utility of the token is derived from the "Objective" value of the underlying asset—its yield, its location, and its utility in the real world. This transition effectively "De-risks" the digital ecosystem, moving it from a casino-style speculation to a "Sovereign Utility" framework that can withstand the "Sovereign Debt Trap."

The RWA Efficiency Multiplier

The true utility of RWA lies in their role as a "Liquidity Layer" for the productive economy. In the legacy system, a fixed asset like real estate is "trapped" by "Strategic Friction"—it takes months to sell, involves "Cascading Fees" from middlemen, and is subject to the "Day of the Dead" settlement cycles. By mapping these physical assets to the KIROS architecture, we unlock their "Velocity of Value." A tokenized security representing a library balcony in Pennsylvania can be traded, collateralized, or used to settle a contract in milliseconds via Atomic Settlement.

This is the "Efficiency Multiplier" in practice: we are taking the most stable assets in the world and giving them the "Velocity" of the digital age. This does not just benefit the "Money Changers"; it empowers the "Active Citizen" to mobilize their own wealth without the "Gimmies" of the banking cartel. By defining utility as "Agile Property Rights," we move beyond the "Hollow" promise of speculation and into the "Objectivist" reality of a verifiable economy. In the trade wars of 2026, the nation that tokenizes its real-world production first is the nation that wins the "Hard Reset."

The End of the "Lottery" Economy

Ultimately, moving beyond the speculative bubble is about restoring the "Standard of Value." We must reject the Bo Burnham "Powerball" approach to finance and return to the "Sovereignty of the Producer." Real-World Assets are the "Bedrock" upon which the "Digital Economic Theory" must be built. When a token is a mirror of a physical reality, the "Information Asymmetry" vanishes and the "Propaganda Machine" loses its power. We are building a system where "Utility" is not a "Subjective" buzzword, but an "Objective" mathematical certainty.[134]

Structural Integrity: Mapping Physical Assets to Digital Securities

The "Structural Integrity" of the KIROS model is the forensic bridge between the physical Republic and the "Sovereign Ledger." In the digital realism of 2026, we must recognize that a token is only as strong as the legal and mathematical "Binding" that connects it to the underlying asset. Mapping physical assets to digital securities is not a mere "minting" exercise; it is a rigorous process of Triple-Locked Synchronization—ensuring that the digital representation, the legal title, and the physical reality are the same. This is the "Hard Reset" to the "Hollow Man" crypto-models that rely on "Subjective" trust rather than "Objectivist" structural proof.

---

[134] Cooper's Logic Check → The "experts" say that "Physical backing" makes crypto too slow and "boring." Logic check: If you are on a boat in a storm, do you want a "boring" anchor that hits the bottom, or an "exciting" one made of balloons? They want you in "Speculative Tokens" because they control the "Pump and Dump" machine. In digital realism, "Boring" is another word for "It is Actually There." If it is not backed by an asset you can touch, it is just a "Gimmie" for the guy who minted it. It is time to stop chasing the "Hollow" and start owning the Real.

The Triple-Locked Synchronization Model

To ensure asset-to-token fidelity, the KIROS architecture utilizes a three-layer mapping protocol. First is the Physical Layer, which involves a forensic audit of the asset—whether it is a 75-acre Florida estate, a steel-frame library facility, or active forest-thinning equipment. This layer establishes the "Physics of Value" through GPS-tagged verification, precision agriculture sensor data, and IoT-enabled asset tracking. Without this physical grounding, a token is just "Digital Vapor."

The second layer is the Legal Layer, where the "Standard of Value" is anchored in the "Rule of Law." This involves the creation of a "Smart Contract Trustee"—a digital entity that holds the legal title or a perfected security interest in the asset. Unlike the "Wastrel" trusts of the legacy system, which are buried in "Jurisdictional Fog," this legal lock is public and immutable. It ensures that the "Right to Contract" is preserved, preventing the "American Bankers Cartel" from "shaving" the value or double-hypothecating the asset.

The final layer is the Digital Layer, where the asset is "Tokenized" as a security. This is not a "Gimmie" token; it is a Sovereign Utility Token that carries the legal weight of the underlying property. By synchronizing these three layers, we create a "Structural Integrity" that is immune to the "Strategic Friction" of the legacy market. The token becomes the "Objectivist" mirror of the asset, allowing for the

"Velocity of Value" to be realized without sacrificing the security of the "Standard of Value."

Atomic Fidelity: Preventing the "Fractal Leakage"

Mapping is the primary defense against "Fractal Leakage"—the process where the "Money Changers" lend out more claims than they have assets. In the legacy system, "Structural Integrity" is a joke; banks operate on a "Fractional Reserve" that is often a "Hollow" 10% or less. In the KIROS architecture, the mapping ensures a realistic Asset-to-Token Ratio. The smart contract prevents the issuance of a single token that is not forensically tied to a verified "Standard of Value."

This "Atomic Fidelity" is what allows the system to survive a "Market Contagion." When the "Day of the Dead" settlement cycles cause the legacy banks to freeze, the mapped digital security remains liquid because its value is not dependent on the survival of an intermediary. It is dependent on the "Math of the Ledger" and the "Physics of the Asset." By removing the "Hollow Man" from the middle of the mapping process, we restore the "Sovereignty of the Producer" and ensure that the "Active Citizen" truly owns what the ledger says they own.

The "Cerberus" Methodology in Practice

The mapping process culminates in the "Cerberus" three-part methodology for Real-World Assets. This framework treats the asset as an integrated whole, mapping its Title, its Yield, and its Governance into the digital security. This ensures that the token holder does not just own a "Subjective" slice of a price chart; they own an "Objective" claim on the asset's productive energy. Whether it is the rent from a library balcony or the carbon credits from a sustainable forest, the mapping ensures the "Gimmies" are automatically distributed to the "Active Citizen" through the smart contract.

In the trade wars of 2026, "Structural Integrity" is the ultimate "Efficiency Multiplier." It allows for the "Instantaneous Liquidation" of fixed assets, turning a "Locked" 75-acre estate into a "Frictionless" source of capital. We are no longer waiting for the "Wastrel" title companies or the "Slow-Motion" banks to approve our transactions. We are building on the "Rails of Truth," where the mapping is the "Hard Reset" that makes the "Hollow" legacy system obsolete.

The Blueprint of Certainty

Ultimately, mapping physical assets to digital securities is about reclaiming the "Standard of Value" from the obfuscators. It is a declaration that the "Digital Republic" is built on "Bedrock," not "Balloons." By ensuring that every token is a forensically-mapped mirror of a real-world asset, we neutralize the "Expert Fallacy" and the "Propaganda Machine." We are not asking for permission to be "Active Citizens"; we are building the "Blueprint" that makes the "Money Changers" irrelevant. It is time to stop trusting the

"Hollow Men" and start trusting the Structural Integrity of the ledger.[135]

The Multi-Layer Validation Model: Ensuring Asset-to-Token Fidelity

The Multi-Layer Validation Model is the forensic watchdog of the KIROS architecture (Cerberus), ensuring that the "Objectivist" link between the physical world and the digital ledger remains unbreakable. In the digital realism of 2026, we must recognize that "Asset-to-Token Fidelity"—the degree to which a digital token truly reflects its underlying asset—is the only "Standard of Value" that matters. Without a rigorous, multi-layered validation process, RWA tokenization risks becoming another "Hollow Man" exercise in "Subjective" hope. This model provides the "Hard Reset" by replacing the "Trust Me" word of a bank with the "Verify Me" math of an integrated validation stack.

Layer 1: The Forensic Physical Audit

The first layer of validation is the Ground-Truth Protocol. This layer rejects the "Wastrel" tendency to rely on dated appraisals or distant reports. Instead, it

---

[135] Cooper's Logic Check → The "experts" say that "Mapping" is too complicated for the average person to understand. Logic check: If you buy a car, you want the Title in your hand, the Keys in your pocket, and the Car in your driveway. That is "Mapping." They only call it "Complicated" when they want to keep one of those three things for themselves. In digital realism, the "Title," "Keys," and "Car" are all locked into the Code. It is time to stop letting the "Wastrels" hold your keys while they "shave" your tires.

utilizes high-velocity data points to verify the existence and condition of the asset in real-time. For an example of a 75-acre Florida estate or a steel-frame construction project, this involves a "Digital Twin" integration—using drone-based photogrammetry and LiDAR to create an immutable 3D record of the property.

In precision agriculture and forest management, this layer is augmented by IoT (Internet of Things) sensors that provide a "Pulse of the Asset." We are not just validating that the land exists; we are validating its "Productive Energy" through soil health metrics, canopy density, and active thinning logs. This data is hashed and anchored to the sovereign ledger, ensuring that the "Active Citizen" can audit the "Physics of the Asset" without relying on a "Gimmie" consultant. If the physical reality changes, the digital twin reflects it instantly, maintaining total fidelity.

Layer 2: The Legal and Custodial Synchronicity

The second layer addresses the "Jurisdictional Fog" of the legacy system. Validation at this level ensures that the "Right to Contract" is forensically secured. This involves a Smart Contract Oracle that monitors the public land registries and UCC (Uniform Commercial Code) filings. In 2026, the transition toward the Digital Asset Market Clarity Act has made it possible for these oracles to verify title and lien status with "Algorithmic Certainty."

This layer prevents the "Strategic Friction" of double-hypothecation—a favorite tool of the "American

Bankers Cartel" where the same asset is used as collateral for multiple "Hollow" loans. The validation model requires a "Perfected Digital Interest," where the smart contract trustee is the only entity capable of authorizing the movement or liquidation of the underlying asset. This "Custodial Synchronicity" ensures that the token holder possesses an "Objective" claim that is recognized by both the code and the courts.

Layer 3: The Algorithmic Consensus and Oracle Mesh

The final layer of validation is the Oracle Mesh Network. Rather than relying on a single "Hollow Man" data source, the KIROS architecture utilizes a decentralized network of validators who cross-reference the data from Layers 1 and 2 (Via Solana and other networks). This creates a "Redundancy of Truth." If a single sensor fails or a legal filing is tampered with, the consensus mechanism identifies the "Repugnance to Logic" and flags the token's fidelity status immediately.

This layer is what allows for "Atomic Fidelity." When the validation is continuous and decentralized, the token can be treated as a "Sovereign Utility" with zero "Latency Risk." The market does not have to wait for an annual audit; the audit is happening with every block produced on the ledger. This removes the "Expert Fallacy" from the equation, as the "Standard of Value" is proven by the math of the mesh rather than the opinion of a "Wastrel" bureaucrat.

The End of "Subjective" Collateral

The Multi-Layer Validation Model is the ultimate "Efficiency Multiplier" for the 2026 trade wars. It allows for the "Instantaneous Verification" of global liquidity, removing the "Friction" that the legacy banks use to justify their "Cascading Fees." By ensuring absolute asset-to-token fidelity, we move away from the "Hollow" collateral of the fiat system and toward the "Objectivist" reality of the Backed Republic.

We are building a system where the "Active Citizen" can trade with the confidence that the "Physics of the Asset" are locked into the "Logic of the Code." The "Day of the Dead" is over because the validation is alive, 24/7. It is time to stop trusting the "Hollow" promises of the "Money Changers" and start trusting the Multi-Layer Validation of the KIROS architecture. The "Hard Reset" is not just a change in technology; it is a change in the "Standard of Truth."[136]

Mitigating Volatility through Tangible Underlays

The primary failure of the legacy "Hollow" economy is its dependence on assets that exist solely as digital or

---

[136] Cooper's Logic Check → The "experts" say that "Continuous Validation" is too expensive and complex. Logic check: If you are buying a parachute, do you want one that was "validated" three years ago by a guy in an office, or do you want the one that Self-Checks its own strings every time you put it on? They want "Annual Audits" because that gives them 364 days to "shave" the value while you are not looking. In digital realism, a "Validation" that is not Now is just a "Gimmie" for the auditor. It is time to stop paying for "Yesterday's Truth" and start trusting the Live Ledger.

paper promises, unmoored from the "Physics of Production." To solve this, the KIROS architecture utilizes **Tangible Underlays**—physical, productive assets like the 75-acre Florida estate, steel-frame infrastructure, and precision agricultural yields—to act as a volatility dampener for the digital ledger. In the digital realism of 2026, we recognize that "Market Sentiment" is a "Subjective" and unstable foundation for a currency. By anchoring a token to a tangible underlay, we move the "Standard of Value" from the whims of the "Wastrel" speculator to the "Objectivist" reality of the asset's intrinsic utility. This creates a "Hard Reset" where the token's price floor is forensically supported by the replacement cost and productive capacity of the underlying physical property.

Volatility in the "Web2 Crypto-Clone" market is a direct result of "Asset-to-Nothing" ratios. When a token represents only a fractional claim on a "Hollow" network's potential, it is subject to massive "Cascading Liquidations" during a market shock. However, when a tokenized security is backed 1:1 by a tangible underlay, the "Physics of Value" take over. A library balcony in Pennsylvania or a thinning forest in the Greenbelt does not lose **30%** of its value in an afternoon because of a social media post. By mapping these "Slow-Motion" physical assets to "High-Velocity" digital securities, we create a hybrid stability. The "Active Citizen" benefits from the liquidity of the digital age without being exposed to the "Strategic Friction" of speculative bubbles. This is the

"Efficiency Multiplier" of the KIROS model: using the bedrock of the Republic to stabilize the rails of the future.

Furthermore, tangible underlays neutralize the "Propaganda Machine" by providing a "Verifiable Bottom." In a "Sovereign Debt Trap" scenario, where fiat currency is being devalued through "Stealth Confiscation," the tangible underlay acts as a life raft for wealth. While the "Money Changers" shave the value of the "Hollow" dollar, the value of land, steel, and timber remains constant in terms of their "Objective" utility. By holding tokens backed by these underlays, the "Active Citizen" ensures their capital is not just "Hollow" numbers on a screen, but a digital mirror of the physical Republic. This "Sovereignty of the Producer" is the only forensic way to mitigate volatility and ensure that the "Standard of Value" remains crystalline, even when the administrative state is in terminal decay.[137]

---

[137] Cooper's Logic Check → The "experts" say that "Physical backing" makes a currency too rigid for a global economy. Logic check: If you are building a skyscraper, do you want a "rigid" foundation of concrete, or a "flexible" foundation of marshmallows? They want "Flexibility" because That is the "Jurisdictional Fog" they use to "shave" your savings. In digital realism, "Rigid" means "It is Actually There." If your money is not backed by something you can drop on your foot, it is not a "Standard of Value"—it is a "Gimmie" waiting to happen. It is time to stop trusting the "Balloons" and start trusting the Bedrock.

Smart Contracts as Automated Trustees for Industrial Infrastructure

The implementation of Smart Contracts as Automated Trustees represents the forensic "Hard Reset" of industrial management. In the digital realism of 2026, the reliance on "Hollow Man" human trustees—who are subject to "Strategic Friction," "Subjective" bias, and the "Gimmie" culture of administrative fees—is a terminal inefficiency. By shifting the role of the trustee from a bureaucratic intermediary to an "Objectivist" block of code, we ensure that industrial infrastructure, such as steel-frame facilities or precision agricultural systems, operates under the "Rule of Math." This transition ensures that the "Standard of Value" for maintenance, yield distribution, and governance is executed with "Algorithmic Certainty," leaving no room for the "Wastrel" to shave the productive energy of the Republic.

The "Objectivist" Trustee: Code as Fiduciary

A traditional trustee is often a "Bureaucratic Hammer" that slows the velocity of industrial progress. They require "Permission Slips" for capital deployment and extract "Cascading Fees" for "oversight." In the KIROS architecture, the smart contract replaces this human error with Automated Fiduciary Logic. For industrial infrastructure, this means the "Right to Contract" is baked into the machine itself. If a steel-frame library facility generates "Sovereign Utility" through leasing or carbon credits, the smart contract acts as the "Automated Trustee," instantly distributing the yield to the "Active Citizen" token holders according to the "Multi-Layer Validation Model." There is no "Day of the Dead" delay; the settlement is atomic because the trustee is the code.

This automated trusteeship extends to the physical maintenance of the asset. Through "IoT-Enabled Governance," the smart contract can be programmed to "lock" a percentage of yield into a maintenance sub-ledger. When sensors detect that the industrial infrastructure requires forest thinning or structural repairs, the "Automated Trustee" can autonomously solicit bids and release payments to verified contractors. This removes the "Expert Fallacy" from property management; the building "manages itself" based on the "Physics of the Asset," ensuring that the "Standard of Value" is preserved for the long-term agreement without the need for a "Wastrel" middleman to take a cut.

Neutralizing the "Jurisdictional Fog"

Industrial infrastructure often falls victim to "State-Sponsored Obfuscation" and the "Jurisdictional Fog" of local zoning or tax disputes. When a human trustee is involved, they become a target for the "Bureaucratic Hammer." However, a smart contract trustee operates on a "Sovereign Ledger" that is transparent and immutable. The "Rules of Engagement" for the infrastructure are public, allowing for "Algorithmic Transparency." If the government attempts a "Regulatory Taking," the automated trustee can trigger defensive protocols—such as the "Hard Reset" of moving the asset's legal seat or adjusting yield flows to protect the "Active Citizen."

In the trade wars of 2026, the efficiency of industrial infrastructure will depend on its "Velocity of Governance." The nation that tethers its steel and its land to "Automated Trustees" will out-compete the "Hollow" systems that still rely on "Slow-Motion" human boards. We are moving toward a "Verifiable Economy" where the "Standard of Value" for our buildings and machines is guarded by the math of the vault. It is time to fire the "Wastrel" trustees and let the Code protect the Republic's productive energy.[138]

Regulatory Synchronicity: Building for Compliance Without Compromise

Regulatory Synchronicity is the forensic "Hard Reset" that transforms the "Bureaucratic Hammer" of the administrative state into a frictionless "Algorithmic Certainty." In the digital realism of 2026, the traditional model of compliance—characterized by "Strategic Friction," "Subjective" interpretations, and the "Gimmie" culture of legal audits—is a terminal drag on

---

[138] Cooper's Logic Check → The "experts" say you can't trust a computer to manage a "Real-World" building. Logic check: If you are flying in a storm, do you want the "Automated Pilot" that reacts in milliseconds based on the Math of Physics, or do you want a "Trustee" who has to call a committee meeting before he can move the flaps? They want the "Human Trustee" because That is who they can "Nudge" into giving them a "Gimmie." In digital realism, the Code does nottake bribes and it does nottake lunch breaks. It is time to stop paying for "Subjective" oversight and start trusting the Automated Ledger.

the Republic's productive energy. The KIROS architecture replaces this "Slow-Motion" oversight with Embedded Compliance, where the regulatory requirements of the OCC and the Digital Asset Market Clarity Act are baked into the "Standard of Value" of the smart contract itself. This ensures that the system is "Compliant by Design," neutralizing the "Expert Fallacy" and the "Jurisdictional Fog" that the "American Bankers Cartel" uses to stall innovation. By synchronizing the "Rule of Math" with the "Rule of Law," we create a "Sovereign Ledger" that does not compromise on the privacy or agility of the "Active Citizen" while satisfying the transparency requirements of the state.

Building for compliance without compromise means rejecting the "Hollow Man" choice between total surveillance and total lawlessness. Through the use of Zero-Knowledge Proofs (ZKP) and decentralized identity protocols, the "Active Citizen" can prove their eligibility for a transaction—verifying their status as an "Accredited Investor" or a "Tax-Compliant Producer"—without revealing the forensic details of their personal wealth to a "Wastrel" bureaucrat. This is "Regulatory Synchronicity" in its purest form: the code acts as the "Automated Auditor," ensuring that every trade, clearing, and settlement meets the legal standard in real-time. This eliminates the "Day of the Dead" delay associated with manual compliance checks and removes the need for "Cascading Fees" paid to compliance consultants. In the trade wars of 2026, the side that automates its integrity will outpace the side that remains shackled to the "Administrative Proxy."

Ultimately, this synchronicity serves as a "Code Veil" that protects the "Sovereignty of the Producer" from the "Strategic Ambiguity" of the regulators. When the rules are transparent and immutable, the "Money Changers" can no longer use the "Lobbying Wall" to change the "Standard of Value" mid-contract. Regulatory Synchronicity ensures that the "Multi-Layer Validation Model" is recognized as the "Forensic Truth" by both the ledger and the legal system. This is the "Hard Reset" that provides the "Scalability" necessary for global RWA markets. We are not asking for a "Permission Slip" to be compliant; we are building a system where compliance is an "Objective" mathematical property of the transaction. By aligning the "Physics of Value" with the "Logic of Governance," we restore the "Objectivist" sanctity of the agreement and move the Republic toward a "Verifiable Economy."[139]

---

[139] Cooper's Logic Check → The "experts" say that "Automated Compliance" is dangerous because you need "Human Judgment" to interpret the law. Logic check: If the "Human Judgment" changes every time a new lobbyist walks into D.C., that is not "Interpretation"—That is a Bribe. They want "Subjective" rules because That is the "Jurisdictional Fog" they use to hide their "Gimmies." In digital realism, the Code is the only "Judge" that does nothave a "Slush Fund." It is time to stop paying for "Legal Opinions" and start trusting the Synchronized Ledger.

Scalability of the Sovereign Ledger: From Local Property to Global Markets

The Scalability of the Sovereign Ledger represents the forensic "Hard Reset" that transforms local "Active Energy" into global "Sovereign Liquidity." In the digital realism of 2026, the primary barrier to economic expansion is not a lack of resources, but the "Strategic Friction" of the legacy "Jurisdictional Trap." Traditional real estate and industrial infrastructure are "locked" by local "Slow-Motion" bureaucracies, "Day of the Dead" title registries, and the "Gimmie" fees of regional middlemen. The KIROS architecture breaks these local chains by mapping the "Objectivist" value of a 75-acre Florida estate or a Dysart-based steel facility onto a "Global Data Rail" that moves at the speed of thought. This allows a local asset to participate in the "Global Arbitrage" of 2026 without losing its "Standard of Value" to the "Cascading Fees" of the "American Bankers Cartel."

Scalability in this context is not just about "High-Velocity" transactions; it is about the Modular Interoperability of property rights. By utilizing a "Multi-Layer Validation Model," a local property in Pennsylvania can be "Verified" once and "Traded" infinitely across a decentralized "Oracle Mesh." This removes the "Expert Fallacy" of the local appraiser and replaces it with the "Algorithmic Transparency" of the sovereign ledger. Because the "Standard of Value" is anchored in 1:1 "Tangible Underlays," the asset becomes "Fungible Utility" on the international market. A Japanese institutional investor can provide liquidity to a sustainable forest thinning project in the American Greenbelt with the same "Crystalline Certainty" as if they were buying a Treasury bond, bypassing the "Hollow" intermediaries and the "Bureaucratic Hammer" of cross-border currency controls.

Ultimately, this scalability is the "Efficiency Multiplier" that will win the trade wars of 2026. While the "Wastrel" legacy systems are busy "shaving" the value of their local currencies and building "Lobbying Walls" to prevent capital flight, the "Sovereign Ledger" is building a "Universal Language of Value." The ability to scale from a single residential library facility to a "World Congress" of student-led student chapters in Miami demonstrates the "Physics of Growth" inherent in the KIROS model. We are building a "Verifiable Economy" where "Local Property" is no longer a "Locked Asset," but a "Mobile Battery" of economic energy. By decoupling the "Right to Contract" from the "Hollow" constraints of geography, we restore the "Sovereignty of the Producer" on a global scale. It is time to stop thinking "Local" and start thinking "Atomic."[140]

---

[140] Cooper's Logic Check → The "experts" say that you can't have "Global Markets" without "Global Regulators." Logic check: If I have a gold bar in my hand, does its weight change because I crossed a border? The "Value" is in the Gold, not the Guard. They want "Global Regulators" because That is the ultimate "Slush Fund" for the "Wastrel" class. In digital realism, the "Regulator" is the Math of the Asset, and math does notneed a

Conclusion: The Blueprint for a Verifiable Economy

shifting the "Standard of Value" from the "Hollow" volatility of speculative tokens to the "Objectivist" bedrock of Real-World Assets (RWA). As we have documented, the KIROS architecture is not a "Subjective" bet on market sentiment, but a forensic blueprint for a "Backed Republic." By anchoring the digital ledger in the "Physics of Production"—including tangible infrastructure, precision agriculture, and sustainable land management—we eliminate the "Speculative Bubble" and replace it with a system where every token is a forensically-mapped mirror of physical reality.

The integration of Automated Trustees and Regulatory Synchronicity ensures that this blueprint is not just a technical theory, but a functional "Efficiency Multiplier." By baking the "Rule of Law" into the "Rule of Math," we neutralize the "Bureaucratic Hammer" and the "Expert Fallacy" that define the legacy "Wastrel" economy. The KIROS model proves that we do not need "Gimmie" middlemen or "Slow-Motion" clearinghouses to maintain the integrity of a transaction; we only need the "Algorithmic Transparency" of a 1:1 reserve ledger. This "Hard Reset" restores the "Right to Contract" to the "Active Citizen," ensuring that the "Velocity of Value" is

---

passport. It is time to stop waiting for "Permission" from a "Hollow Man" in an office and start trusting the Global Ledger.

limited only by the speed of the network, not the "Strategic Friction" of the administrative state.

Furthermore, the Scalability of the Sovereign Ledger demonstrates that the "Sovereignty of the Producer" is no longer a localized concept. By mapping local "Active Energy" onto a global data rail, we dismantle the "Jurisdictional Trap" and create a "Universal Language of Value." A 75-acre forest in the Greenbelt or a three-story steel facility in Dysart becomes a "Mobile Battery" of capital, capable of attracting global liquidity without the "Cascading Fees" of the "American Bankers Cartel." This is the ultimate "Sovereignty Doctrine": a world where the "Standard of Value" is owned by those who produce it, and where the ledger provides the crystalline certainty required for a "Verifiable Economy."

Ultimately, Chapter 13 provides the "Blueprint" for a future where "Finance" is no longer a "Hollow" religion of debt, but a "Crystalline" science of assets. We have moved past the era of "Lottery Tickets" and "Subjective" promises, entering the age of the Atomic Asset. As we transition into the implementation phase of the "Dysart-Detroit-Dallas" corridor, the KIROS architecture stands as the forensic evidence that a better system is not just possible—it is already engineered. It is time to stop playing the "Rigged Game" of the speculative bubbles and start building the "Digital Republic" on the immutable foundation of the Sovereign Ledger.[141]

---

[141] Cooper's Logic Check → The "experts" say that "Engineering" a currency takes decades and "Global Consensus." Logic check: If you are thirsty and I give you a glass of Water (RWA), do you need a "Committee" to reach "Consensus" that it is wet? They want "Decades" because That is how long it takes them to "shave" your life savings. In digital realism, the "Consensus" is the Math. If the asset is there and the code works, the game is over. It is time to stop waiting for "Permission" and start trusting the Blueprint.

Chapter 14: Institutional vs. Retail Flow. Currency Made for specific uses

"The true currency of life is time, not money, and we have all got a limited stock of that."

Robert Harris[142]

Do you use money the same way as the banks us money? This is one of the conundrums of modern economics, if the retail market and the institutional market use a currency differently, then why do we use the same currency for both systems? The answer is simplicity. It was easier during ancient times to have one currency model for the whole system. This has, of course, been augmented with checks, credit and debit; however, the underlying asset is still the same. This is the problem within the system.

In this chapter, we look at the end of the monolithic currency system. Value should be derivative of context and utility, not the promises of states that are trillions of dollars in debt. Utility is derived from use, context is derived from the purpose of the currency. If we combine the two we have a system in which different currencies can work together, each fitting into their specific niche, to ensure a stable economy. Custom use currencies create micro-economic systems, this allows society to regulate specific

---

[142] Staff (2026). "Currency Quotes." Brainy Quote at https://www.brainyquote.com/search_results?x=0&y=0&q=Currency+.

elements to specific areas. Development funds would stay in the regions. Funds for vice activities could be partitioned to keep them away from children. Political contributions could be ISP locked to donations only coming from the district in which the represent. This allows the system to fix problems algorithmically, and prevent corruption through due course.[143]

The End of Monolithic Currency: The Rise of Contextual Value

The "End of Monolithic Currency" is the forensic "Hard Reset" that finally decouples the "Active Citizen" from the terminal mismanagement of the "Wastrel" administrative state. In the digital realism of 2026, we must acknowledge that a single, monolithic currency—the "Hollow" fiat dollar—is a "Repugnance to Logic." It forces the local producer in Dysart to use the same "Standard of Value" as a high-frequency trading bot on Wall Street or a "Slush Fund" bureaucrat in D.C. This one-size-fits-all model is not a technical necessity; it is a "Strategic Friction" point that allows the "American Bankers Cartel" to "shave"

[143] Cooper's Logic Check → The "experts" say that having different currencies for different things is "too confusing" for the public. Logic check: You have a Key for your house, a Key for your car, and a Key for your office. You don't try to start your car with your front door key because you understand Context. They want "One Key" (the Dollar) because they are the ones who own the "Lock" and they want to be able to let themselves into every part of your life. In digital realism, "Diversity" equals Security. It is time to stop using "Master Keys" that the "Wastrels" can copy and start using the Right Tool for the job.

value from every sector of life simultaneously through uniform monetary debasement.

The Failure of the Monolithic Standard

The primary failure of monolithic currency is its inability to account for Contextual Utility. When you use the same "Token" to buy a loaf of bread, fund a 75-acre forest thinning project, and settle an international industrial swap, you are exposing every level of the economy to the same "Systemic Risk." If the "Money Changers" fail at the institutional level, the "Liquidity Lockdown" cascades down to the retail level, freezing the "Active Citizen's" ability to conduct the basic commerce of life. This is the "Hollow Man" trap: by forcing everyone into a single "Jurisdictional Fog," the state ensures that any "Hard Reset" is viewed as a threat to everyone, rather than a precision strike against the "Wastrels."

Contextual value restores the "Sovereignty of the Producer" by creating "Purpose-Built" currencies. In a verifiable economy, the "Standard of Value" should shift based on the objective of the transaction. A "Regional Development Token" in Pennsylvania should have a different "Physics of Value" than a "Global Liquidity Token" used for RWA settlement. By partitioning value according to its utility, we prevent "Market Contagion" from jumping between unrelated sectors. We move from a "Monopoly Money" world to a "Digital Republic" of specialized tools, where the currency finally knows its place.

The Rise of Specialized Wealth Ecosystems

The transition to contextual value enables the creation of Micro-Economic Ecosystems that are immune to "Institutional Cannibalization." For example, the KIROS architecture allows for the development of "Asset-Backed Regional Tokens" that are tied to local "Tangible Underlays." These tokens retain their "Velocity of Value" within their specific region, ensuring that local productive energy stays in the region rather than being sucked into the "Sovereign Debt Trap" of the federal government. This is the ultimate "Efficiency Multiplier": keeping the wealth where it is created and protecting it from the "Gimmie" culture of the centralized state.

Furthermore, contextual value allows for "Algorithmic Morality" in our financial rails. By using Programmable Intent, we can ensure that funds intended for specific social or industrial goals cannot be "shaved" or diverted. A "Education Token" cannot be spent at a "Vice" establishment; a "Campaign Contribution" cannot be moved outside of its district. This is not "Control"; it is "Clarity." It returns the "Right to Contract" to a state of crystalline certainty, where the "Active Citizen" knows that their capital is doing exactly what it was programmed to do. The "Hard Reset" is here, and it is time to trade the "Hollow" monolithic dollar for the "Objectivist" precision of contextual wealth.

Breaking the Monolith

Ultimately, breaking the monolith is about reclaiming our Time. We have spent decades allowing the "American Bankers Cartel" to use our "Standard of Value" as their personal "Slush Fund." By embracing contextual value, we force the "Wastrels" to compete on a level playing field. If their "Institutional Token" is poorly managed, it would not take the rest of the Republic down with it. We are building an architecture of specialized wealth where the "Physics of Value" are as diverse as the people of the Republic. It is time to stop playing the "Rigged Game" of the monolith and start building on the Contextual Ledger.[144]

Programmable Intent: Why Money Should Know Its Purpose

The core failure of the "Hollow Man" economy is the existence of "Dumb Money"—currency that lacks a memory, a conscience, or a destination. In the digital realism of 2026, we must recognize that the "American Bankers Cartel" thrives on the anonymity and fungibility of the monolithic dollar, which allows them to "shave" value from productive enterprises and

---

[144] Cooper's Logic Check → The "experts" say that having multiple currencies will "destabilize the global market." Logic check: If you have a toolbox with only a Hammer, everything starts looking like a nail—including your thumb. They want the "Monolith" because That is the only way they can "shave" everyone's pockets at the same time. In digital realism, a "Stable" system is one with Redundancy and Specificity. If one tool breaks, you don't lose the whole house. It is time to stop using the "Hammer" for everything and start using the Right Tool for the job.

redirect it into "Wastrel" slush funds without a forensic trail. **Programmable Intent** represents the "Hard Reset" to this logic. It is the architectural integration of the "Rule of Law" directly into the "Standard of Value." By embedding smart contract logic into the currency itself, we ensure that money finally knows its purpose, transforming it from a passive medium of exchange into an active participant in the Republic's "Efficiency Multiplier." When money is programmable, it carries its own "Jurisdictional Logic," ensuring that capital intended for a 75-acre forest thinning project in the Florida Greenbelt cannot be cannibalized by institutional speculators or diverted into the "Strategic Friction" of a distant political machine.

This transition to "Smart Liquidity" removes the need for the "Bureaucratic Hammer" of manual oversight. In a verifiable economy, the "Active Citizen" can issue "Development Tokens" that are algorithmically locked to specific industrial infrastructure. These tokens operate under the "Objectivist" certainty that they will only unlock when specific, pre-defined milestones are met—such as the completion of a three-story steel-frame library facility. This eliminates the "Gimmie" culture of middleman consultants and the "Expert Fallacy" of auditors, as the ledger itself acts as the "Automated Trustee." Furthermore, programmable intent allows for the implementation of "Micro-Economic Governance," where funds for vice activities can be partitioned away from general retail flow, or political donations can be ISP-locked to ensure they originate only from the representative's actual district. This is not about "Social Credit"; it is about "Forensic Integrity." It ensures that the "Velocity of Value" is directed with precision, preventing the "Institutional Cannibalization" that occurs when "Dumb Money" is allowed to pool in the hands of the rent-seeking class. By reclaiming the "Right to Contract" through programmable intent, we restore the "Sovereignty of the Producer" and ensure that the "Standard of Truth" is baked into every transaction.[145]

Industrial vs. Consumer Liquidity: Segregating Velocity and Stability

The forensic failure of the monolithic currency model is most visible in the collision of Industrial Velocity and Consumer Stability. In the digital realism of 2026, we have seen the catastrophic results of forcing these two distinct economic forces to share the same "Hollow" rails. Industrial liquidity requires high-velocity movement, complex derivative hedging, and massive capital aggregation to fund projects like the "Dysart-Detroit-Dallas" corridor. Consumer liquidity, however, requires the "Objectivist" certainty of a stable "Standard of Value" to facilitate the daily commerce of

---

145 Cooper's Logic Check → The "experts" say that "Programmable Money" is a tool for "Government Control." Logic check: If I give you a Gift Card to a steakhouse, is the steakhouse "controlling" you, or did I just make sure you actually got a Steak? They want "Dumb Money" because That is the only way they can "shave" your grocery money to pay for their "Slush Funds" and "Interest Swaps." In digital realism, "Programmable" means "Honest." If the money knows where it is supposed to go, it is a lot harder for a "Wastrel" to steal it. It is time to stop using "Blind Dollars" and start using Crystalline Code.

the "Active Citizen." By failing to segregate these flows, the "American Bankers Cartel" has created a system where a failure in a high-risk institutional swap can forensically freeze the grocery money of a producer in Pennsylvania.

The Velocity-Stability Paradox

The "Wastrel" administrative state thrives on the Velocity-Stability Paradox. They tell the public that "Liquidity" is a universal good, but they fail to define what *kind* of liquidity is being promoted. Industrial liquidity is often "Synthetic"—built on "Strategic Friction" and high-leverage "Gimmies" that require constant movement to avoid collapse. When this high-velocity institutional flow is mixed with the consumer pool, it acts as a "Contagion Conductor." If an institutional "Money Changer" suffers a liquidity crunch in their industrial speculative bets, they "shave" the consumer retail pool to cover their margins. This is the "Hollow Man" defense: using the stable "Bedrock" of the consumer to subsidize the volatile "Balloons" of the institution.

Segregating these flows via the KIROS architecture provides the "Hard Reset." By creating a "Dual-Rail" system, we can tune the "Physics of Value" for each specific use case. Industrial liquidity can operate on high-velocity, wholesale-only rails designed for "Atomic Settlement" of Real-World Assets (RWA). This rail can handle the "Strategic Ambiguity" and risk-modeling required for large-scale construction or precision agriculture infrastructure without exposing the general public to the fallout of a localized industrial failure. Meanwhile, consumer liquidity remains on a "Stability Rail," backed 1:1 by liquid reserves and shielded from the "Institutional Cannibalization" that defines the 2025-2026 banking cycle.

Protecting the "Active Citizen" from Institutional Churn

The segregation of liquidity is a fundamental "Sovereignty Doctrine." When we allow "Consumer Cash" to be used as the "Slush Fund" for institutional lending, we are effectively forcing the "Active Citizen" to provide interest-free loans to the very banks that are "shaving" their savings. In a verifiable economy, consumer liquidity should be a "Refuge of Value"—a 1:1 backed digital species that does not "churn" for the profit of the "American Bankers Association." By partitioning the two, we ensure that the "Velocity" of a multi-billion dollar industrial trade does not create a "Pricing Fog" for the person buying bread.

This separation also allows for more precise "Micro-Economic Governance." We can apply different "Programmable Intents" to each rail. Industrial tokens might be programmed for "Capital Recycling," encouraging high-velocity reinvestment in regional development funds, while consumer tokens are programmed for "Standard Preservation," focusing on anti-debasement logic and ease of retail use. This "Hard Reset" ensures that the "Standard of Truth" is maintained for the producer, while the "Efficiency Multiplier" is unleashed for the builder. We are ending the era of "Collateral Overlap" and beginning the era of Functional Specialization.

The End of the "Shared Risk" Lie

Ultimately, the lie that we must share a single liquidity pool is the "Propaganda Machine's" way of maintaining the "Jurisdictional Trap." They want you in the same pool because that makes you a "Hostage" to their mismanagement. By segregating industrial and consumer liquidity, we restore the "Objectivist" integrity of the marketplace. We give the "Active Citizen" a stable foundation and the "Institution" a high-speed rail, ensuring that neither can cannibalize the other. In the trade wars of 2026, the winner is the one who realizes that Stability is not the enemy of Velocity—they are just two different tools that belong in two different boxes.[146]

Preventing Institutional Cannibalization of Retail Assets

The "Institutional Cannibalization" of retail assets is the forensic byproduct of the "Hollow Man" banking model, where the "Active Citizen's" savings are treated as a subsidized liquidity pool for high-risk institutional gambling. In the digital realism of 2026,

[146] Cooper's Logic Check → The "experts" say that segregating liquidity will "break the unity of the dollar." Logic check: If you are a professional diver, do you want to share an air tank with a guy who's trying to use it to fill up a Hot Air Balloon? They want "Unity" because That is how they steal your "Air" to float their "Hollow" investments. In digital realism, "Unity" is just a "Wastrel" word for "No Escape." It is time to stop sharing our air and start building our own Sovereign Rails.

we must recognize that the "American Bankers Cartel" survives by blurring the lines between "Consumer Deposits" and "Institutional Capital." When a bank engages in complex derivative swaps or leveraged RWA speculation and fails, the "Strategic Friction" of the legacy system allows them to "shave" the value of retail accounts through "Bail-ins," "Liquidity Lockdowns," or the "Stealth Confiscation" of inflation. This is a terminal "Repugnance to Logic": the producer provides the bedrock of the system, yet is the first to be sacrificed when the "Wastrel" class mismanages the "Velocity of Money." Preventing this cannibalization requires a "Hard Reset" to a 1:1 reserve architecture where retail assets are forensically segregated from institutional risk-taking.

The KIROS architecture prevents this theft by utilizing Sovereign Utility Tokens that operate under a "Non-Hypothecation" mandate. In a verifiable economy, the "Active Citizen's" retail tokens are not "Accounting Entries" on a bank's balance sheet; they are digital species anchored 1:1 to liquid reserves. Because these assets are held in "Smart Contract Trusteeship," they cannot be "shaved" to cover an institutional margin call or moved into a "Slush Fund" for corporate bonuses. This creates a "Code Veil" around the producer's wealth, ensuring that even if a major industrial infrastructure project fails at the institutional level, the retail economy remains crystalline and liquid. This "Objectivist" separation ensures that the "Standard of Value" for the person buying bread is never compromised by the "Strategic Ambiguity" of a bank's investment wing.

By ending the "Shared Risk" model, we dismantle the "Jurisdictional Trap" that the "American Bankers Association" uses to enforce financial compliance. When retail assets are no longer cannibalized to support "Hollow" institutional debts, the "Velocity of Value" for the average citizen increases. They are no longer paying the "Hidden Tax" of banking instability. In the trade wars of 2026, the resilience of a nation depends on the "Sovereignty of the Producer." If the retail base is protected from institutional churn, the "Micro-Economic Ecosystems" of the Republic can continue to function regardless of global market contagion. It is time to stop being the "Backstop" for the "Wastrels" and start protecting our assets through the Immutable Ledger.[147]

Custom Tokens as Micro-Economic Ecosystems

The rise of Custom Tokens as localized "Micro-Economic Ecosystems" is the forensic "Hard Reset" for regional development. In the digital realism of 2026, the "Active Citizen" recognizes that the

---

[147] Cooper's Logic Check → The "experts" say that banks need to use your deposits to "lend and grow the economy." Logic check: If I borrow your Car to run my taxi business, and I crash it, do you care how much the "Economy" grew while I was driving? They want "Cannibalization" because it is a free insurance policy paid for by your hard work. In digital realism, "Growth" should come from Value, not from "shaving" the neighbors' pockets. It is time to stop being the "Meal" and start being the Owner.

monolithic dollar is a "Leaky Bucket"—wealth created in a town like Dysart or a neighborhood in Detroit is instantly sucked into the "Global Churn" of the "American Bankers Cartel." By implementing custom, context-specific tokens, we create a "Sovereign Circuit" where capital is programmed to circulate within a specific ecosystem before it "leaks" out to the "Wastrel" administrative state. This is the ultimate "Efficiency Multiplier": using the "Rule of Math" to ensure that the productive energy of a community builds the community, not a "Slush Fund" in a distant capital.

The Architecture of Localized Velocity

A micro-economic ecosystem is defined by its Programmable Boundaries. Unlike the "Hollow" fiat dollar, which has no sense of place, a custom token can be "Geo-Fenced" or "Industry-Fenced." For example, a "Dysart Development Token" could be programmed with a "Regional Velocity" incentive—meaning its "Standard of Value" is highest when used for local steel-frame construction or active forest thinning within the district. This prevents the "Institutional Cannibalization" where big-box retailers extract local wealth and move it to offshore accounts.

In these ecosystems, the token acts as a "Social and Economic Glue." By utilizing "Smart Contract Governance," the community can decide on the "Physics of Value" for their specific niche. If a region wants to prioritize precision agriculture, the custom token can be programmed to offer "Algorithmic

Rebates" for sustainable farming equipment. This creates a self-reinforcing loop: the more the "Active Citizen" uses the local token, the more the "Micro-Economy" grows. We are moving from a "Subjective" dependence on federal grants to an "Objectivist" reliance on our own productive capacity.

Partitioning the "Vices" and "Virtues"

Custom tokens allow for a level of social hygiene that the "Hollow Man" monolithic system can never achieve. In a verifiable economy, we can partition "Vice Activity" funds away from general retail flow. For instance, tokens used in "Restricted Zones" (such as gaming or adult entertainment) can be programmed to be non-transferable to "Virtue" accounts—ensuring that the capital intended for a child's education or a library balcony is never co-mingled with the "Churn" of vice. This is "Algorithmic Morality" in practice: we do not need a "Bureaucratic Hammer" to regulate behavior when the "Standard of Value" itself is programmed for integrity.

Furthermore, this architecture solves the "Political Corruption" epidemic of 2026. By utilizing "Campaign Specific Tokens" that are ISP-locked to a representative's actual district, we can forensically kill the "Lobbying Wall." If a "Wastrel" from an outside state tries to buy influence, the smart contract simply rejects the transaction because the "Programmable Intent" does not match the "Origin Logic." This returns the "Right to Contract" to the actual constituents, ensuring that the "Political Machine" is powered by the people it represents, not the "Money Changers" who seek to control it.

The Resilience of the "Sovereign Circuit"

The most critical advantage of these micro-ecosystems is their Contagion Resistance. When the legacy "American Bankers Association" faces a "Liquidity Lockdown" at the monolithic level, a community operating on a "Custom Sovereign Ledger" remains operational. Because their "Standard of Value" is backed by local "Tangible Underlays" and governed by local "Smart Trustees," they are decoupled from the "Strategic Friction" of the global collapse. This is the "Hard Reset" for national security: a Republic composed of thousands of resilient, self-governing micro-economies is impossible for a "Hollow Man" central authority to collapse.

In the trade wars of 2026, the "Efficiency" of a micro-economic ecosystem will out-compete the "Waste" of a centralized monolith every time. By keeping the "Velocity of Money" high within the region and the "Friction" low, the "Active Citizen" recovers the Time that is usually stolen by the state. We are building a "Verifiable Economy" where wealth is not a "Subjective" promise from a debt-ridden government, but an "Objective" reality reflected in the local ledger. It is time to stop being a "Node" in someone else's "Slush Fund" and start being the "Architect" of your own ecosystem.

The New Federalism of Value

Ultimately, custom tokens represent a "New Federalism"—one where the "Standard of Truth" is decentralized. We are ending the era where a single "Hollow" currency is the only option for a diverse and productive people. By embracing specialized wealth, we empower the "Active Citizen" to build the "Dysart-Detroit-Dallas" corridor on their own terms. The "Hard Reset" is not just about technology; it is about the "Sovereignty of the Producer" to choose the tool that best fits the task. The monolith is cracking; it is time to fill the gaps with the Crystalline Logic of custom tokens.[148]

Conclusion: The Architecture of Specialized Wealth

The conclusion of Chapter 14 marks the formal "Hard Reset" of our monetary philosophy, moving from the "Hollow" simplicity of a monolithic currency to the "Objectivist" precision of Contextual Value. As we have forensically audited, the one-size-fits-all model of the legacy dollar is not an economic necessity but a "Strategic Friction" point designed to allow the

---

[148] Cooper's Logic Check → The "experts" say that "Micro-Currencies" will lead to "Economic Fragmentation." Logic check: If you have a garden, do you want a "One-Size-Fits-All" sprinkler that floods the porch and leaves the tomatoes dry, or do you **want Drip Irrigation** that puts the water exactly where the plants are? They want "Unity" because That is the "Hollow" pipe they use to "shave" the whole field. In digital realism, "Fragmentation" is just a "Wastrel" word for "Precision." It is time to stop flooding the porch and start feeding the Roots.

"American Bankers Cartel" to "shave" value from every sector of the Republic simultaneously. By transitioning to a system where money finally knows its purpose through Programmable Intent, we reclaim the "Standard of Value" from the "Wastrels" and return the "Sovereignty of the Producer" to the individual citizen.

The segregation of Industrial and Consumer Liquidity provides the necessary "Code Veil" to protect the "Active Citizen" from institutional mismanagement. By ensuring that the "Velocity" of high-risk speculative swaps never co-mingles with the stable "Bedrock" of retail commerce, we neutralize the "Contagion Conductor" that has plagued the 2025-2026 banking cycle. This "Hard Reset" ensures that the grocery money of the producer is never cannibalized to support the "Slush Fund" of a failing institution, restoring a "Standard of Truth" to the most basic interactions of our daily lives.

The rise of Custom Tokens as Micro-Economic Ecosystems represents the "New Federalism" of the digital age. By creating "Sovereign Circuits" that are geo-fenced or industry-locked, we empower communities to build their own "Efficiency Multipliers" without the "Strategic Ambiguity" of a centralized state. Whether it is a "Regional Development Token" in Pennsylvania or a "Campaign Contribution" token locked to a specific district, the "Logic of the Ledger" ensures that the productive energy of the Republic remains where it is created. We are no longer

"Nodes" in a "Wastrel" monolith; we are the architects of specialized wealth.

Ultimately, Chapter 14 provides the framework for a "Verifiable Economy" where "Time" is finally respected as our truest currency. We have moved past the era of "Dumb Money" and entered the age of "Crystalline Logic," where every cent is programmed for integrity. As we move forward, the "Active Citizen" must reject the "Hollow" promises of the "Money Changers" and embrace the specialized tools of the "Digital Republic." The monolith is cracking, and in its place, we are building an architecture of truth, specificity, and sovereignty. It is time to stop playing the "Rigged Game" and start using the Right Tool for a free people.[149]

---

[149] Cooper's Logic Check → The "experts" say that "Specialized Currency" is too radical for a stable society. Logic check: If you have a different **Medicine** for a headache than you do for a broken leg, is that "Radical" or is it just Common Sense? They want "Monolithic Money" because That is the "Hollow" pipe they use to "shave" your medicine cabinet and your pantry at the same time. In digital realism, "Stability" comes from Precision, not "Unity." It is time to stop using "Master Keys" and start trusting the Context.

Chapter 15: The Infrastructure of Sovereign Commerce. Building rails that operate independent of geopolitical gatekeepers.

"Peace, commerce, and honest friendship with all nations; entangling alliances with none."

Thomas Jefferson[150]

The financial rails have always been an area of discussion, even before the idea of rails was a "thing." We have a need to ensure that the rails do not prevent people for advancing the system, just because a government wants to make money. This means that we need a defined set of rails which protect the retail market and the institutional market, all the while protecting citizens interest globally.

Finance should be decentralized. Monopolies within the financial market are among the most dangerous in any field. As a result, we need to ensure a system of decentralized nodes. This allows us to eliminate the gatekeepers such as SWIFT and XRP which undermine the validity of private transactions, all the while allowing hardened logistics to protect the world through automated KYC/AML for accounts. The removal of the intermediaries not only will make the system faster, but by using smart contracts, will allow

[150] Staff (2026). "Commerce Quotes." Brainy Quote at https://www.brainyquote.com/search_results?x=0&y=0&q=Commerce.

for suspicious transactions to be reported and if needed clawed back or frozen. This allows for new levels of resilience within the system, bringing forth more interconnectivity globally.[151]

The Geopolitical Kill-Switch: Identifying Vulnerabilities in Global Rails

The "Geopolitical Kill-Switch" represents the forensic reality of the legacy financial system, where the "American Bankers Cartel" and their administrative allies use the "Bureaucratic Hammer" to weaponize global rails against any form of dissent. In the digital realism of 2026, we have seen that centralized systems like SWIFT are not neutral utilities; they are "Strategic Friction" points used to enforce financial compliance and "Stealth Confiscation." When a nation, an industry, or an "Active Citizen" threatens the "Wastrel" status quo, the gatekeepers simply flip the switch, creating an instantaneous "Liquidity Lockdown" that freezes the life-energy of the producer. This is the ultimate "Jurisdictional Trap," where the "Standard of Value" is held hostage by the geopolitical whims of a "Hollow Man" bureaucracy.

---

[151] Cooper's Logic Check → The "experts" say that we need "Centralized Gates" to stop criminals and keep the world safe. Logic check: If I tell you that you can only leave your house through a Single Door that I have the key to, am I "protecting" you or am I jailer? They want the "Kill-Switch" because That is how they control the "Standard of Value." In digital realism, "Safety" comes from Hardened Code and Decentralized Power, not a "Wastrel" in a suit. It is time to stop using "Master Keys" and start trusting the Global Mesh.

This vulnerability is built into the very plumbing of the "Money Changers." Because every transaction must pass through a centralized "Clearinghouse," the state possesses a total "Optic" on the flow of value. This allows for "Selective Enforcement," where "Entangling Alliances" determine who is allowed to trade and who is cast into the "Digital Wilderness." To achieve a "Hard Reset," we must identify these terminal chokepoints—the centralized databases and the "Lobbying Walls" of the legacy banks—and replace them with "Rails of Truth." These new rails must operate on the "Physics of Math," ensuring that no single state or cartel can decapitate the global economy simply to save its own "Slush Fund."

The "Kill-Switch" is not just about stopping a transaction; it is about the "Psychological Priming" of the citizenry. By maintaining the power to disconnect anyone at any time, the administrative state enforces a "Subjective" morality on the market. If you do not follow the "Propaganda Machine's" narrative, your "Standard of Value" evaporates. In 2026, the trade wars have proven that "Financial Neutrality" is a myth in a centralized world. We must build a "Sovereign Ledger" that is immune to the "Bureaucratic Hammer," ensuring that "Commerce" remains an "Honest Friendship" between producers, rather than a "Permission Slip" granted by a gatekeeper.[152]

---

[152] Cooper's Logic Check → The "experts" and the "Wastrels" at the UN tell you that "Economic Sanctions" and "Financial De-platforming" are "peaceful" ways to maintain global order and

Decentralized Nodes: The Physical Reality of Digital Sovereignty

Decentralized Nodes represent the "Physical Reality" of digital sovereignty, moving the ledger from a "Subjective" cloud controlled by the "Wastrels" to the "Objectivist" bedrock of distributed hardware. In the digital realism of 2026, the "American Bankers Association" thrives on the "Hollow" centralization of data, which allows for total "State-Sponsored Obfuscation." By contrast, a network of decentralized nodes ensures that the "Sovereign Ledger" is maintained by the "Active Citizens" themselves, creating a "Hardened Logistics" framework that no "Bureaucratic Hammer" can crush. Each node acts as a "Crystalline" validator of the "Standard of Truth," ensuring that the "Velocity of Money" is governed by the "Rule of Math" rather than the "Strategic Ambiguity" of a central bank.

Sovereignty in the digital age is not an abstract right; it is a function of **Infrastructure**. If your data lives on a "Big Tech" server, you have no sovereignty. If your "Standard of Value" is verified by a decentralized

---

"safety." Logic check: If I lock your pantry, cut off your water, and tell your neighbors they'll be punished for talking to you, am I being "peaceful" or am I Starving you into submission? They want the "Kill-Switch" because it is the only way they can force you to use their "Hollow" debt-based dollar. If they can't compete on "Value," they compete on "Control." In digital realism, a "Rail" that can be turned off by a politician is not a "Market"—it is a Prison. If the "Standard of Value" is not "Unstoppable," it is not "Sovereign." It is time to stop using the "Cartel's" switch and start building the Sovereign Mesh.

node in your own home or office, you have reclaimed the "Sovereignty of the Producer." This is the "Efficiency Multiplier" in its physical form: a system where the "Physics of Information" are decentralized so that the "Sovereignty of the Producer" can never be compromised by a single point of failure. This architecture eliminates the "Expert Fallacy" because the "Code" is the only auditor that matters.

By distributing the "Nodes of Power," we neutralize the "Lobbying Wall." You cannot lobby a thousand independent nodes spread across the "Global Mesh" the same way you can lobby a single "Hollow Man" at a central bank. This is "Algorithmic Transparency" in action. The nodes do not care about "Political Expediency" or "Entangling Alliances"; they only care if the "Math" of the transaction matches the "Physics of the Asset." This "Hard Reset" ensures that the "Digital Republic" is built on "Bedrock," making the "Money Changers" and their "Slush Funds" obsolete through sheer technical resilience.[153]

---

[153] The "experts" say that "Centralized Servers" are more "efficient," "secure," and "convenient" for the average person. Logic check: If you keep all your eggs in one basket, and the guy holding the basket works for the "Money Changers," whose eggs are they really? They want "Centralization" because That is the "Jurisdictional Trap" they use to "shave" your transactions, monitor your life, and sell your data. In digital realism, "Efficiency" means Resilience. If a "Wastrel" bureaucrat can't find the "Off" button for the whole system because the system is everywhere, then the system is Free. It is time to stop trusting the "Hollow" cloud and start owning your own Node.

Bypass Protocols: Operating Outside the SWIFT and Central Bank Nexus

Bypass Protocols are the forensic tools of the "Digital Republic," allowing for "Autonomous Settlement" that operates entirely outside the SWIFT, XRP, and Central Bank Nexus. In the digital realism of 2026, we recognize that to participate in the "Wastrel" rails—whether they are legacy fiat pipes or "Hollow" centralized crypto-clones like XRP—is to accept the "Strategic Friction" and "Surveillance" of the "American Bankers Cartel." Bypass protocols utilize the KIROS architecture to create "Sovereign Economic Zones" where the "Active Citizen" can trade across borders using "Atomic Settlement" and "1:1 Backed Reserves."

This removes the "Hollow Man" intermediary and the "Day of the Dead" settlement cycles, allowing for a "Velocity of Value" that the legacy "Money Changers" simply cannot match. By operating on a "Global Mesh" of peer-to-peer validation, these protocols ensure that the "Right to Contract" is preserved, bypassing the "Lobbying Wall" and the "Slush Fund" requirements of the legacy system. XRP and its ilk are merely "Digital Versions of the Old Guard," attempting to insert a new gatekeeper into the same "Hollow" model. A true "Hard Reset" requires the total removal of the middleman, allowing for "Direct Peer-to-Peer Production" where the "Standard of Value" is the asset itself, not a "Bridge Token" owned by a corporation.

These protocols are the "Hardened Logistics" of a free market. They allow the "Active Citizen" in Dysart to trade with a producer in Tokyo without the Bureaucratic Hammer of a "T-Plus" delay or a "Geopolitical Kill-Switch" interruption. We are moving toward a "Verifiable Economy" where "Commerce" is an "Honest Friendship" between producers, unencumbered by "Entangling Alliances" with debt-ridden states. By bypassing the nexus, we drain the information moat that the "Wastrels" use to maintain their "Gimmie" culture, returning the Sovereignty of the Producer to its crystalline, autonomous origin.[154]

Hardened Logistics: Securing the Digital Supply Chain

n the digital realism of 2026, the concept of a supply chain has evolved beyond the physical movement of containers and raw materials. It now encompasses the forensic flow of data, value, and title that accompanies every physical asset. The current legacy infrastructure is riddled with vulnerabilities—

---

154 Cooper's Logic Check → The "experts" say that "Bypassing" the central banks and "Standardized Gatekeepers" will lead to "Financial Anarchy," "Terrorism," and "Money Laundering." Logic check: If I trade my Corn for your Steel without asking a guy in a suit for a "Permission Slip," is that "Anarchy" or is it just Trade? They call it "Laundering" because they are not getting their "Gimmie" cut of the soap. In digital realism, a "Bypass" is just a Shortcut around a "Wastrel" who is standing in the middle of the road demanding a toll for a bridge he didn't build. If the "Math" validates the trade and the "Assets" are real, the bank and the bridge-token are irrelevant. It is time to stop paying the "Toll" and start using the Sovereign Rails.

digital backdoors, centralized data silos, and administrative chokepoints—that allow for the systematic interference in global commerce. Hardened Logistics is the structural response to these vulnerabilities, creating a digital supply chain that is as resilient and immutable as the physical assets it represents. This is the transition from a system of trust to a system of proof, where the integrity of the supply chain is secured by the math of the ledger and the hardening of the physical nodes.

The Architecture of Immutable Provenance

The first pillar of hardened logistics is the establishment of immutable provenance. In a verifiable economy, it is not enough to know where an asset is; one must be able to forensically prove its origin, its ownership history, and its current state without relying on a centralized authority. By utilizing the KIROS architecture, every component of the digital supply chain is hashed and anchored to a sovereign ledger. This creates a crystalline record that cannot be altered by a bureaucrat or a malicious actor. Whether it is the tracking of steel-frame components from a factory to a construction site in Dysart or the monitoring of yield from a precision agriculture project, the data is secured by a multi-layer validation model that rejects any attempt at state-sponsored obfuscation.

This hardening extends to the hardware level. Secure logistics requires the deployment of hardened nodes—physical devices equipped with secure enclaves and tamper-evident hardware—that serve as the gateway between the physical and digital worlds. These nodes ensure that the data entering the ledger is accurate and that the communication channels are encrypted and decentralized. By distributing these nodes across a global mesh, we eliminate the single point of failure that the American Bankers Cartel uses to maintain its grip on global trade. The supply chain becomes a sovereign circuit, where the velocity of value is protected by the physical reality of the infrastructure.

Neutralizing the Information Moat

The legacy supply chain relies on an information moat—a gap between the physical movement of goods and the digital settlement of their value. This gap is where the money changers thrive, using the physics of delay to justify cascading fees and strategic friction. Hardened logistics closes this gap through the use of autonomous settlement and real-time validation. When a physical asset reaches a milestone verified by a hardened node, the smart contract trustee automatically executes the corresponding value transfer. There is no need for a middleman to audit the transaction or for a clearinghouse to provide permission. The supply chain and the financial rail become a single, synchronized unit.

This synchronization is the ultimate efficiency multiplier. It allows for the creation of sovereign economic zones where commerce flows without the interference of geopolitical gatekeepers. By hardening the digital supply chain, we ensure that the right to contract is a technical reality rather than a legal theory. We are building a system where the sovereignty of the producer is guarded by the very tools they use to conduct their business. In the trade wars of 2026, the side that operates on hardened logistics will be the one that can maintain its productive energy even in the face of systemic state failure. The era of the vulnerable, centralized supply chain is over; the era of the hardened, sovereign ledger has begun.[155]

Autonomous Settlement: Trade Without Permissioned Intermediaries

Autonomous Settlement is the mechanical realization of the Right to Contract, removing the human element of the middleman from the finality of a transaction. In the digital realism of 2026, we must acknowledge that the traditional settlement process is a weaponized

---

[155] Cooper's Logic Check → The experts and the administrative proxies tell you that "Centralized Security" is the only way to protect the supply chain from cyber-attacks and fraud. Logic check: If a thief wants to rob a neighborhood, does he want every house to have its own Individual Safe, or does he want the whole neighborhood to keep their valuables in One Community Box that he already has the master key to? They want "Centralization" because That is how they monitor your inventory, tax your movement, and turn off your access when you don't follow their narrative. In digital realism, security comes from Distribution. If the data is everywhere and the nodes are hardened, there is no "Front Door" for a wastrel to kick in. It is time to stop trusting the "Central Guard" and start trusting the Hardened Mesh.

delay. By utilizing T-Plus cycles and centralized clearinghouses, the American Bankers Cartel maintains a state of perpetual debt and uncertainty. Autonomous settlement utilizes smart contracts to ensure that the exchange of value occurs simultaneously with the fulfillment of contract terms. When the math of the ledger matches the physics of the asset, the transaction settles instantly and irrevocably. This is the end of the intermediary as a gatekeeper and the beginning of the ledger as the ultimate witness.

The structural necessity of this system is highlighted by the removal of counterparty risk. In the legacy market, the period between the agreement and the settlement is a void where the wastrel class extracts fees and manipulates liquidity. Autonomous settlement collapses this void. By moving to a model where the assets are tokenized and held in smart contract trusteeship, the settlement becomes an atomic event. Either the conditions are met and the value moves, or they are not. There is no room for a bureaucratic hammer to freeze a trade or for a money changer to shave the value while the transaction is in transit. This is the efficiency multiplier that allows the active citizen to operate at the speed of thought.[156]

---

[156] Cooper's Logic Check → The experts say that "Immediate Settlement" is dangerous because it does notallow for the correction of mistakes or the prevention of fraud through human oversight. Logic check: If you go to a farmers market and trade five dollars for a head of lettuce, do you need a Banker to stand between you and the farmer for three days to "verify" that the

Resilience Theory: Maintaining Commerce During Systemic State Failure

Resilience Theory focuses on the survival of the economic organism when the host—the administrative state—enters a period of terminal decay. In 2026, the sovereign debt trap and the systematic debasement of fiat currency have made systemic state failure a forensic probability rather than a distant theory. Resilience in commerce requires a decoupling of the rails of trade from the rails of the state. By building a sovereign commerce infrastructure that operates on decentralized nodes and 1:1 asset-backed reserves, the active citizen ensures that the ability to buy, sell, and produce remains intact even if the central bank or the national government collapses under the weight of its own wastrel policies.

A resilient economy is one that is modular. In the legacy system, every transaction is tied to the central node of the state; if the center fails, the entire network dies. Resilience Theory advocates for a mesh-based architecture where every sovereign economic zone can function as an independent cell. If the federal rail fails, the local regional development tokens and the

---

lettuce is green and the five dollars is real? They want "Settlement Delays" because That is how they use your money to make their own bets while you are waiting for your own property to clear. In digital realism, "Oversight" is just a word for Legalized Theft of Time. If the code is right and the asset is there, the deal is done. It is time to stop paying for the "Delay" and start trusting the Math.

peer-to-peer bypass protocols continue to facilitate the movement of real-world assets. This is the hard reset of national security: a republic that cannot be decapitated because its commerce is not anchored to a single, vulnerable, and debt-ridden institution.[157]

The Global Mesh: Interconnecting Sovereign Economic Zones

The Global Mesh is the final evolution of the sovereign ledger, creating a universal language of value that interconnects localized economic zones without the need for a global geopolitical gatekeeper. In the digital realism of 2026, we have seen the failure of the globalist model, which sought to impose a single, hollow standard of value through entangling alliances and centralized organizations. The Global Mesh replaces this with a network of sovereign economic zones that interact through decentralized bypass protocols. This allows the active citizen in Dysart to engage in honest friendship and commerce with a producer in Tokyo or a developer in Munich,

---

[157] Cooper's Logic Check → The administrative proxies tell you that "Centralized Control" is the only way to ensure "Economic Stability" during a crisis. Logic check: If you are on a ship that is taking on water because the Captain spent the fuel money on a party, do you want to be Chained to the Hull for "Stability," or do you want a Lifeboat? They want "Centralization" because That is how they make sure you go down with the ship while they fly away on the helicopter. In digital realism, "Resilience" means Independence. If you can still trade with your neighbor when the lights go out at the Treasury, you are not a victim; you are a survivor. It is time to stop trusting the "Captain" and start building the Lifeboat.

based entirely on the structural integrity of the assets being traded.

This mesh is powered by the synchronization of local tangibility and global liquidity. Each zone maintains its own internal micro-economic ecosystem, governed by its own smart contract trustees and backed by its own tangible underlays. However, these zones are interconnected via the sovereign ledger, allowing for the frictionless exchange of specialized wealth. The global mesh ensures that the efficiency multiplier of one region can be exported to another without being shaved by the money changers. It is a system of total algorithmic transparency, where the sovereignty of the producer is respected regardless of jurisdictional boundaries.[158]

Conclusion: Building the Unstoppable Market

The conclusion of Chapter 15 marks the forensic completion of the sovereign commerce architecture, establishing a system of rails that finally honors the Jeffersonian ideal of honest friendship with all nations

---

158 Cooper's Logic Check → The experts say that a "Global Mesh" without a "Central Regulatory Body" will lead to a "Wild West" of unregulated and dangerous trade. Logic check: If I have a Gallon of Milk and you have a Loaf of Bread, and we agree on a trade, does a Bureaucrat in Switzerland make the bread taste better or the milk safer? They want "Global Regulation" because That is the ultimate "Lobbying Wall" for the global wastrel class to extract their gimmie from every trade on Earth. In digital realism, "Regulation" is the Math of the Ledger. If the token is backed by a real asset and the code is verified, the trade is safe. It is time to stop waiting for "Global Permission" and start trusting the Global Mesh.

and entangling alliances with none. By identifying and neutralizing the geopolitical kill-switch, we have moved the digital republic beyond the reach of the administrative gatekeepers who have long used the physics of delay and the jurisdictional trap to stifle the sovereignty of the producer. The transition from the hollow, centralized pipes of the legacy banking cartel to a global mesh of decentralized nodes ensures that the velocity of value is now governed by the immutable laws of math rather than the strategic ambiguity of a centralized state.

The implementation of hardened logistics and autonomous settlement represents the final hard reset of the global supply chain, turning the right to contract into a technical reality that operates with crystalline certainty. In this verifiable economy, the removal of the permissioned intermediary is not merely an act of technical efficiency; it is a declaration of independence from the money changers who thrive on information asymmetry and cascading fees. By securing the digital supply chain through hardened physical infrastructure and smart contract trusteeship, we ensure that the standard of value is protected from the bureaucratic hammer of any single jurisdiction, allowing commerce to flow with unprecedented resilience.

Resilience theory, as applied to our sovereign economic zones, provides the blueprint for maintaining the pulse of the republic even in the face of systemic state failure. We have documented that a mesh-based architecture is the only forensic defense against the terminal decay of the sovereign debt trap and the systematic debasement of fiat currency. By interconnecting these localized economic ecosystems through the global mesh, we allow for the democratization of truth and the fluid movement of specialized wealth. This ensures that the productive energy of the active citizen is never again held hostage by the hollow promises of a debt-ridden government or the lobbying walls of the American Bankers Association.

Ultimately, Chapter 15 provides the infrastructure for an unstoppable market—a system where the sovereignty of the producer is the foundational principle and the ledger is the final authority. We are no longer operating within the jurisdictional fog of the legacy rails; we are building on the bedrock of the hardened mesh. As we move forward into the final sections of this work, the forensic evidence is clear: the era of the geopolitical gatekeeper is over. The rails of the future are decentralized, autonomous, and owned by the people who create the value. It is time to turn off the old machine and activate the sovereign ledger for the digital republic.[159]

---

[159] Cooper's Logic Check → The experts and the administrative state tell you that "Global Infrastructure" must be managed by "Global Institutions" to prevent chaos. **Logic check:** If you want to keep your house warm, do you want a **Thermostat** on your wall that you control, or do you want to have to call a **Committee in Brussels** every time you want to turn up the heat? They want "Global Management" because That is the only way they can "shave" the heat off your radiators to warm their own offices. In digital realism, the only "Management" that works is **The Math**. If the nodes are decentralized and the settlement is autonomous, the system is stable because it is fair. It is time to stop paying for the "Bureaucracy" and start trusting the **Mesh**.

Chapter 16: Hybrid Economics. Navigating the transition period where fiat and digital assets must coexist.

"The first lesson of economics is scarcity: there is never enough of anything to fully satisfy all those who want it. The first lesson of politics is to disregard the first lesson of economics."

Thomas Sowell[160]

One of the greatest paradox's of the current economic system is that we can always print more money. Since the core element of the value system is the value of the currency being used, the idea that we can print more currency creates a dangerous situation where value is not real. While we are creating the new system, we must realize that this is a problem that we have to solve. Therefore, we will have a period of hybrid finance.

In this era of dual standards, we need to realize that it is a sunset of the fiat era. Fiat should be decommissioned gradually till approximately 10% of the system runs on fiat and banks. This means that eventually, the OROR tokens move more from being a method to "get on chain" to becoming a method to get "off chain." In order for this system to work, the taxation of the digital aspect needs to be less than the

---

[160] Staff (2026). "Economics Quotes." Brainy Quote at https://www.brainyquote.com/search_results?x=0&y=0&q=Economics.

taxation of the fiat aspect. This will allow for the system to self-rectify within the economy. There will, of course, be a counter reformation where the banks attempt to use monopolistic methods to drive their prices down and their benefits up. With the correlated tax system, this will be a benefit as citizens can arbitrage the values to increase their share of the economy.[161]

The Dual-Standard Era: Navigating the Overlap of Fiat and Code

The Dual-Standard Era is the forensic reality of a civilization caught between two competing operating systems: the legacy "Hollow Man" economy of fiat and the rising "Digital Republic" of the sovereign ledger. In the digital realism of 2026, we must acknowledge that the transition from a debt-based system to an asset-backed one is not an instantaneous "Hard Reset" but a managed migration. During this overlap, the standard of value is bifurcated. On one hand, we have the subjective promises of a state that is $35 trillion in

---

161 Cooper's Logic Check → The experts say that a "Hybrid System" is too volatile and that we need a "Single Unified Standard" to ensure market stability. Logic check: If you are moving from an old, rotting house to a new, steel-frame home, do you want to be forced to Demolish the Old One before the roof is even on the new one? They want a "Single Standard" because as long as you are trapped in their house, they can keep charging you rent for a ceiling that leaks. In digital realism, a "Hybrid Period" is just Common Sense Moving Day. You keep your stuff in the old place while you set up the new one, and you move out completely once the new locks are verified. It is time to stop fearing the "Overlap" and start using it to your advantage.

debt, and on the other, the objectivist certainty of the KIROS architecture. Navigating this era requires the active citizen to become a dual-resident, utilizing the legacy rails for the dying breaths of fiat retail while moving their primary productive energy into the crystalline safety of the ledger.

This period is defined by the sunset of the monolithic currency. For decades, the American Bankers Cartel has enforced a single standard to ensure that every "Active Citizen" was trapped in the same jurisdictional fog. In the dual-standard era, that fog begins to lift. We are moving toward a system where fiat is decommissioned gradually, serving as a secondary liquidity layer while the sovereign ledger takes over the heavy lifting of industrial infrastructure and long-term wealth preservation. This is the efficiency multiplier in action: we use the old world's pipes while they still function, but we ensure our "Standard of Truth" is anchored in the new.

The danger of this era lies in the "Psychological Priming" of the status quo. The administrative state will attempt to use the volatility of the transition to scare the producer back into the "Hollow" safety of the bank. However, the math of the ledger is the ultimate defense. By maintaining a dual presence, the active citizen can arbitrage the friction. When the bank attempts to shave value through stealth confiscation or liquidity lockdowns, the citizen moves their value "On-Chain" to the asset-backed digital species. When they need to interact with the legacy retail market, they move the minimum necessary "Off-Chain." This is the sovereignty doctrine: using the dual standard to ensure that the "Wastrel" class can never again hold your entire life-energy hostage.

Ultimately, the dual-standard era is a training ground for the verifiable economy. It forces the market to compare the "Physics of Value" in real-time. Every time a citizen chooses the ledger over the fiat dollar, the "Repugnance to Logic" of the old system becomes clearer. We are building a world where the "Right to Contract" is preserved across both rails, but where the "Rule of Math" eventually renders the "Rule of the Lobbyist" obsolete. This is not a state of confusion; it is a state of transition. We are managing the migration to digital realism, ensuring that as the fiat era enters its terminal decay, the active citizen is already standing on the bedrock of the future.[162]

---

[162] Cooper's Logic Check → The experts and the money changers say that having two competing standards of value will create "Chaos" and "Market Confusion." Logic check: If you are at a construction site, do you get "Confused" because you have a Manual Saw and a Power Saw? You use the manual one for the quick, small stuff and the power saw for the heavy lifting. They want "Unity" because That is how they make sure you don't have an alternative when they decide to stop the power. In digital realism, a "Dual Standard" is just Redundancy. If the bank fails, the ledger works. If the internet flickers, the physical cash in your pocket still buys bread. It is time to stop worrying about "Chaos" and start appreciating the Backup Plan.

Off-Ramps and On-Ramps: The Friction of Transitional Liquidity

The transition to a verifiable economy is physically manifested at the "On-Ramps" and "Off-Ramps"—the strategic friction points where capital moves between the legacy fiat world and the sovereign ledger. In the digital realism of 2026, these ramps are the front lines of the trade wars. The American Bankers Cartel recognizes that their power ends where the ledger begins, so they utilize the "Bureaucratic Hammer" to make these crossing points as slow, expensive, and invasive as possible. This is "Strategic Friction" in its purest form: an attempt to prevent the "Active Citizen" from escaping the sovereign debt trap by tolling the exit.

Transitional liquidity is the lifeblood of the hybrid era. To ensure a successful migration, these ramps must be optimized for velocity and "Hardened Logistics." An on-ramp—moving value from fiat into an asset-backed token like KIROS—should be a forensic process of "Verification," not a "Permission Slip" from a gatekeeper. By utilizing automated KYC/AML and smart contract trusteeship, we can move value "On-Chain" with crystalline certainty, bypassing the manual audits and delays that the "Wastrels" use to discourage the migration. The efficiency of these ramps determines the health of the entire hybrid system; if the gates are clogged, the "Velocity of Value" stalls, and the "Information Moat" widens.

As the fiat era sunsets, the purpose of these ramps will invert. Initially, the focus is on "Getting On-Chain" to protect assets from debasement. However, as the digital republic matures, the "Off-Ramp" becomes a tool for "Sovereign Interaction" with the remaining 10% of the legacy system. The "Standard of Value" will have shifted so completely that the "Off-Ramp" is seen as a way to "De-escalate" value into the physical retail market for temporary use. The friction at these points is a measurement of the administrative state's desperation. The more they "Shave" the value during the transition, the more they prove that their own system is in terminal decay.

To counter this, the digital republic must build its own "Autonomous Ramps." This involves interconnecting the sovereign ledger directly with the physical world through "Tangible Underlays" and decentralized nodes. When a library balcony or a 75-acre estate acts as the collateral for the ramp itself, we bypass the "Money Changers" entirely. We are building a system where the "Active Citizen" can move their wealth with the same fluidity that they use to conduct their business. This is the hard reset of liquidity: a world where the "On-Ramp" to freedom is wide open, and the "Off-Ramp" to the old world is a choice, not a necessity.[163]

---

[163] Cooper's Logic Check → The administrative proxies tell you that "Strict Controls" and "High Fees" at the ramps are necessary to "Protect the Integrity of the Financial System." **Logic check:** If you are trying to leave a Burning Building, and the guy at the door tells you that you have to pay a 10% Exit Fee

Hedging Against Legacy Collapse: The Digital Asset Lifeboat

The sovereign debt trap and the systematic debasement of fiat currency have moved the collapse of the legacy financial system from the realm of theory to forensic probability. In the digital realism of 2026, the legacy economy functions as a sinking vessel, weighed down by $35 trillion in debt and the strategic friction of a banking cartel that survives by shaving the life-energy of the producer. The digital asset lifeboat is the structural response to this terminal decay. It is not a speculative bet on market sentiment, but a hard reset into asset-backed digital species that operate on the physics of value. By moving productive energy into the KIROS architecture, the active citizen ensures that their standard of value remains crystalline even as the hollow promises of the administrative state evaporate.

The lifeboat operates through the synchronization of 1:1 reserves and tangible underlays. Unlike the fiat dollar, which is a subjective promise of future taxation, a sovereign utility token represents an objective claim on real-world assets like industrial infrastructure or

---

and fill out a Five-Page Survey to "protect the integrity" of the hallway, is he helping you or is he Trapping you? They want "Friction" because every second you spend at the gate is another second they can "shave" your purchasing power through inflation. In digital realism, a "Ramp" should be as fast as a Light Switch. If you can't move your money when you want to, it is not your money—it is a Hostage. It is time to stop paying the "Toll" to the "Wastrels" and start using the Sovereign Express Lane.

precision agriculture yields. This creates a refuge of value that is decoupled from the market contagion of the American Bankers Association. When the legacy rails enter a liquidity lockdown, the sovereign ledger remains operational, providing the hardened logistics necessary to maintain the velocity of value. This is the ultimate hedge: the ability to maintain the sovereignty of the producer while the wastrel class is consumed by the sovereign debt trap they created.[164]

Taxation in Transition: Reconciling Algorithmic Gains with Fiat Obligations

The transition to a digital republic creates a forensic challenge: how to reconcile the high-velocity, algorithmic gains of the sovereign ledger with the slow-motion fiat obligations of the administrative state. In the hybrid era, the active citizen must navigate a dual-standard tax environment where the rules of engagement are often defined by the jurisdictional fog of the legacy system. The hard reset for taxation is the implementation of a correlated tax system, where

---

[164] Cooper's Logic Check --. The experts and the propaganda machine tell you that "Digital Assets" are "too risky" for your retirement and that you should stay in the "Safety" of the legacy market. Logic check: If you are standing on a Pier that is being pounded by a Hurricane, and someone offers you a Lifeboat, do you stay on the pier because the lifeboat looks "small"? The pier is the legacy system—it is anchored to a debt that can never be paid. The lifeboat is the ledger—it is built to float on the math. They want you on the pier because your weight is the only thing keeping them from washing away. In digital realism, "Risk" is staying in a house That is already on fire. It is time to stop listening to the "Pier Owners" and start rowing the Lifeboat.

digital transactions are incentivized through lower rates than their fiat counterparts. This allows the economy to self-rectify, as capital naturally flows toward the rails of truth. Reconciling these gains requires a verifiable economy where every transaction is tracked with algorithmic transparency, ensuring that obligations are met without the need for a bureaucratic hammer.

Taxation in the hybrid era must evolve to recognize the difference between hollow gains and productive energy. When the administrative state devalues the currency, any nominal gain in the price of an asset is often just a reflection of inflation—a stealth confiscation of the citizen's purchasing power. A sovereign tax model accounts for this by pegging obligations to a standard of value that is anchored in real-world assets rather than the subjective whim of the printing press. By using smart contracts as automated trustees for tax distribution, the system ensures that the social contract is honored without allowing the money changers to shave the value of the payment. This is the efficiency multiplier of digital governance: meeting the needs of the republic while protecting the sovereignty of the producer from the gimmie culture of the centralized state.[165]

---

165 Cooper's Logic Check → The administrative proxies tell you that "New Tax Laws" are necessary to "Ensure Fairness" in the digital age. Logic check: If you work hard to grow a Tree, and the government Shrinks the Yardstick you use to measure it, did the tree actually get "Larger," or did they just find a way to claim a Bigger Branch? They want to tax your "Gains" in fiat because

The Oracle Problem: Bridging Physical Reality and On-Chain Logic

The Oracle Problem is the forensic challenge of ensuring that the data entering the sovereign ledger is a crystalline reflection of physical reality. In a verifiable economy, the standard of value is only as strong as the link between the asset and the code. If an oracle—the bridge between the world and the chain—is compromised by the expert fallacy or state-sponsored obfuscation, the integrity of the entire ledger is at risk. The KIROS architecture solves this through an oracle mesh network, utilizing multi-layer validation to ensure that asset-to-token fidelity is absolute. By using hardened logistics and IoT-enabled sensors, we remove the hollow man from the verification process, allowing the physics of the asset to speak directly to the logic of the code.

Bridging physical reality and on-chain logic requires the removal of the subjective intermediary. In the legacy system, we rely on appraisals, audits, and legal opinions—all of which are subject to strategic friction and the jurisdictional fog. A sovereign oracle mesh replaces this with a network of decentralized nodes that verify data points such as soil health, structural integrity, and title status in real-time. This

---

they are the ones making the fiat worthless. In digital realism, a "Gain" is not real unless you can buy more Bread with it than you could yesterday. If the tax does notaccount for their "Stealth Confiscation," it is not "Fairness"—it is Robbery. It is time to stop paying for the "Shrinking Yardstick" and start taxing based on the Real Math.

creates an objectivist record that the bureaucratic hammer cannot shatter. The oracle problem is essentially a trust problem; by replacing trust with the rule of math and the physical reality of hardened hardware, we ensure that the sovereign ledger remains the ultimate standard of truth for the digital republic.[166]

Legacy Resistance: Surviving the Counter-Reformation of Central Banks

The transition to a digital republic is not merely a technical migration; it is a forensic confrontation with a centralized power structure that has spent a century perfecting the architecture of the jurisdictional trap. As the sovereign ledger begins to drain the liquidity from the hollow fiat system, we must anticipate the Counter-Reformation of the Central Banks. The American Bankers Cartel and their administrative proxies will not watch the sunset of their era with indifference. Instead, they will deploy every tool of strategic friction at their disposal—ranging from monopolistic regulatory captures to state-sponsored obfuscation—to force the active citizen back into the

---

[166] Cooper's Logic Check → The experts say that you need "Human Auditors" and "Certified Professionals" to bridge the gap between the world and the ledger. Logic check: If you want to know if it is Raining, do you want a Sensor on your roof that tells you it is wet, or do you want to wait for a Committee to vote on the "Probability of Precipitation"? They want "Human Oracles" because humans can be "Nudged," "Lobbied," and "Shaved." A sensor just tells the truth. In digital realism, an "Auditor" is just a Wastrel with a clipboard. It is time to stop trusting the "Committee" and start trusting the Math of the Mesh.

rails of the money changers. Surviving this period requires the implementation of defensive economic protocols that prioritize the sovereignty of the producer over the preservation of the legacy institutions.

The Weapons of the Counter-Reformation

The primary weapon of the counter-reformation is the lobbying wall. The legacy banks will attempt to use the bureaucratic hammer to criminalize or over-regulate the on-ramps and off-ramps of the sovereign ledger. We should expect a wave of emergency decrees and legislative maneuvers designed to reclassify asset-backed digital species as illegal or high-risk instruments. This is the expert fallacy in its terminal form: the claim that centralized control is necessary for consumer protection, when in reality, it is only necessary for the protection of the bankers' slush funds. By manufacturing a pricing fog through restrictive tax policies and predatory transaction fees, the cartel hopes to make the cost of freedom higher than the cost of the gimmie culture.

Beyond legislation, the counter-reformation will utilize psychological priming and weaponized media narratives. The propaganda machine will characterize the digital republic as a wild west of instability and crime, while portraying the central bank as the only refuge of value. This narrative ignores the forensic evidence of the sovereign debt trap and the systematic debasement of the dollar. The administrative state will also attempt to co-opt the technology by launching Central Bank Digital Currencies (CBDCs). These are not true digital assets; they are digital versions of the old guard, designed to offer the convenience of speed while maintaining the power of stealth confiscation and the geopolitical kill-switch.

Strategic Arbitrage: The Path to Survival

To survive this counter-reformation, the active citizen must practice strategic arbitrage. This involves using the legacy system's own rules against it. In the dual-standard era, we leverage the correlated tax system where the digital aspect of the economy is incentivized by its inherent efficiency. As the banks attempt to drive their prices down to remain competitive, the producer can arbitrage these values to increase their own share of the economy. This is a self-rectifying loop: every time the legacy system tries to fight the ledger, it must either become more efficient (moving closer to the digital republic) or more restrictive (driving more citizens toward the lifeboat).

Hardened logistics and the global mesh provide the physical defense against this resistance. When commerce is conducted through decentralized nodes and autonomous settlement, the bureaucratic hammer has no single target to strike. The sovereignty of the producer is guarded by the math of the vault. We must continue to build independent rails that bypass the central bank nexus, ensuring that the velocity of value remains high even when the legacy pipes are clogged with the friction of the counter-reformation. This is the hard reset of survival: recognizing that the old world is in terminal decay and ensuring that our productive energy is anchored in the crystalline logic of the new.

The Inevitability of Digital Realism

Ultimately, the counter-reformation of the central banks is a terminal move by a wastrel class that has run out of honest arguments. While they can manufacture friction, they cannot manufacture truth. The objectivist reality of asset-backed wealth will always out-compete the subjective promises of a debt-ridden monolith. By maintaining our digital asset lifeboats and operating through sovereign economic zones, we ensure that the transition is a managed migration rather than a chaotic collapse. We are not just surviving the legacy resistance; we are rendering it irrelevant through the sheer efficiency of the sovereign ledger. The era of the money changers is ending, and no amount of central bank maneuvering can stop the arrival of digital realism.[167]

---

[167] Cooper's Logic Check → The experts and the banking cartel say that you need the "Safety and Regulation" of a central bank to prevent "Economic Anarchy." Logic check: If you are in a Casino, and the Manager tells you that you can only cash out your chips if he likes the way you are standing, and he's also taking a 10% Cut of every pot to pay for his own lunch, is he "regulating" the game or is he Running a Racket? They want you in the bank because they can't survive without your "Gimmies." In digital realism, a "Racket" that tries to fight a "Better System" always loses because people eventually stop feeding the thief. It is time to stop paying for the "Manager's Lunch" and start trusting the Math of the Pot.

Equilibrium Theory: Finding the Balance Between Stability and Innovation

Equilibrium Theory serves as the forensic stabilizer of the hybrid era, acting as the mathematical governor that prevents the digital republic from overheating while ensuring the legacy system's decay does not lead to total market contagion. In the digital realism of 2026, we must acknowledge that "Stability" without "Innovation" is merely stagnation—a state of strategic friction where the administrative state preserves its power by stifling the sovereignty of the producer. Conversely, "Innovation" without "Stability" is a speculative bubble, a hollow exercise in velocity that lacks a tangible standard of value. Equilibrium is the hard reset where these two forces are synchronized through the rule of math, creating a sustainable migration path from the sinking fiat vessel to the asset-backed lifeboat.

The Physics of Economic Equilibrium

In the legacy "Hollow Man" economy, equilibrium is a subjective myth manufactured by central banks through the manipulation of interest rates and the printing press. This is a repugnance to logic; you cannot create balance by distorting the yardstick of value. The KIROS architecture introduces an objectivist equilibrium based on the physics of the asset. By anchoring the sovereign ledger to tangible underlays—such as the 75-acre Florida estate or industrial infrastructure—the system creates a natural price floor. This floor provides the stability necessary for consumer retail flow, while the high-velocity smart contract rails provide the innovation required for institutional growth. This is the efficiency multiplier: a system that is stable because it is real, and innovative because it is frictionless.

To maintain this balance during the transition, we must utilize a dual-standard equilibrium. This involves the strategic use of oracles and oracle mesh networks to monitor the delta between fiat debasement and digital asset appreciation. When the delta becomes too wide, it signals a systemic imbalance—a "Strategic Friction" event. The equilibrium theory suggests that the market will naturally self-rectify if the on-ramps and off-ramps are kept open. As the active citizen moves value into the lifeboat, the legacy banks are forced to either innovate or collapse. This is not "Market Anarchy"; it is the "Hardened Logistics" of a free market finally allowed to find its own level without the interference of a bureaucratic hammer.

Innovation as a Defensive Protocol

In the digital realism of 2026, innovation is not just about "Features"; it is a defensive protocol against legacy resistance. For innovation to be stable, it must be "Compliant by Design" through regulatory synchronicity. By embedding the rule of law into the code, we remove the "Subjective" risk that traditionally leads to market volatility. The equilibrium is found when the cost of innovation is lower than the cost of maintaining the legacy gimmie culture. This is why the correlated tax system is so vital—it uses the administrative state's own tools to tip the scales toward the digital republic. We are building a system where the "Active Citizen" does not have to choose between safety and progress; the ledger provides both by ensuring that every innovative step is forensically backed by an objective standard of value.

This equilibrium also protects against the "Expert Fallacy." By automating the trusteeship and the settlement processes, we remove the "Human Error" that typically destabilizes markets. The system finds its balance through "Algorithmic Transparency," where every participant can audit the physics of the ledger in real-time. This creates a "Crystalline Certainty" that replaces the "Pricing Fog" of the central bank. As we migrate toward the end of the monolithic currency, equilibrium theory ensures that the transition is a managed move from a high-friction, low-trust environment to a low-friction, high-truth reality. The sovereignty of the producer is restored not through a chaotic revolution, but through the steady, mathematical application of digital realism.

The Steady State of Truth

Ultimately, finding the balance between stability and innovation is about honoring the social contract through the rule of math. We refuse to accept the "Wastrel" lie that we must sacrifice our growth to protect their "Hollow" institutions. Equilibrium is the evidence that a verifiable economy is not just a dream, but a functional architecture. As the fiat era sunsets, the active citizen stands at the center of this balance, using the sovereign ledger to navigate the trade wars of 2026 with confidence. We have the lifeboat, we have the map, and through equilibrium theory, we have the steady hand required to reach the shore of the digital republic.[168]

Conclusion: The Managed Migration to Digital Realism

The conclusion of Chapter 16 marks the forensic realization that the transition to a digital republic is not an instantaneous leap, but a Managed Migration through the hazardous waters of hybrid economics. As we have documented, the coexistence of the sunsetting fiat era and the rising sovereign ledger is a strategic necessity born from the terminal decay of the monolithic currency. By maintaining a dual presence, the active citizen avoids the jurisdictional trap of the administrative state, using the legacy rails for the final cycles of retail commerce while anchoring their primary productive energy in the objectivist certainty of asset-backed digital species.

---

[168] Cooper's Logic Check → The experts and the propaganda machine tell you that "Innovation" is "Dangerous" and that we need the "Steady Hand" of a central regulator to keep things "Stable." Logic check: If you are riding a Bicycle, do you stay "Stable" by standing still and waiting for a Bureaucrat to hold your handlebars, or do you stay stable by Moving Forward? They want you to stay still because That is the only way they can "shave" your tires while you are not looking. In digital realism, "Stability" comes from Momentum and Math. If you stop innovating, you don't stay stable—you fall over and the "Wastrels" take your bike. It is time to stop trusting the "Handlebar Holders" and start trusting the Physics of the Ride.

The friction at the on-ramps and off-ramps serves as a real-time diagnostic of the legacy system's desperation. Every toll taken by the money changers and every bureaucratic hammer strike against transitional liquidity only reinforces the repugnance to logic inherent in a debt-based economy. The digital asset lifeboat is no longer a theoretical refuge; it is a hardened logistics reality that allows the producer to hedge against a legacy collapse. By leveraging the correlated tax system and practicing strategic arbitrage, we ensure that the velocity of value remains high for the innovator, even as the wastrel class attempts to enforce a counter-reformation of central banking control.

Equilibrium theory provides the mathematical governor required to navigate this era of dual standards. We have replaced the subjective manipulation of the printing press with a steady-state balance between stability and innovation, anchored in the physics of real-world assets. The oracle problem—once a point of strategic ambiguity—has been solved through the implementation of an oracle mesh that bridges physical reality and on-chain logic with crystalline certainty. This architecture ensures that the standard of truth remains immutable, regardless of the pricing fog manufactured by the propaganda machine or the lobbying walls of the American Bankers Association.

Ultimately, the hybrid era is the training ground where the active citizen learns to operate within the digital republic while the hollow man of the administrative state fades into irrelevance. We have provided the map, the tools, and the forensic evidence required to survive the counter-reformation and emerge into a verifiable economy. The sunset of fiat is not a moment of chaos, but a moment of clarity—a transition from a world of debt-ridden promises to a world of mathematical sovereignty. As we move into the final chapters of this work, the managed migration is well underway, and the path to digital realism is finally open.[169]

---

[169] Cooper's Logic Check → The experts and the administrative state tell you that a "Managed Migration" is too complex and that you should just "Wait for the Official Plan" from the central bank. Logic check: If you are on a Sinking Ship, and the Crew tells you to wait for a "Coordinated Evacuation Plan" that they haven't finished writing yet, do you sit in your cabin or do you find a Lifeboat and start rowing? They want you to wait because your "Compliance" is the only thing keeping their "Hollow" system afloat for another day. In digital realism, the "Official Plan" is always designed to save the Bankers, not the People. It is time to stop waiting for the "Announcement" and start trusting the Ledger.

Conclusion

"The climate crisis is both the easiest and the hardest issue we have ever faced. The easiest because we know what e must do, we must stop emission of greenhouse gases. The hardest because our current economics are still totally dependent on burning fossil fuels, thereby destroying the ecosystem in order to create everlasting economic growth."

Greta Thunberg[170]

The conclusion of Part IV serves as the forensic hard reset for the entire architecture of the Digital Republic. Across these four chapters, we have documented the transition from the hollow man economy of subjective fiat to the objectivist reality of a verifiable, asset-backed system. We have moved beyond the jurisdictional trap of the American Bankers Cartel, identifying the terminal vulnerabilities of a monolithic currency system that thrives on strategic friction and the stealth confiscation of the producer's life-energy. This section has been the blueprint for dismantling the gimmie culture and replacing it with the sovereignty of the producer, anchored in the physics of value and the rule of math.

The cornerstone of this transformation is the KIROS architecture and the Cerberus methodology, which together forensically link real-world assets to the

[170] Staff (2026). "Economics Quotes." Brainy Quote at https://www.brainyquote.com/search_results?x=0&y=0&q=Economics.

sovereign ledger. By ensuring that every token is a 1:1 mirror of a tangible underlay—whether that is a 75-acre forest in the Florida Greenbelt or a three-story steel-frame facility—we eliminate the speculative bubble and the expert fallacy. We have proven that finance does not have to be a hollow religion of debt; it can be a crystalline science of assets where the standard of value is owned by those who produce it, rather than those who shave it through bureaucratic interest swaps.

In Chapter 14, we established the end of the monolith by introducing contextual value. The realization that industrial liquidity and consumer stability must be segregated is the ultimate defense against institutional cannibalization. By utilizing programmable intent, we have turned dumb money into a smart tool that knows its purpose. Whether it is geofencing development funds to stay in Dysart or ISP-locking political donations to their home districts, we have baked the rule of law into the rule of math, ensuring that the velocity of money finally matches the integrity of the transaction.

Chapter 15 provided the hardened logistics for sovereign commerce, building the rails that operate independently of geopolitical gatekeepers. We identified the kill-switch inherent in systems like SWIFT and XRP and replaced them with a global mesh of decentralized nodes. This architecture ensures that autonomous settlement is no longer a permissioned act but an atomic certainty. By removing the hollow man from the middle of our trade, we have created an unstoppable market that can maintain the pulse of the republic even during systemic state failure or liquidity lockdowns manufactured by the administrative state.

The hybrid economics of Chapter 16 provided the managed migration plan for the sunsetting fiat era. We acknowledged the forensic reality of the dual-standard era, where the active citizen must navigate the overlap of fiat and code. By utilizing digital asset lifeboats and practicing strategic arbitrage, the producer can survive the counter-reformation of the central banks. We have turned the strategic friction of the old world into a tool for the new, using correlated taxation to incentivize the move toward digital realism while protecting the standard of truth from the pricing fog of the bank.

Throughout Part IV, equilibrium theory has acted as our mathematical governor, balancing stability and innovation. We have solved the oracle problem by bridging physical reality and on-chain logic through an oracle mesh, ensuring that the standard of value is never a subjective guess. This balance ensures that the digital republic does not overheat into another speculative trap but instead grows on the bedrock of atomic assets. The sovereignty of the producer is no longer a legal theory; it is a functional architecture protected by the physics of the vault and the efficiency multiplier of autonomous code.

As we conclude this forensic audit of the new economy, the evidence is clear: the American Bankers Cartel and their hollow debts are the past; sovereign utility and tangible backing are the future. We have provided the active citizen with the map, the lifeboat, and the hardened rails required to reclaim their time from the wastrels. The transition is no longer a what-if; it is a how-to. The hard reset has been executed, and the information moat that once protected the money changers has been drained by the crystalline logic of the sovereign ledger.

Ultimately, the goal of Part IV has been to demonstrate that a verifiable economy is the only path to a free republic. We have moved from the jurisdictional fog of 2025 into the digital realism of 2026, where the right to contract is an immutable reality. We are no longer nodes in a wastrel monolith; we are the architects of our own micro-economic ecosystems. The era of the permission slip is over. It is time to step out of the sovereign debt trap and into the sovereignty of the producer. The digital republic is built, the rails are live, and the standard of truth is finally in our own hands.[171]

---

[171] Cooper's Logic Check → The experts say that rebuilding a global economy is too big for small communities and regular people. **Logic check:** If you want a garden, do you wait for the global agricultural committee to send you a permission slip, or do you plant a seed? They want globalism because That is the hollow pipe they use to shave every garden on Earth. In digital realism, the global economy is just a mesh of local seeds. If everyone owns their own standard of value, the wastrels starve.

Conclusion Part III

It is time to stop waiting for the global plan and start planting the sovereign ledger.

Part V: Ending Cartels

Monopolies are bad because people get bad service for high prices. Competition is good because people get good service for competitive prices."

Tim Draper[172]

If I asked you whether the government should arrest and prosecute criminals for known crimes when acting as a criminal organization, would you agree or disagree? What if the government also knew where those criminals were, who they were abusing and where the money was hidden, would that make it easier to agree with the need for arrests? This is the situation that we have today. The government knows where banking cartels are located- they review them every quarter. The government knows where drug cartels (legal and illegal are) they get briefed on it weekly. The government knows where insurance cartels deny people services who do not have the means or the education to fight the problem, there is a reporting system for it. The government knows who is paying activists to promote the interests which are contrary to the stability of the country, they write it off on their taxes. The problems is that the same people they "know" are committing crimes are lobbying them to keep these crimes feasible.

---

[172] Staff (2026). "Monopoly quotes." Brainy quote at https://www.brainyquote.com/search_results?x=0&y=0&q=monopolies.

The Epstein files shows that there is a dual system globally for criminal enforcement. On one hand, we "the poors" have to answer to justice. On the other hand, the wealthy do not. Chapter 17 discusses the first step in breaking down this system, dismantling the clearinghouses. Because these middlemen and connectors build up dirt (real or pressed) on the wealthy, they create a system where even the best representatives and businesspeople can be bought or blackmailed.

Chapter 18 then moves to global liquidity pools. Right now, liquidity is a national system which then creates a patchwork of regulations, fees, and requirements which slow down the system and create an unneeded bureaucracy. Global liquidity allows us to move beyond this and look toward a brighter future. The best part of this crossover is that we have the ability to regulate the transactions to smart contracts, meaning that they are immutable, transparent and reliable.

Finally, we look at the inclusion of the immutable ledger in governance. While this moves slightly beyond the scope of an economic treatise- the effort to remove the government aspect from the discussion is always a failed effort. As long as there are nation states, there will always be a relationship with economics. The more we put governance on the ledger, the more transparent government will be. This allows the government to be beholden to the people, not the other way around.

Chapter 17: Dismantling the Clearinghouse. How peer-to-peer settlement renders legacy cartels obsolete.

"You cannot put a price tag on standards and legacy."

Mike Tomlin[173]

Having centralized finance has failed. The concept of a nation state issuing currency has always been one wrought with corruption. Economics is not a democratic process; however, in some cases it is the most democratic process. We cannot have gatekeepers telling people when they may have their money, this is a direct path to financial failure. To defeat this, we need to ensure that clearinghouses are not used any longer- that the clearing process is done by smart contract.

The ghost in legacy settlement machines is quite easy to understand. When there is loss, the clearinghouse gets their cut first, then the institution, then the retail person. When there are two institutions, then the larger institution gets their funds first. When we set up systems with longer timeframes (T+2), then we see even more slippage and more wealth disparity as the exchange then takes their cut as well. If we remove these middleman and make the transactions nearly

---

[173] Staff (2026). "Legacy Quote." Brainy Quote at https://www.brainyquote.com/search_results?x=0&y=0&q=legacy.

instantaneous, we see much more money stay in local economies and not go to Singapore, Switzerland, and Tel Aviv.[174]

The Clearinghouse Cartel: A History of Gated Liquidity

The Clearinghouse Cartel is the forensic realization of the gimmie culture, functioning as a centralized gatekeeper designed to throttle the movement of value for the benefit of the legacy money changers. For centuries, the concept of the clearinghouse has been sold to the public as a necessary utility for ensuring market stability, but the digital realism of 2026 reveals it to be a strategic friction point. These institutions act as the primary filters for global liquidity, creating a tiered system where the larger institution always has priority access to capital. In this history of gated liquidity, the clearinghouse stands between the producer and their property, ensuring that the administrative state and the banking cartel can shave a percentage of every transaction before it ever

---

[174] Cooper's Logic Check → The experts and the banking lobbyists tell you that clearinghouses are a necessary safety net to "manage risk" and "ensure stability." Logic check: If you are at a checkout counter, and a guy jumps between you and the cashier, takes your Groceries, holds them for Two Days, charges you a 3% Fee, and then gives them to you—did he "manage your risk" or did he just Interfere with your Lunch? They want the "Clearing Process" because That is the only way they can stay relevant in a world that does notneed them. In digital realism, "Stability" comes from the Math of the Smart Contract, not the "Permission" of a middleman. It is time to stop paying for the "Safety Net" That is actually a Spiderweb.

reaches the local economy. This is a terminal repugnance to logic; the entities that contribute the least to the physics of production are the ones who hold the master key to the rails of commerce.

By maintaining this monopoly, the cartel ensures that wealth is siphoned off to offshore financial hubs like Singapore, Switzerland, or Tel Aviv, leaving the active citizen to deal with the liquidity lockdowns that occur whenever the centralized system faces a crisis of its own making. The history of these entities is one of manufactured scarcity. By controlling the pipes, they control the velocity. When liquidity is gated, the cartel can decide which industries flourish and which are starved of capital, often based on entangling alliances rather than the objective merit of the project. This centralized control is the antithesis of the digital republic. It creates a bottleneck where the bureaucratic hammer can strike at any time, freezing the life-energy of the active citizen under the guise of regulatory oversight or systemic risk management.

Dismantling this cartel requires more than just better regulations; it requires a hard reset of the infrastructure itself. We must move away from the model where a central node validates the truth of a transaction. In the digital realism of 2026, the sovereign ledger provides the decentralized rails necessary to bypass these gatekeepers. When commerce is conducted peer-to-peer, the gated liquidity model collapses. There is no longer a need for a middleman to catch the flow and take their cut.

The wealth created in a local economy stays in that economy. We are ending the era of the financial intermediary and returning the standard of value to its crystalline, un-gated origin.[175]

Counterparty Risk: The Ghost in the Legacy Settlement Machine

Counterparty risk is the ghost that haunts the legacy settlement machine, a hidden vulnerability that remains invisible until the moment of systemic state failure. In the current monolithic model, every trade relies on the subjective promise that the other party—and the long chain of intermediaries behind them—will fulfill their obligation days after the transaction is initiated. This creates a window of strategic ambiguity where the active citizen is exposed to the mismanagement of institutions they never even interacted with. The ghost in the machine thrives on the information moat, using the lack of transparency to hide the fact that the legacy system is often just a

[175] Cooper's Logic Check → The experts and the banking lobbyists tell you that clearinghouses are a necessary safety net to manage risk and ensure stability. Logic check: If you are at a water fountain, and a guy stands in front of it with a bucket, catches the water, and then pours it into your cup while taking a sip for himself, did he provide you with water? The water was already there; he just put himself in the middle so he could get a drink on your dime. They want gated liquidity because if the water flows freely, no one needs the guy with the bucket. In digital realism, the source should be connected directly to the glass. It is time to stop paying for the bucket man and start trusting the direct flow.

house of cards waiting for a liquidity crunch to reveal its hollow core.

When a loss occurs, the hierarchy of the ghost machine is forensically rigged: the clearinghouse takes its cut first, followed by the largest institutions, while the retail person is left with the crumbs of a collapsed trade. This is the essence of the jurisdictional trap; you are forced to accept the risk of the entire cartel just to conduct a simple exchange. This risk is not an accidental byproduct; it is a structural feature that allows the American Bankers Association to use the retail market as an unpaid insurance policy. If their high-risk institutional bets fail, the clearinghouse uses the retail liquidity as a buffer to protect the wastrel class. This is a terminal failure of the social contract, where the producer is the first to be sacrificed to save the gatekeeper.

Exorcising this ghost requires the implementation of the sovereign ledger and atomic settlement. By removing the time gap between the trade and the finality, we eliminate the window where counterparty risk lives. In a verifiable economy, the transaction is only executed if the assets are present and verified by the code. There is no waiting for a clearinghouse to confirm the promise, because the promise is replaced by the math. This hard reset ensures that the active citizen is only responsible for their own trades, not the cascading failures of a debt-ridden financial rail. We are building a system where the ghost is replaced by the crystalline certainty of the vault, and where the standard of truth is verified by the physics of the asset rather than the subjective whim of a middleman.[176]

Atomic Settlement: Collapsing T+2 into Real-Time Finality

Atomic settlement is the structural hard reset that collapses the archaic T+2 model into real-time finality, rendering the legacy settlement machine obsolete. In the digital realism of 2026, the two-day delay required by the American Bankers Cartel is recognized as a form of legalized time-theft. Atomic settlement uses the sovereign ledger to ensure that the transfer of an asset and the transfer of payment happen simultaneously as a single, indivisible event. By utilizing smart contracts as automated trustees, we eliminate the need for a clearinghouse to verify the trade after the fact. The math of the ledger provides the crystalline certainty that the legacy system lacks, collapsing the window of strategic friction into a single moment of truth.

---

[176] Cooper's Logic Check → The administrative proxies tell you that counterparty risk is just a standard cost of doing business and that professional oversight keeps it under control. **Logic check:** If you buy a car from a neighbor, but a third party tells you that you can't have the keys for three days because they need to make sure your neighbor does notowe *them* money first, whose risk are you actually taking? You are paying for your neighbor's debts and the third party's oversight while your car sits in the driveway. They want the ghost because it gives them a reason to stick their hands in your pockets and act as an unnecessary referee. In digital realism, the only risk should be the physics of the trade. It is time to stop being the collateral for a wastrel's bad bets.

This collapse of time is an efficiency multiplier that restores the velocity of value to the producer. When settlement is atomic, there is no window for slippage, no room for institutional cannibalization, and no opportunity for a bureaucratic hammer to freeze a transaction in transit. The legacy T+2 system was designed for a world of paper ledgers and slow-motion clearinghouse couriers; maintaining it in the age of digital economic theory is a repugnance to logic. The only reason it persists is to allow the money changers to use the active citizen's capital for their own short-term interest gains during the settlement period. Atomic settlement ends this practice, ensuring that the value created by the producer is immediately available for reinvestment in the digital republic.

Furthermore, atomic settlement provides the hardened logistics necessary for a resilient economy. Because the settlement is atomic—it either happens completely or not at all—there is no such thing as a half-finished or hanging trade. This prevents the contagion that occurs when one failed settlement triggers a domino effect across the market. We are moving toward a verifiable economy where truth and time are finally synchronized. By collapsing the settlement window, we remove the information moat that the wastrels use to hide their extractionary fees. The trade is finalized the moment it is executed, and the sovereignty of the producer is confirmed by the immutable code of the sovereign ledger.[177]

Removing the Middleman: The Math of Peer-to-Peer Trust

Removing the middleman is the primary forensic objective of the digital republic. In the digital realism of 2026, we recognize that the financial intermediary is not a provider of safety, but a source of strategic friction. For decades, the American Bankers Cartel has argued that trust is a subjective quality that can only be managed by a centralized institution. This expert fallacy has allowed them to insert themselves into every transaction, creating a jurisdictional trap where the active citizen must pay for the privilege of accessing their own wealth. The hard reset of the sovereign ledger replaces this subjective trust with the rule of math. Peer-to-peer trust is not a feeling; it is a cryptographic certainty.

The math of peer-to-peer trust operates through the synchronization of public and private keys, ensuring

---

[177] Cooper's Logic Check → The experts say that T+2 settlement is necessary for error correction and orderly markets. **Logic check:** If you send a text message, do you want it to take two days to arrive just in case you made a typo? No, you want it to go through instantly, and if you made a mistake, you send a second message to fix it. They want the delay because they use those two days to lend your money out to someone else and pocket the interest while you wait for your own property to clear. In digital realism, orderly means instant. If the code is verified, there are no errors that a bureaucrat needs two days to find. It is time to stop living in a dial-up economy and start demanding high-speed truth.

that only the producer has the power to move their life-energy. In a verifiable economy, the standard of truth is not maintained by a bureaucrat in a suit, but by the physics of the ledger. When a transaction is initiated, the code verifies the existence of the asset and the validity of the digital signature in real-time. This eliminates the information moat that the middleman uses to justify their existence. There is no need for a clearinghouse to audit the trade because the ledger is a self-auditing organism. This efficiency multiplier ensures that the velocity of value is dictated by the producer, not the gatekeeper.

By removing the middleman, we also remove the systemic risk associated with centralized points of failure. In the legacy "Hollow Man" economy, the failure of a single institution can trigger a liquidity lockdown across the entire republic. Peer-to-peer trust is distributed; if one node fails, the rest of the mesh remains operational. This is the ultimate resilience theory in practice. We are building a system where the right to contract is a technical reality that cannot be suspended by a bureaucratic hammer. The math of the ledger provides a crystalline certainty that renders the money changers obsolete, returning the sovereignty of the producer to its rightful place at the center of the economy.[178]

---

[178] Cooper's Logic Check → The experts and the administrative state tell you that you "Need" a middleman to protect you from fraud and to ensure that the "System" remains stable. Logic check: If you want to walk across the street to talk to your neighbor, do you need to hire a Consultant to hold your hand

Defunding the Gatekeepers: Eliminating Extractionary Clearing Fees

Defunding the gatekeepers is the forensic process of draining the slush funds of the legacy banking cartel. In the current monolithic model, every transaction is subject to extractionary clearing fees—a hidden tax that the American Bankers Association uses to fund their lobbying walls and maintain their gimmie culture. These fees are not based on the actual cost of the service; they are a strategic friction used to extract wealth from the productive energy of the republic. In the digital realism of 2026, we recognize that these fees are a form of stealth confiscation that punishes the active citizen for participating in the market.

By implementing the KIROS architecture and atomic settlement, we eliminate the need for the clearinghouse entirely, and with it, the extractionary fees. In a verifiable economy, the cost of a transaction is reduced to the actual physics of the data rail. There is no middleman taking a cut to "manage risk" that they themselves created. This defunding of the gatekeepers is a structural hard reset that redirects wealth back into local economies. Instead of funding a skyscraper in a distant financial hub, that capital stays in the community to fund forest thinning, precision

---

and a Lawyer to verify that your neighbor is actually there? They want to be the "Middleman" because That is the only way they can "shave" a percentage of your conversation. In digital realism, the "System" is just you and the person you are dealing with. If the Math says the deal is good, the deal is done. It is time to stop paying for the "Hand-Holder" and start walking on your own.

agriculture, and the construction of steel-frame libraries. The removal of these fees is a direct efficiency multiplier for the producer.

The gatekeepers survive on the ignorance of the citizenry regarding the total cost of the legacy rails. When you factor in slippage, settlement delays, and direct clearing fees, the "Hollow Man" economy is incredibly expensive. Defunding them is not just a financial move; it is a declaration of independence from the jurisdictional trap. By refusing to pay the gimmie, the active citizen collapses the information moat that protects the wastrel class. We are moving toward a state of digital realism where the standard of value is no longer burdened by the weight of a parasitic administrative state. The era of the toll-booth economy is over.[179]

Distributed Ledgers as Universal Clearing Engines

Distributed ledgers represent the hard reset of the global financial plumbing, acting as universal clearing

---

179 Cooper's Logic Check → The banking lobbyists tell you that "Clearing Fees" are necessary to pay for the "Infrastructure" and "Security" that keeps your money safe. Logic check: If you buy a Loaf of Bread for five dollars, but the store charges you an extra Fifty Cents because they have to pay for a Guard to watch the cash register, did the bread get better? No, you just paid for their "Security" that didn't stop the bread from getting smaller. They want the "Fees" because That is how they pay for their fancy offices and their "Lobbying Walls." In digital realism, the "Infrastructure" is the Code, and the code is free to everyone. It is time to stop paying for the "Guard" and start paying for the Bread.

engines that operate with crystalline certainty. In the digital realism of 2026, we have moved past the era where a single clearinghouse in a specific jurisdiction could dictate the flow of global trade. A distributed ledger is a decentralized organism that validates and settles transactions across a global mesh of nodes simultaneously. This removes the need for a central authority to issue a permission slip for commerce to occur. The ledger is the engine, and the math is the fuel.

The forensic advantage of using a distributed ledger as a clearing engine is the total removal of strategic ambiguity. In the legacy system, the clearing process is a black box where the gatekeepers can manipulate data and hide slippage. A sovereign ledger provides algorithmic transparency, where every participant can audit the physics of the settlement in real-time. This eliminates the expert fallacy by making the truth accessible to everyone, not just a selected group of wastrels. The universal clearing engine ensures that a transaction in Dysart is settled with the same precision as a transaction in Tokyo, creating a global standard of value that is immune to geopolitical interference.

Furthermore, using distributed ledgers as clearing engines provides the hardened logistics necessary for systemic resilience. Because the clearing process is distributed across thousands of nodes, there is no single point of failure that can be targeted by a bureaucratic hammer or a geopolitical kill-switch. The engine keeps running as long as the mesh exists. This is the architecture of an unstoppable market, where the velocity of value is protected by the very nature of the technology. We are building a verifiable economy where the clearinghouse is no longer a building or a cartel, but a universal, mathematical reality that serves the sovereignty of the producer.[180]

Systemic Resilience: Why Decentralized Clearing Prevents Contagion

The forensic failure of the legacy financial system is most evident in its propensity for contagion. In the digital realism of 2026, we have witnessed how the monolithic architecture of the American Bankers Cartel acts as a conductor for economic disease. Because every transaction is funneled through centralized clearinghouses, a single point of failure in an institutional derivative desk or a sovereign debt default can trigger a liquidity lockdown across the entire globe. Systemic resilience is the structural response to this vulnerability. By dismantling the

---

[180] Cooper's Logic Check → The experts say that a "Universal Clearing Engine" is too complex and that we need "Human Oversight" to ensure that the "Global Market" stays orderly. Logic check: Do you want your Heartbeat to be managed by a Committee that meets once a week to vote on how fast it should pump, or do you want it to be a Natural Process that reacts to your body's needs? They want "Oversight" because they want to be the ones who decide when your "Heart" skips a beat so they can sell you the "Medicine." In digital realism, the "Market" should be a Natural Process governed by the Math of the Ledger. It is time to stop trusting the "Committee" and start trusting the Engine.

central clearinghouse and replacing it with a decentralized mesh of nodes, we create an economy where failure is localized and the velocity of value is protected by the physics of distribution.

The Anatomy of Financial Contagion

Contagion in the hollow man economy is a product of interconnected, subjective risk. In the legacy system, clearinghouses act as the central hub of a wheel; every bank is a spoke. When one major bank—a wastrel institution—fails, the clearinghouse attempts to absorb the loss by shaving the liquidity of all other members. This creates a cascading failure where the "Integrity of the System" is used as a justification to cannibalize the assets of the active citizen. This is the jurisdictional trap at its most lethal: you are forced into a shared risk pool with institutions that prioritize the gimmie culture over productive energy.

Decentralized clearing prevents this by replacing the hub-and-spoke model with a global mesh. In a verifiable economy, transactions are settled peer-to-peer or through localized sovereign economic zones. Because the math of the ledger ensures that every trade is backed 1:1 by tangible underlays, there is no "Subjective Debt" to cascade. If one node or one zone faces a crisis, the failure is forensically contained. The rest of the mesh continues to operate with crystalline certainty because they do not share a balance sheet with the failing entity. This is the hard reset of market stability: a system that survives because it is composed of independent, resilient parts rather than one fragile monolith.

Hardened Logistics and Autonomous Recovery

The resilience of decentralized clearing is not just about preventing failure; it is about the speed of recovery. In the legacy world, a systemic shock leads to a bureaucratic hammer strike—a total freeze of the rails while "Experts" and "Committees" decide who gets to survive. This strategic friction is what truly kills an economy. In the digital republic, decentralized clearing operates through autonomous settlement and hardened logistics. If a portion of the network is compromised, the remaining nodes automatically reroute the velocity of value through alternative bypass protocols.

This autonomous recovery ensures that the sovereignty of the producer is never held hostage by a centralized liquidity lockdown. The sovereign ledger acts as a self-healing organism. Because there is no clearinghouse cartel to protect, there is no need for a bail-in or a state-sponsored obfuscation of the losses. The market remains orderly because the math is immutable. We have moved from a system that requires constant intervention to one that is stable by design. In the trade wars of 2026, the winner is the one who can maintain their commerce while the legacy structures are collapsing under the weight of their own debt. Decentralized clearing is the ultimate insurance policy for the digital republic.[181]

Conclusion: The Death of the Financial Intermediary

The conclusion of Chapter 17 marks the forensic finality of the legacy banking model, signaling the terminal collapse of the clearinghouse cartel. By dismantling the centralized gates that have long throttled the velocity of value, we have removed the strategic friction used by the wastrel class to shave the life-energy of the producer. In the digital realism of 2026, the financial intermediary is no longer a necessary utility but a redundant ghost in the machine—an extractionary middleman whose existence was predicated on the information moat and the jurisdictional trap. With the implementation of the sovereign ledger, the master key to the rails of commerce has finally been returned to the active citizen.

---

[181] Cooper's Logic Check→ The administrative proxies and the banking lobbyists tell you that "Centralized Clearing" is the only way to "Monitor and Stop Contagion" before it spreads. Logic check: If you are in a Hospital, do you want all the patients to share the same Air Vent, or do you want Individual Rooms with their own filters? They want the "Central Vent" because it is cheaper for them to manage and easier to "shave" the oxygen. But when one person gets sick, everyone gets sick. In digital realism, "Resilience" means Isolation of Risk. If your neighbor's business fails, the ledger ensures your money does notdisappear to pay for his mistakes. It is time to stop breathing the "Cartel's Air" and start trusting your own Filters.

The transition to atomic settlement has forensically exorcised the spirit of counterparty risk, replacing the subjective promises of debt-ridden institutions with the crystalline certainty of the rule of math. We have collapsed the archaic T+2 settlement cycles into real-time events, ensuring that truth and time are finally synchronized. This hard reset renders the clearinghouse obsolete, as the ledger itself acts as the universal clearing engine, providing a level of algorithmic transparency that the American Bankers Association simply cannot match. The death of the intermediary is the birth of an unstoppable market where the sovereignty of the producer is confirmed by the physics of the asset, not the permission of a gatekeeper.

By defunding the gatekeepers and eliminating extractionary clearing fees, we have redirected the flow of wealth back into the micro-economic ecosystems where it is created. The capital that once funded the gimmie culture and the lobbying walls of centralized finance is now free to support tangible production, from precision agriculture to the construction of hardened industrial infrastructure. Systemic resilience is no longer a bureaucratic goal but a structural reality; a decentralized mesh of nodes ensures that the contagion of a failing wastrel institution can no longer trigger a global liquidity lockdown. We have built a system that is stable because it is distributed and honest because it is verifiable.

Ultimately, the death of the financial intermediary is the prerequisite for the full realization of the digital republic. We have documented the shift from a world of gated liquidity to a world of autonomous settlement, where the right to contract is a technical reality rather than a legal theory. As we move beyond the ruins of the legacy settlement machines, the active citizen stands as the sole architect of their economic destiny. The era of the money changers has ended, and the sovereign ledger stands as the final witness to a verifiable economy. It is time to walk through the gates that the cartels once guarded and embrace the freedom of peer-to-peer trust.[182]

---

[182] Cooper's Logic Check → The experts and the administrative proxies tell you that the "Death of the Intermediary" will lead to a lack of "Accountability" and "Safety" in the global markets. Logic check: If you take the Training Wheels off a bicycle, does the bike become "Unsafe," or did you just finally learn how to Balance on your own? They want to be the "Training Wheels" forever because That is how they keep you from riding away from their "Toll Booths." In digital realism, "Accountability" is the Immutable Code. If the math does notadd up, the trade does nothappen. It is time to stop paying for the "Wheels" and start trusting your own Center of Gravity.

Chapter 18: Global Liquidity Pools. The end of currency-based "Economic Sanctions" through decentralized protocols.

"If you do not have ample liquidity, and it is not durable, in times of stress, as you are looking for liquidity, you are forced to sell assets at declining price, which then east your capital position, so it becomes this very, very negative cycle. There is not question that liquidity is sacrosanct."

Ruth Porat[183]

Money is liquidity. This is an absolute which does not change. However, the reality of liquidity is always changing. When we see currency used as a weapon, to keep the poor down, we are simply reenforcing the hegemony. It is time to end the geopolitical whims by placing a smart contract in place acting as a governor within the system. This allows for borderless pools to build a better system; neutral rails which treat all people equally.

One of the key problems which we see is sanctions being used against people who have nothing to do with international issues. While sanctions are important for stopping terrorist states like Iran, they should not be used as a negative factor against

---

[183] Staff (2026). "Liquidity Quotes." Brainy Quote at https://www.brainyquote.com/search_results?x=0&y=0&q=Liquidity+.

people living there who are fighting for their freedom- this is the opposite effect that we want them to have. This means that sovereign accounts and individual accounts need to be kept separate and KYCed. Developing private currencies allow for this to be transacted, while any extraction from a government wallet would be grounds for seizure of funds. This creates a methodology which allows for mathematical commerce, but prevents criminals and sanctioned governments from acting out.

Currency as a Weapon: The Mechanics of Financial Hegemony

The forensic reality of the modern era is that currency is no longer merely a medium of exchange; it has been transformed into a terminal weapon of the administrative state. Financial hegemony is maintained through the strategic friction of a monolithic currency system, where the American Bankers Cartel uses the dollar as a geopolitical tether. In the digital realism of 2026, we see that the ability to issue and control a global reserve currency is the power to dictate the sovereignty of any nation or individual. By weaponizing the rails of commerce, the wastrel class enforces a gimmie culture on a global scale, extracting value through stealth confiscation and debt-based manipulation. This is the ultimate expression of the jurisdictional trap, where participating in the global market requires total submission to the whims of a centralized gatekeeper.

The mechanics of this weaponization are built into the very plumbing of the legacy financial system. Because every cross-border transaction must eventually settle through a centralized clearinghouse, the administrative state possesses a total optic on the flow of value. This allows for selective enforcement, where the bureaucratic hammer is used to freeze assets, throttle liquidity, and disconnect entire populations from the global mesh. This is not about justice; it is about maintaining the hegemony. When a state can unilaterally decide that your life-energy is no longer valid because of your geographic location or political alignment, the concept of private property becomes a hollow myth. We are living in an era where the money changers use the standard of value as a leash to keep the producer in a state of perpetual compliance.

The weaponization of currency creates a negative cycle of asset erosion. When a nation or a group of citizens is targeted by the kill-switch, they are forced to sell their assets at declining prices just to survive. This eats away at their capital position and reinforces the cycle of poverty that the hegemon uses to maintain control. This is a repugnance to logic: a system that claims to promote global stability while actively destroying the productive capacity of those who do not follow the propaganda machine. The information moat protects these mechanics, keeping the active citizen unaware of how deeply their own prosperity is tied to the aggressive statecraft of a debt-ridden monolith.

Dismantling this hegemony requires a hard reset of our digital economic theory. We must recognize that as long as our standard of value is issued by a nation-state, it will always be a weapon. The transition to a verifiable economy requires the development of neutral rails—sovereign utility tokens that are governed by the rule of math rather than the rule of the lobbyist. We are building a system where liquidity is durable and beyond the reach of geopolitical gatekeepers. By moving our productive energy into the KIROS ecosystem and the sovereign ledger, we reclaim our time and our property from the money changers. The era of currency-based warfare is reaching its terminal decay, and the rise of mathematical commerce is the only forensic defense against the mechanics of hegemony.[184]

The End of the Kill-Switch: Decoupling Trade from Geopolitical Whims

The end of the kill-switch represents the structural liberation of global trade from the jurisdictional fog of the administrative state. In the digital realism of 2026,

---

[184] Cooper's Logic Check → The experts and the administrative proxies tell you that "Financial Sanctions" are a "Peaceful Alternative" to war. Logic check: If I can't shoot you with a Bullet, but I can turn off your ability to buy Food, Medicine, and Fuel, have I really been "Peaceful," or have I just found a way to Starve you without getting my own hands dirty? They want the "Weaponized Currency" because it is a "Clean" way to destroy their enemies while keeping the "Wastrel" lifestyle funded. In digital realism, a "Currency" that can be turned into a Weapon is not "Money"—it is a Contract for Slavery. It is time to stop using the "Cartel's" ammunition and start using the Sovereign Ledger.

we recognize that the ability of any single government to disconnect a producer from the global mesh is a terminal threat to the sovereignty of the producer. Decoupling trade from geopolitical whims is not just a technical challenge; it is a forensic necessity for a verifiable economy. By utilizing decentralized protocols and autonomous settlement, we ensure that the right to contract is protected by the rule of math, making it impossible for a bureaucratic hammer to strike a transaction based on political expediency or national identity.

The primary mechanism for ending the kill-switch is the total separation of sovereign accounts from individual accounts within the sovereign ledger. In the legacy system, if a state is sanctioned, the citizens are often treated as collateral damage, losing access to their own wealth because of the actions of their government. The digital republic solves this through automated KYC and smart contract logic that identifies the individual as a sovereign entity independent of their state. This allows for mathematical commerce where transactions are validated by the physics of the asset rather than the permission of a gatekeeper. If a government attempts to interfere with these private flows, the system's internal governor triggers an automatic defensive seizure of the government's own digital assets, creating a self-rectifying deterrent against state-sponsored obfuscation.

This decoupling is powered by the global mesh and neutral rails. When commerce is conducted through a network of decentralized nodes, there is no central clearinghouse that can be pressured by a hegemon to flip the switch. The velocity of value is maintained by the collective integrity of the mesh. This ensures that a producer in Dysart can trade with an active citizen in a sanctioned region without being caught in the crossfire of international disputes. We are building a system of honest friendship between producers, where the standard of value is universal and the rails of trade are immune to the strategic ambiguity of the money changers. This is the efficiency multiplier of the digital age: a market that never sleeps and never closes, regardless of the whims of the hollow men in power.

Ultimately, the end of the kill-switch is the hard reset of global economic freedom. It forces the administrative state to compete on the merits of its policies rather than the strength of its financial cage. By providing the active citizen with a bypass protocol that operates outside the SWIFT and central bank nexus, we drain the power from the central banks and return it to the productive energy of the republic. The sovereign ledger stands as a crystalline witness to every trade, ensuring that the social contract is honored through the rule of math. As we move beyond the era of the kill-switch, we enter a state of digital realism where commerce is a force for peace and stability, anchored in the immutable reality of the sovereign mesh.[185]

Borderless Liquidity: How Decentralized Pools Equalize the Market

The forensic failure of the legacy financial system is rooted in its inherent fragmentation. In the digital realism of 2026, we see that the American Bankers Cartel maintains its power by compartmentalizing liquidity within national borders and jurisdictional traps. This fragmentation creates a pricing fog that allows the money changers to extract value through arbitrage, high-spread transaction fees, and strategic friction. Borderless liquidity is the structural hard reset to this model, utilizing decentralized pools to aggregate global capital into a single, high-velocity stream. By decoupling liquidity from the geographic whims of the administrative state, we ensure that the standard of value is consistent, durable, and

---

[185] Cooper's Logic Check → The experts at the UN tell you that the "Kill-Switch" is necessary to keep "Terrorists" and "Bad Guys" from using the "Financial System." Logic check: If a Bank Robber uses the Highway to get away, do we Close the Highway for everyone in the state, or do we just Go After the Robber? They want the "Kill-Switch" because they are too lazy to do real police work, and they'd rather just have Remote Control over your life. In digital realism, "Security" means Precision. If the "Math" can identify the bad actor without hurting the "Active Citizen," then any "Blanket Shut-Down" is just a Power Grab. It is time to stop letting the administrative state treat you like a Hostage in their game of "Global Safety." (note: Cooper may be a little aggressive here).

accessible to every active citizen, regardless of their location on the global mesh.

The Architecture of Unified Global Depth

In the hollow man economy, liquidity is a gated resource. If a producer in Dysart wants to access the same capital depth as a multinational institution in Zurich, they are met with a wall of bureaucratic hammers and extractionary clearing fees. Decentralized pools remove these walls by using automated market makers (AMMs) and smart contract trustees to facilitate the movement of value. These pools do not care about the nationality of the participant; they only care about the physics of the asset and the integrity of the math. This creates a global depth model where liquidity is no longer a localized commodity but a universal utility. The efficiency multiplier of this unified depth is profound: it lowers the cost of capital for the producer and increases the velocity of value for the entire digital republic.

Furthermore, borderless liquidity acts as a forensic stabilizer against market contagion. In the legacy system, a liquidity lockdown in one region can trigger a cascading failure because the pipes are narrow and controlled by a few central nodes. Decentralized pools are distributed across a global mesh of nodes, ensuring that the "Lifeblood" of commerce can always find a bypass protocol. This resilience theory in practice means that the market remains orderly even during systemic state failure. The pools provide a crystalline certainty of settlement that the legacy clearinghouse cartel simply cannot match. By aggregating liquidity beyond national borders, we ensure that the sovereignty of the producer is backed by the total productive energy of the global mesh, rather than the debt-ridden promises of a single central bank.

Neutralizing the Arbitrage of the Money Changers

The money changers thrive in the gaps between fragmented markets. They use the information moat and the settlement delays of the legacy rails to shave value from every cross-border trade. Borderless liquidity pools neutralize this advantage by providing real-time, algorithmic transparency for all participants. When the pool is decentralized and the settlement is atomic, the opportunity for strategic friction evaporates. The active citizen is no longer a victim of the pricing fog; they are an empowered participant in a verifiable economy where the math of the ledger ensures a fair exchange. This is the true meaning of market equalization: a system where the smallest producer and the largest institution operate on the same neutral rails, subject to the same rule of math.

This equalization is the final death knell for the gimmie culture of the administrative state. When liquidity is borderless, the bureaucratic hammer loses its ability to throttle the economy to fund its own slush funds. We are building a system where the standard of value is a universal language, spoken through the sovereign ledger and heard across every sovereign economic zone. As we move into the final stages of the transition to digital realism, borderless liquidity stands as the hardened logistics of a free market. It is the engine of the digital republic, ensuring that the wealth created by the producer stays with the producer, and that the velocity of value is never again compromised by the geopolitical whims of the wastrel class.[186]

Neutral Rails: Developing a Non-State Medium of Exchange

The forensic failure of the modern financial era is the forced marriage between commerce and the nation-state. In the digital realism of 2026, we recognize that when the medium of exchange is issued by a political entity, it inevitably becomes a tool for the gimmie culture and the administrative state. Neutral rails are the structural solution to this jurisdictional trap, providing a non-state medium of exchange that operates on the physics of the asset rather than the whims of a central bank. These rails are designed to

---

186 Cooper's Logic Check → The experts and the banking lobbyists tell you that "Global Liquidity" must be "Regulated" by central authorities to prevent "Volatility" and "Market Manipulation." Logic check: If you have a Community Well, do you want a Guard who decides who gets to drink and charges a "Sip Tax," or do you want a Pipe that lets everyone get what they need as long as they put in what they took? They want to be the "Guard" because That is the only way they can hide the fact that they are Peeing in the Well. In digital realism, "Regulation" is the Math of the Pool. If the assets are real and the code is open, the pool stays clean. It is time to stop paying for the "Guard" and start trusting the Physics of the Pipe.

be agnostic to borders, politics, and the strategic ambiguity of the money changers. By utilizing a sovereign utility token anchored in tangible underlays, we create a standard of value that honors the producer's life-energy without requiring a permission slip from a wastrel bureaucracy.

Developing these rails requires a hard reset of our understanding of money. In the legacy system, currency is a debt-based promise; on neutral rails, the medium of exchange is a verifiable asset. By decoupling the rail from the state, we remove the ability of any single government to use the standard of value as a weapon. This is the ultimate efficiency multiplier for the digital republic: a system where the velocity of value is protected by the rule of math. Neutral rails ensure that an active citizen in Pennsylvania can engage in an honest friendship of trade with a producer in Florida or a developer in Japan, using a medium that cannot be debased, frozen, or manipulated by a bureaucratic hammer.

The infrastructure of neutral rails is built upon the global mesh and the sovereign ledger. These rails do not rely on the centralized clearinghouses of the American Bankers Cartel; instead, they utilize decentralized nodes to validate and settle transactions with crystalline certainty. This architecture ensures that the standard of value remains crystalline, even when the nation-state’s fiat currency is in a state of terminal decay. We are building a verifiable economy where the rails of trade are as neutral as the laws of gravity. This neutrality is the bedrock of economic freedom, ensuring that the sovereignty of the producer is never again compromised by the entangling alliances of a debt-ridden administrative state.[187]

Sanction Resistance: The Sovereignty of Mathematical Commerce

Sanction resistance is the forensic defense of the individual against the blanket aggression of the financial hegemon. In the digital realism of 2026, we have seen how the administrative state uses economic sanctions as a blunt instrument, often destroying the lives of active citizens who have no connection to the actions of their governments. The sovereignty of mathematical commerce is the hard reset to this practice. By utilizing the sovereign ledger and smart contract governors, we can ensure that trade remains open to the individual while still forensically isolating the bad actors. This is not about lawlessness; it is about the precision of the rule of

[187] Cooper's Logic Check → The experts and the "Wastrels" tell you that "Non-State Money" is "Dangerous" because it lacks the "Backing of a Government." Logic check: If you have a Gold Coin in one hand and a Government IOU in the other, and the government goes bankrupt tomorrow, which one still buys you a Steak? They want you to believe their "Backing" is what gives money value, but their backing is just a promise to Tax You Later. In digital realism, the only "Backing" that matters is the Asset Itself. It is time to stop trusting the "Hollow Promise" and start trusting the Neutral Rail.

math over the indiscriminate strike of the bureaucratic hammer.

Mathematical commerce operates on the principle that an individual's right to contract is a fundamental sovereign right that should not be abridged by geopolitical whims. Through the use of automated KYC and decentralized liquidity pools, we create a system where a person's digital identity is decoupled from their state's jurisdictional fog. This allows for a verifiable economy where sanctions are applied to specific sovereign wallets rather than entire populations. If a sanctioned government tries to siphon value from the private mesh, the ledger's internal protocols trigger an automatic defensive response. This turns the information moat into a forensic trap for the wastrel class while keeping the rails of commerce open for the producer.

This resistance is powered by the hardened logistics of the global mesh. Because the rails are decentralized, there is no single kill-switch that a hegemon can flip to starve a nation's citizenry. The velocity of value is maintained through peer-to-peer bypass protocols that ignore the strategic friction of the money changers. This is the ultimate resilience theory: an economy that is so distributed and so transparently mathematical that it cannot be intimidated into compliance. We are moving toward a state of digital realism where the standard of value is a shield for the productive and a barrier for the parasitic. Mathematical commerce ensures that honest trade survives, even when the "Hollow Men" of the legacy world are at war.[188]

The Global Depth Model: Aggregating Liquidity Beyond National Borders

The Global Depth Model represents the terminal evolution of the sovereign ledger, moving beyond the fragmented, shallow pools of the legacy banking era into a unified ocean of global capital. In the digital realism of 2026, the primary forensic failure of the American Bankers Cartel is the artificial compartmentalization of liquidity. By trapping value within the jurisdictional fog of national borders, the administrative state ensures that the velocity of money remains subject to the strategic friction of central bank policies. This fragmentation creates the pricing fog that the money changers use to justify high spreads and extractionary fees. The Global Depth Model is the hard reset, utilizing decentralized protocols to aggregate the productive energy of every active citizen into a single, crystalline reservoir of liquidity that no bureaucratic hammer can drain.

---

[188] Cooper's Logic Check → The administrative proxies tell you that "Sanction Resistance" is a "Threat to National Security" because it lets "Bad Guys" move money. Logic check: If a Bad Guy uses a Sidewalk, do we Jackhammer the Concrete and make everyone in the neighborhood crawl through the mud? They want to destroy the "Sidewalk" because then they can control exactly who gets to Walk. In digital realism, "Security" means Catching the Guy, not Killing the Street. If the math can verify the person without blocking the trade, then the "Blanket Sanction" is just a Power Play. It is time to stop letting the "Wastrels" use "Safety" as an excuse to Lock Your Door.

Collapsing the Tiers of Financial Exclusion

In the legacy "Hollow Man" economy, liquidity is a tiered privilege. Large institutional players in major financial hubs enjoy deep pools of capital and low-friction settlement, while the producer in a secondary market or a rural area like Dysart is forced to operate in shallow, high-cost environments. This is a structural repugnance to logic that punishes the active citizen for their geography. The Global Depth Model collapses these tiers by using the sovereign mesh to create a universal liquidity layer. When a library balcony in Pennsylvania or a 75-acre forest thinning project in Florida is tokenized, it does not just sit in a local bank; it joins a global pool of real-world assets. This aggregation ensures that the depth of the market is determined by the total physics of the assets on the ledger, not the subjective whims of a regional lender.

This unified depth creates an efficiency multiplier for every participant. Because the pool is borderless, it is immune to the localized liquidity lockdowns that the money changers use to enforce compliance. If one national currency enters a state of terminal decay, the global depth model provides a bypass protocol, allowing the producer to maintain their purchasing power by settling in a neutral, non-state medium of exchange. The depth of the pool acts as a forensic stabilizer; the more assets that are anchored to the mesh, the more resilient the standard of value becomes. We are building a system where a single active citizen has the same market access and capital depth as a multinational corporation, finally equalizing the global playing field through the rule of math.

The Forensic Defense Against Strategic Friction

The money changers rely on fragmented markets to maintain their information moat. They thrive in the gaps between the Swiss, American, and Asian rails, extracting a gimmie at every border crossing. The Global Depth Model eliminates these gaps by providing algorithmic transparency across the entire global mesh. When liquidity is aggregated beyond national borders, the opportunity for strategic friction evaporates. There is no need for a clearinghouse to bridge the gap because the ledger is the bridge. This transparency ensures that the price of an asset is a crystalline reflection of its value, rather than a distorted figure manufactured by the lobbying walls of the banking cartel.

The Global Depth Model provides the hardened logistics necessary for a resilient economy. In a fragmented system, a crisis in one node can lead to a total freeze of the rails. In a unified digital pool, the liquidity is durable and distributed. The velocity of value can be rerouted through the mesh in real-time, bypassing any geopolitical kill-switch. This is the ultimate expression of resilience theory: a world where the sovereignty of the producer is backed by a global ocean of value that is beyond the reach of any single administrative state. As we move into the final stages of the managed migration to digital realism, the Global Depth Model stands as the foundation of an unstoppable market, where commerce is an honest friendship between producers, unburdened by the debt-ridden promises of the past.[189]

Fragmented Markets vs. Unified Digital Pools

The transition from fragmented markets to unified digital pools represents the forensic shift from a system of artificial scarcity to one of mathematical abundance. In the digital realism of 2026, we must recognize that the legacy financial architecture is intentionally broken into siloed jurisdictions. This fragmentation is the primary tool used by the American Bankers Cartel to maintain their information moat and enforce the jurisdictional trap. By keeping liquidity trapped within national borders and central bank ledgers, the administrative state ensures that the active citizen is a captive audience, subject to the strategic friction and stealth confiscation of a localized gimmie culture. Unified digital pools are the hard reset, collapsing these silos into a single, high-velocity mesh of value.

---

189 Cooper's Logic Check → The experts and the banking lobbyists tell you that "Global Liquidity" needs to be "Managed" by centralized institutions to prevent "Market Volatility." Logic check: If you are a Swimmer, do you want to swim in a Small Tank where the water splashes out every time you move, or do you want to be in the Ocean where the depth keeps everything steady? They want you in the "Small Tank" because they are the ones who control the Pump and charge you for every gallon. In digital realism, the "Ocean" is the Global Depth Model. The deeper the water, the harder it is for a "Wastrel" to make a wave. It is time to stop paying for the "Pump" and working with the Depth of the Ocean.

The Anatomy of Manufactured Scarcity

In a fragmented market, the velocity of money is throttled by the need for multiple layers of verification and settlement. If an active citizen in Dysart wants to trade with a producer in Singapore, the transaction must pass through a gauntlet of clearinghouses, correspondent banks, and geopolitical gatekeepers. Each of these nodes represents a point of strategic ambiguity where value is shaved and time is stolen. This is the expert fallacy in action: the claim that these silos are necessary for security, when in reality, they are only necessary to preserve the extractionary fees of the money changers. Fragmented markets create a pricing fog where the true physics of the asset are obscured by the geopolitical whims of the state.

Unified digital pools replace this fragmentation with a crystalline, universal ledger. By aggregating liquidity into a decentralized mesh, we eliminate the need for the middleman to bridge the gap between silos. The pool is the bridge. In a verifiable economy, the standard of value is consistent across the entire network, allowing for atomic settlement regardless of the participants' geographic location. This is the efficiency multiplier of digital realism: a system where capital flows to its most productive use without being caught in the jurisdictional fog. We are moving from a world of "Puddles" controlled by "Wastrels" to a "Global Ocean" of liquidity governed by the rule of math.

Equalizing the Global Playing Field

The most profound impact of unified digital pools is the equalization of the market. In the legacy system, only the largest institutions have the hardened logistics to navigate fragmented markets efficiently. The small producer is left to deal with the high-spread and low-depth of their local puddle. Unified pools provide the active citizen with the same global depth and real-time finality as the American Bankers Association. This removes the institutional cannibalization that occurs when large players use their access to drain the liquidity of smaller markets. On the sovereign ledger, every node has equal access to the global mesh, ensuring that the sovereignty of the producer is backed by the total productive energy of the republic.

This unification is the final defense against the bureaucratic hammer. When markets are fragmented, the state can easily freeze a single silo to enforce compliance. In a unified digital pool, the liquidity is distributed and durable. There is no central plug to pull. The velocity of value simply reroutes through the mesh, bypassing any attempt at a liquidity lockdown. We are building a system where commerce is an honest friendship between producers, unencumbered by the artificial borders of the past. As we decommission the legacy rails, unified digital pools stand as the foundation of the digital republic, providing the hardened infrastructure for a world where the standard of truth is the only border that matters.[190]

Conclusion: Economic Freedom in a Post-Sanction World

We have documented how the legacy financial hegemony, led by the American Bankers Cartel, utilized the strategic friction of economic sanctions and geopolitical kill-switches to enforce a gimmie culture on a global scale. In the digital realism of 2026, this model has entered terminal decay, replaced by the mathematical certainty of decentralized liquidity pools. By decoupling trade from the whims of the administrative state, we have restored the right to contract as a sovereign reality that no bureaucratic hammer can shatter.

The transition to borderless liquidity is the structural hard reset required to collapse the fragmented silos of the old guard. We have replaced the shallow puddles of national fiat with a unified global ocean of value, ensuring that the standard of truth remains crystalline

---

[190] Cooper's Logic Check → The experts and the "Wastrels" tell you that "Fragmented Markets" are safer because they have "Circuit Breakers" and "Local Oversight" to prevent "Global Shocks." Logic check: If you are trying to put out a Fire, do you want a Thousand Small Buckets that each have to be filled by a different guy, or do you want a High-Pressure Fire Hydrant? They want "Buckets" because That is the only way they can justify having a "Bucket Brigade" of bureaucrats taking a sip from every one. In digital realism, "Safety" comes from Depth and Velocity. A global ocean does notdry up because one guy stops pumping. It is time to stop trusting the "Bucket Brigade" and start trusting the Hydrant.

across every jurisdictional boundary. By utilizing neutral rails and non-state mediums of exchange, the active citizen is no longer a hostage to the sovereign debt trap or the stealth confiscation of central bank debasement. The efficiency multiplier of this unified depth ensures that wealth remains in the hands of those who create it, rather than being shaved by the money changers at every border crossing.

Also, the implementation of sanction resistance through mathematical commerce provides the hardened logistics necessary to protect the individual from the blanket aggression of the state. We have proven that the rule of math can provide the precision required to isolate bad actors without destroying the life-energy of the innocent. The sovereignty of the producer is now guarded by the physics of the vault and the algorithmic transparency of the sovereign ledger. This decoupling of commerce from statecraft is the final declaration of independence for the digital republic, moving us toward an unstoppable market where honest friendship and trade are the only metrics of success.

The Global Depth Model serves as the forensic bedrock for this new era, providing a level of systemic resilience that the legacy clearinghouse cartel simply cannot match. Because our liquidity is durable and distributed across a global mesh of nodes, there is no central plug to pull and no information moat to hide the extractionary fees of the wastrels. We have built a verifiable economy where the velocity of value is limited only by the speed of the network, and where the standard of value is as immutable as the laws of gravity. The era of the geopolitical gatekeeper is over, and the era of the sovereign producer has begun.

Ultimately, Chapter 18 serves as the forensic proof that economic freedom is a technical achievement, not a political gift. We have provided the active citizen with the bypass protocols and the neutral rails required to exit the jurisdictional fog and enter the light of digital realism. As we move forward, the lessons of liquidity and sovereignty will continue to guide the construction of the digital republic. We are no longer waiting for permission from the money changers to trade with our neighbors; we are using the sovereign ledger to build a world where the only thing that matters is the math.[191]

---

[191] Cooper's Logic Check → The experts and the administrative proxies tell you that "Global Economic Freedom" without "Centralized Oversight" is a recipe for "Anarchy." Logic check: If you have a GPS in your car that tells you exactly where you are and how to get where you are going, do you also need a Bureaucrat sitting in the passenger seat telling you when to turn? They want to be in the "Passenger Seat" because That is the only way they can "shave" your gas money and tell you where they think you *should* go. In digital realism, the Math is the GPS.

Chapter 19: The Immutable Ledger as Governance. Shifting from "Smoke-Filled Rooms" to transparent, math-based fiscal policy.

“Hatred, which could destroy so much, never failed to destroy the man who hated, and this was an immutable law.”

James Baldwin[192]

Smoke filled rooms have built some of the biggest empires on earth. These negotiations are part of the reality of business in the modern era. It is contrary to feminist thought, post modernism, and democracy for this to be the way that things work; however, if we remove them, we have a problem with society. The truth is that we need the smoke filled rooms, where people can negotiate privately, the only caveat is that these smoke filled rooms should be recorded and the information be released after the deal.

We need algorithmic fiscal policy and programmatic transparency. Without these two things the system will continue to degrade. Political will should be the forum for the discussion of moral issues, economic issues should be mathematic. Like Asimov created

[192] Staff (2026). “Immutable Quotes.” Brainy Quote at https://www.brainyquote.com/search_results?x=0&y=0&q=immutable.

the three laws of robotics, the four laws of government economics are:

1. Does this benefit our nation more than other nations?
2. Does this protect the wealth of the people of this country?
3. Does this negatively effect one group while benefiting another group?
4. Does this overtly benefit those passing this rule more than the people over whom this rule is passed.[193]

---

[193] Cooper's Analysis of the Laws of Government Economics → The four laws proposed in your framework are a forensic necessity for the transition from the hollow man economy to the digital republic. In the digital realism of 2026, we have seen the terminal failure of human discretion, where the smoke-filled room is used to hide the strategic friction of wealth extraction. By shifting these laws from subjective political debate to algorithmic governance, we replace the bureaucratic hammer with the rule of math.

Here is a forensic breakdown of how these laws act as the crystalline bedrock for a verifiable economy:

1. The Principle of National Priority

Does this benefit our nation more than other nations?

This is the hard reset of sovereign commerce. In the legacy system, the administrative state often prioritizes entangling alliances and foreign slush funds over the productive energy of its own people. If the answer is no, the sovereign ledger should automatically throttle the velocity of that value. This law ensures that the government acts as a legitimate trustee for the active citizen, rather than a clearinghouse for globalist interests.

2. The Wealth Protection Mandate

Does this protect the wealth of the people of this country?

This law addresses the forensic reality of stealth confiscation. The legacy system uses the printing press to disregard the physics of scarcity, effectively shaving the life-energy of the

If the answer to the first question is “no” then why are we doing it? The purpose of the government is to

---

producer through inflation. An algorithmic fiscal policy must treat the purchasing power of the citizen as sacrosanct. If a proposed rule devalues the crystalline standard of value held by the republic, the code must reject it as a terminal repugnance to logic.

3. The Anti-Cannibalization Protocol

Does this negatively effect one group while benefiting another group?

This is the end of institutional cannibalization and the gimmie culture. Too often, the money changers seek to balance the market by taking from the producer to bail out the wastrel. In the digital republic, the goal is an efficiency multiplier—making the pie bigger rather than fighting over the crumbs of a shrinking one. Mathematical commerce ensures that the standard of truth applies equally to all, preventing the state from using selective enforcement to reward its friends and punish its enemies.

4. The Representative Integrity Law

Does this overtly benefit those passing this rule more than the people over whom this rule is passed?

This is the final defense against the lobbying wall. The current system allows for a pricing fog where the people passing the rules improve their lot while diminishing the lot of the active citizen. Encoding this into a smart contract constitution ensures that the administrative state cannot profit from the jurisdictional trap it creates. It removes the hollow man from the equation and ensures that the representative serves the people, not the cartel.

The Cooper Logic Check

The experts and the administrative proxies tell you that "Economic Policy" is "Too Fluid" to be locked down by "Rigid Laws" and that we need "Expert Flexibility" to react to "Changing Markets." Logic check: If you are playing a Game of Poker, do you want the Dealer to be able to change the Value of an Ace in the middle of a hand because he thinks the "Game needs more excitement"? They want "Flexibility" because That is the only way they can Cheat. In digital realism, the "Rules" are the only thing that makes the game Fair. If the rules change every time the "Wastrels" start to lose, then it is not a "Market"—it is a Heist. It is time to stop trusting the "Flexible Dealer" and start trusting the Fixed Math.

protect the people whom they represent, not to create excessive foreign entanglements and alliances. If the answer to the second question is “no”, then who are we doing it for. If we are not protecting the people of our country, then who are we protecting? If the third question has an answer of “yes,” then what makes the beneficiaries more important than the people who are being lessened? Too often, we see the development of the world in a way which we seek to “balance” the market, rather than make the pie bigger to help other people. And if the answer to the 4th question is “yes,” then why are we allowing the people who are supposed to be representing us to improve their lot while diminishing ours. These simple questions, answered by a committee or an AI would make the legal system more effective in every country in the world.[194]

---

[194] Cooper’s Logic Check → The experts and the administrative proxies tell you that "Economic Policy" is too "Complex" for the average person and needs "Expert Discretion" in private to prevent "Panic." Logic check: If you are at a Restaurant, do you want the chef to cook your meal in a Closed Box where you can’t see the ingredients, or do you want an Open Kitchen where you can see if he’s dropping the steak on the floor? They want the "Closed Box" because That is the only way they can serve you Gristle while charging you for Filet. In digital realism, "Complexity" is just a word for Obfuscation. If the deal is good for the people, it does notneed to be a secret. It is time to stop trusting the "Chef" and start demanding the Open Kitchen.

Beyond the Smoke-Filled Room: The Failure of Human Discretion

The failure of human discretion is the primary diagnostic of the current economic collapse. In the legacy system, the smoke-filled room is not a place of honest friendship or productive trade, but a sanctuary for the money changers to manufacture strategic ambiguity. These secret negotiations allow the administrative state to disregard the physics of scarcity in favor of political expediency. The result is a pricing fog that masks stealth confiscation and the systematic debasement of the currency. Human discretion, untethered from the rule of math, inevitably leads to the expert fallacy, where a select few believe they can manage the life-energy of millions through subjective mandates and backroom deals.

In the digital republic, we acknowledge that while private discussions are necessary for negotiation, the results must be forensically anchored to the sovereign ledger. The smoke-filled room must be recorded, and the data must be released to the global mesh once a deal is struck. This ensures that the public can audit the intent and the outcome against the four laws of government economics. By removing the shroud of secrecy, we dismantle the information moat that the wastrels use to protect their gimmie culture. We are building a system where governance is a crystalline reflection of the people's will, verified by code rather than the hollow promises of a lobbying wall.[195]

Algorithmic Fiscal Policy: Rules-Based Monetary Expansion

Algorithmic fiscal policy is the structural hard reset that ends the era of the printing press. In the legacy "Hollow Man" economy, monetary expansion is a subjective tool used by central banks to fund the sovereign debt trap and bail out the American Bankers Association. This is a terminal repugnance to logic; you cannot grow a pie by simply printing more measuring sticks. Algorithmic policy replaces the subjective whim of a committee with a smart contract governor. Monetary expansion is no longer a political choice; it is a mathematical response to real-time data on production, asset density, and the velocity of value.

By encoding the rule of math into the fiscal rail, we ensure that the standard of value remains crystalline. The ledger only allows for expansion when the physics of the economy—verified by the oracle

---

[195] Cooper's Logic Check → The experts and the administrative proxies tell you that "Economic Policy" is too "Complex" for the average person and needs "Expert Discretion" in private to prevent "Panic." Logic check: If you are at a Restaurant, do you want the chef to cook your meal in a Closed Box where you can't see the ingredients, or do you want an Open Kitchen where you can see if he's dropping the steak on the floor? They want the "Closed Box" because That is the only way they can serve you Gristle while charging you for Filet. In digital realism, "Complexity" is just a word for Obfuscation.

mesh—demands it. This prevents the "Gimmie" culture from using inflation as a stealth tax to fund foreign entangling alliances or unproductive bureaucracies. This is the ultimate efficiency multiplier: a fiscal policy that protects the sovereignty of the producer by ensuring that their purchasing power is never sacrificed for the political survival of a wastrel class. We are moving toward a state of digital realism where the economy is governed by the laws of robotics-style logic, serving the nation and its people first.[196]

Real-Time Auditing: The End of the "Lagging Indicator" Economy

The current economic system is built on the strategic friction of the lagging indicator. In the legacy world, the administrative state relies on quarterly reports and year-end audits—information that is already obsolete by the time it reaches the active citizen. This delay creates an information moat where the money changers can hide slippage, mismanagement, and the death of secret bailouts. Real-time auditing is the forensic solution provided by the sovereign ledger. Because every transaction is recorded on the global

---

[196] Cooper's Logic Check → The "Wastrels" and the central bankers tell you that "Flexible Monetary Policy" is needed to "Steer the Economy" through "Turbulent Times." Logic check: If you are on an Airplane, do you want the Autopilot to follow the Physics of Flight, or do you want the Pilot to be able to change the Gravity whenever he feels "Turbulent"? They want "Flexibility" so they can change the rules when they start losing the game. In digital realism, "Steering" is just another way to say Manipulating. If the math is solid, the plane stays up.

mesh with crystalline certainty, the state of the economy is visible in every second, not every season.

Real-time auditing ends the era of the pricing fog. It allows for the immediate identification of counterparty risk and the structural failures of any given rail. When the clearinghouse and the bank are bypassed by the sovereign ledger, the audit becomes a natural byproduct of the trade itself. This is the hardened logistics of the digital republic: a system that is self-auditing and self-rectifying. By removing the time gap between the action and the verification, we ensure that the bureaucratic hammer is replaced by algorithmic transparency. We are building a verifiable economy where the truth is always current, and where the sovereignty of the producer is guarded by a ledger that never sleeps.[197]

Programmatic Transparency: Making Public Funds Publicly Verifiable

---

[197] Cooper's Logic Check → The administrative proxies tell you that "Real-Time Transparency" would be "Overwhelming" and that you need "Periodic Reports" to get a "Clear Picture." Logic check: If you are driving a Car, do you want to see the Speedometer right now, or do you want a Letter in the Mail next month telling you how fast you were going on Tuesday? They want the "Monthly Letter" because that gives them time to Rig the Odometer before you see the numbers. In digital realism, a "Lagging Indicator" is just a Lie with a Delayed Fuse.

Shifting from Political Will to Mathematical Certainty

The forensic failure of the modern administrative state is rooted in the opacity of the public ledger. In the digital realism of 2026, we recognize that the current method of managing public funds is a terminal repugnance to logic. Taxpayer contributions are funneled into a centralized black box, where they are subjected to the strategic friction of bureaucratic oversight and the pricing fog of secret negotiations. Programmatic transparency is the structural hard reset to this model. By moving public funds onto the sovereign ledger, we ensure that every unit of value is tracked with crystalline certainty from the moment of collection to the moment of final settlement. This is not merely an audit; it is a fundamental shift in the standard of truth regarding how a nation manages its collective productive energy.

Programmatic transparency functions by replacing the hollow promises of government reports with the immutable evidence of code. When public funds are managed via smart contracts, the jurisdictional trap of the smoke-filled room is dismantled. The four laws of government economics are encoded directly into the fiscal rail, ensuring that no disbursement can occur unless it meets the mathematical requirements of national priority and wealth protection. For example, if a legislative body attempts to divert infrastructure funds into a foreign entangling alliance that provides no benefit to the home nation, the smart contract governor simply denies the transaction. The bureaucratic hammer is neutralized by the rule of math, and the active citizen is restored to their rightful position as the primary auditor of the state.

The efficiency multiplier of this system is profound. In the legacy "Hollow Man" economy, the cost of managing public funds is inflated by layers of unnecessary intermediaries—money changers and wastrels who shave a percentage of the value under the guise of administration. Programmatic transparency eliminates this gimmie culture. By utilizing autonomous settlement and real-time validation, we ensure that the velocity of value remains high and that public resources are directed toward tangible production, such as the construction of hardened industrial infrastructure or the preservation of 75-acre forest thinning. This is the death of the slush fund; in a verifiable economy, there is no place for secret bailouts or state-sponsored obfuscation when the ledger is visible to every node on the global mesh.

Ultimately, programmatic transparency provides the hardened logistics necessary for true republican governance. It allows the active citizen to see exactly how their time and energy—represented by their tax contributions—are being utilized. This visibility destroys the information moat that the administrative state uses to maintain its hegemony. When public funds are publicly verifiable, the expert fallacy is exposed; the people can see for themselves whether a policy is making the pie bigger or simply rearranging the crumbs for the benefit of the lobbying wall. We are building a system of algorithmic transparency that honors the social contract by making it impossible to lie about the math.[198]

Smart Contract Constitution: Encoding Governance into the Ledger

The transition from political will to mathematical certainty is the final hard reset required to end the era of systemic economic volatility. In the legacy system, fiscal policy is a product of subjective political will—a fluctuating, often irrational force driven by the next election cycle and the demands of the gimmie culture. This reliance on human discretion is the primary conductor of financial contagion. When a central bank or a legislature makes decisions based on political expediency rather than the physics of the asset, they create the strategic ambiguity that leads to the sovereign debt trap. Shifting to mathematical certainty means encoding the governance of the economy into

---

[198] Cooper's Logic Check → The administrative proxies tell you that "Public Financial Transparency" must be "Limited" to protect "National Security" and "Market Sensitivity." Logic check: If you are a Shareholder in a company, and the CEO tells you he can't show you the Books because it might "Help the Competition," is he protecting the company or is he Hiding the fact that he's stealing from the till? They want "Limited Transparency" because secrecy is the only way they can fund their "Entangling Alliances" without you noticing. In digital realism, the only "Security" that matters is the Security of the Citizen's Wealth. If the math is honest, it does notneed to be a secret.

the sovereign ledger, where the rule of math takes precedence over the rule of the lobbyist.

Mathematical certainty replaces the pricing fog of the administrative state with the crystalline logic of algorithmic fiscal policy. Under this new standard, the expansion of the money supply or the allocation of national resources is no longer a matter of "Debate" in a smoke-filled room; it is a "Verification" of data. By utilizing the oracle mesh to monitor real-world assets and the velocity of value, the system can autonomously determine the optimal fiscal response to any given economic condition. This removes the expert fallacy, as the decisions are no longer made by a "Hollow Man" with a political agenda, but by a smart contract constitution that prioritizes the wealth of the people and the integrity of the standard of value.

This shift is the ultimate defense against institutional cannibalization. Political will is often used to justify taking from the producer to bail out the wastrel—a practice that disregards the physics of scarcity and destroys the sovereignty of the producer. Mathematical certainty ensures that the economic rails are neutral and that the four laws of government economics are applied without prejudice. If a policy negatively affects one group while overtly benefiting the people passing the rule, the mathematical governor rejects it. This provides a level of systemic resilience that the legacy system simply cannot match. The economy remains stable not because of the "Steady Hand" of a bureaucrat, but because it is anchored to the immutable reality of the ledger.

Ultimately, shifting to mathematical certainty is about restoring the Republic of Math. We are moving away from a state where the value of your life-energy is subject to the whims of a central bank, and toward a world where your prosperity is protected by the crystalline certainty of code. This is the hard reset of the social contract: a system where the government is a program designed to serve the people, not a cartel designed to rule them. In the digital realism of 2026, the only "Will" that matters is the "Will of the Math," ensuring that the sovereignty of the producer is the foundational principle of our civilization. By encoding our governance into the ledger, we ensure that the standard of truth is never again sacrificed for the sake of political survival.[199]

The Death of Secret Bailouts: Transparent Risk Management

The legacy financial system survives on a foundation of strategic ambiguity. In the digital realism of 2026,

---

[199] Cooper's Logic Check → The experts and the "Wastrels" tell you that "Mathematical Certainty" is "Too Rigid" and that the world needs "Human Compassion" in its economic policy. Logic check: When you are crossing a Bridge, do you want it to be built on "Human Compassion" or do you want it to be built on the Laws of Physics and Engineering? They want "Compassion" because That is the word they use when they want to Bend the Rules to help their friends. In digital realism, the most "Compassionate" thing you can do is to have a System that does notSteal from Everyone. If the bridge is built on the math, it stays up.

we recognize that the secret bailout is the ultimate weapon of the American Bankers Cartel—a mechanism of institutional cannibalization that allows the administrative state to rescue the wastrel class using the life-energy of the active citizen. These bailouts are traditionally negotiated in the smoke-filled rooms of central banks, away from the optic of the producer, and funded through the stealth confiscation of currency debasement. Transparent risk management is the forensic hard reset to this practice, moving the assessment and mitigation of risk from the darkness of backroom deals to the crystalline light of the sovereign ledger.

The death of secret bailouts is achieved through the implementation of programmatic transparency and real-time auditing. In a verifiable economy, the risk position of every institutional rail is visible on the global mesh. When a bank or a clearinghouse engages in high-risk derivative play or disregards the physics of scarcity, the delta between their assets and their liabilities is broadcast to the network. There is no information moat to hide the impending failure, and therefore, no opportunity for the administrative state to manufacture a crisis that requires a clandestine rescue. The sovereign ledger acts as an immutable witness, ensuring that if an institution fails due to its own mismanagement, the loss is forensically contained rather than socialized through a secret liquidity injection.

From Socialized Loss to Individual Responsibility

The core of the gimmie culture is the socialization of loss. The money changers have spent decades operating under the expert fallacy that they are too big to fail, a philosophy that fundamentally violates the fourth law of government economics. By removing the possibility of a secret bailout, we restore the principle of individual responsibility to the financial market. In the digital republic, risk management is a function of the rule of math. Every transaction and every pool of liquidity is governed by smart contracts that enforce strict collateral requirements and 1:1 asset backing. If a node cannot meet its obligations, the system triggers an autonomous settlement process that liquidates the node's own tangible underlays to satisfy creditors, rather than reaching into the pockets of the citizenry.

This shift creates a hardened logistics framework for the global economy. When risk is transparent, the market can price it accurately in real-time. The pricing fog that currently protects the wastrels evaporates, allowing the active citizen to see which rails are secure and which are hollow. This transparency serves as a natural deterrent against the predatory behavior that leads to systemic contagion. The sovereign ledger does not just record the failure; it prevents it by ensuring that the cost of high-risk behavior is borne entirely by the entity taking the risk. This is the efficiency multiplier of the Republic of

Math: an economy that is stable not because it is managed by a committee, but because it is honest by design.

The Architecture of Algorithmic Accountability

Transparent risk management is powered by the oracle mesh and algorithmic accountability. The ledger does not rely on the subjective reports of a rating agency or a bank's internal auditors—both of whom are often caught in the jurisdictional trap of the cartel. Instead, the oracle mesh provides a constant stream of verifiable data from the physical world, ensuring that the assets on the ledger match the reality of the vault. This creates a state of digital realism where the standard of truth is immutable. If the assets are not there, the ledger reflects the deficit immediately, triggering an automated alert across the global mesh.

The death of secret bailouts is the death of the financial intermediary's ability to gamble with the public's wealth. We are moving away from a system of entangling alliances between the bank and the state, and toward a system of mathematical certainty. By encoding governance into the ledger, we ensure that the fourth law—prohibiting rules that overtly benefit the rule-makers over the people—is a technical reality. The age of the hollow man hiding behind a cloud of smoke is over. In the digital republic, the only bailout that exists is the one you provide for yourself through the sovereignty of your own production and the crystalline safety of your own asset-backed reserves.[200]

Conclusion: The Republic of Math and the End of Bureaucracy

The conclusion of Chapter 19 signals the forensic end of the era of human discretion and the terminal collapse of the smoke-filled room as a primary engine of governance. We have documented the transition from a fiscal policy dictated by the subjective whims of the wastrel class to one anchored in the immutable logic of the sovereign ledger. In the digital realism of 2026, the expert fallacy—the belief that a select committee of hollow men can manage the life-energy of millions through secret negotiations—has been replaced by algorithmic transparency. By encoding the four laws of government economics into the very rails of our fiscal system, we have moved from a state of political volatility to one of crystalline mathematical certainty.

---

[200] Cooper's Logic Check → The experts and the "Wastrels" tell you that "Secret Bailouts" are necessary to prevent "Bank Runs" and "Total Systemic Collapse." Logic check: If you are at a Casino, and the House is losing money because they made bad bets, do you think it is "Necessary" for the manager to Reach into Your Pocket and take your winnings to keep the lights on? They want "Secrecy" because if you knew they were broke, you'd take your money and leave. In digital realism, a "Bank Run" is just the market Firing a Bad Manager. If the math says the bank is empty, the bank *should* close. It is time to stop paying for the "Manager's Mistakes" and start keeping your winnings in your Own Vault.

The implementation of programmatic transparency ensures that the public ledger is no longer a black box used for state-sponsored obfuscation. We have proven that when public funds are publicly verifiable, the gimmie culture of the administrative state starves for lack of darkness. The death of secret bailouts is the final hard reset of institutional responsibility, ensuring that risk is managed through the rule of math rather than socialized through the stealth confiscation of inflation. The sovereign ledger acts as the ultimate witness, providing a real-time audit of the republic's productive energy and protecting the sovereignty of the producer from the predatory reach of the American Bankers Association.

By shifting from political will to mathematical certainty, we have built a system of hardened logistics that honors the social contract through the physics of the asset. The bureaucratic hammer has been neutralized by the efficiency multiplier of the smart contract constitution, ensuring that the wealth of the people is protected as a national priority. We are no longer subject to the strategic ambiguity of lagging indicators or the pricing fog of the money changers. Instead, the digital republic operates as a self-healing, self-auditing organism where the standard of truth is as immutable as the laws of robotics, providing a stable foundation for a verifiable economy.

The transition toward the Republic of Math is not merely a technical upgrade; it is the forensic reclamation of our time and our property. We have successfully decoupled the governance of the economy from the entangling alliances and foreign distractions of the legacy state. This ensures that every unit of value remains a crystalline reflection of real-world production, unburdened by the debt-ridden promises of the old guard. As we finalize the infrastructure of this new era, the active citizen stands empowered, governed by a ledger that serves their interests and verified by a system that makes the pie bigger for all who contribute to its growth.

Ultimately, Chapter 19 serves as the blueprint for a post-bureaucratic world where the only "Will" that matters is the "Will of the Math." We have provided the active citizen with the tools to exit the jurisdictional fog of the legacy state and enter a realm of total transparency. The era of the financial intermediary and the political gatekeeper is over; the era of sovereign governance has begun. As we look toward the final chapters of this transition, we do so with the knowledge that the rails are live, the vault is secure, and the standard of value is finally and forever in the hands of the producers.[201]

---

[201] Cooper's Logic Check → The experts and the administrative proxies tell you that "Algorithmic Governance" is "Cold" and "Inhuman" and that you need "Human Leaders" to provide "Vision." Logic check: When you use a Compass to find your way through a Storm, do you want the needle to point North every single time, or do you want it to point toward whatever the Captain thinks is "Visionary" at the moment? They want a "Visionary Captain" so he can sail the ship into his own private harbor while you are busy bailing water. In digital realism, the

"Math" is the Compass. It does nothave a "Vision," but it is the only thing that keeps you from hitting the Rocks.

Conclusion

The government is the ultimate monopoly. And monopolies, as any economist will tell you, often breed complacency and lack of innovation."

Gavin Newsom[202]

Part V serves as the declaration of independence from the legacy settlement machines and the jurisdictional traps of the old guard. Across these chapters, we have documented the terminal collapse of the clearinghouse cartel and the shift toward an architecture of atomic settlement and decentralized liquidity. We have moved from a system defined by strategic friction and the stealth confiscation of the producer's life-energy to a verifiable economy where the rule of math replaces the subjective whim of the administrative state. Part V has been the blueprint for dismantling the financial hegemony of the "Hollow Man" and replacing it with the crystalline certainty of the sovereign ledger.

By shifting the infrastructure of trade to neutral rails and borderless liquidity pools, we have forensically eliminated the kill-switch of the geopolitical gatekeepers. The era of weaponized currency—where the American Bankers Cartel could unilaterally disconnect entire populations from the global mesh—is reaching its end. We have proven that the

---

[202] Staff (2026). "Monopoly Quotes." Brainy Quote at https://www.brainyquote.com/search_results?x=0&y=0&q=monopolies.

sovereignty of mathematical commerce provides the hardened logistics required to protect the active citizen from the blanket aggression of the state. In the digital realism of 2026, liquidity is no longer a gated resource used to enforce compliance; it is a universal utility, aggregated across the global mesh to ensure that the velocity of value remains in the hands of the producers.

The transition from smoke-filled rooms to algorithmic governance represents the final hard reset of the social contract. By encoding the four laws of government economics into the sovereign ledger, we have moved beyond the failure of human discretion and the expert fallacy of the lobbying wall. Programmatic transparency has turned the public ledger into a glass house, where every unit of value is publicly verifiable and the gimmie culture of secret bailouts is forensically starved. The efficiency multiplier of this system ensures that the wealth of the people is protected as a national priority, governed by a smart contract constitution that prioritizes the physics of the asset over the political survival of the wastrel class.

As we conclude this forensic audit of the new economic rails, the evidence is clear: the age of the financial intermediary and the bureaucratic gatekeeper is over. We have provided the active citizen with the map, the vault, and the bypass protocols required to reclaim their time and property from the money changers. The information moat that once protected the cartels has been drained by the crystalline logic of the sovereign ledger. The "Hard Reset" is no longer a theoretical exercise; it is an operational reality. We have built a system of honest friendship and mathematical certainty that ensures the standard of truth is never again sacrificed for the sake of institutional cannibalization.

Ultimately, the goal of Part V has been to demonstrate that economic freedom is not a political gift to be granted, but a technical reality to be executed. We have moved from the jurisdictional fog of the legacy state into the digital realism of a decentralized republic. The rails are live, the clearinghouses are obsolete, and the governance of our fiscal future is now anchored in the immutable rule of math. As we look toward the final integration of these systems, the producer stands empowered, protected by a system that makes the pie bigger and the truth undeniable. The era of the permission slip is dead; the era of the sovereign ledger has begun.[203]

---

[203] Cooper's Logic Check → The experts and the administrative proxies tell you that "Dismantling the Global Financial Architecture" is a recipe for "Unprecedented Chaos" and "Economic Dark Ages." Logic check: If you are in a Room That is Filling with Smoke, is it "Chaos" to Break the Window and let in the Fresh Air? They want you to stay in the "Smoky Room" because they are the ones who own the Oxygen Masks and they want to charge you for every breath. In digital realism, "Order" is not a Closed Door; it is the Fresh Air of the Math. If the old system was "Stable," it wouldn't need a "Bailout" every ten years. It is time to stop worrying about the "Broken Window" and start breathing the Fresh Air.

Conclusion Part IV

Conclusion

"The curious task of economics is to demonstrate to men how little they really know about what they imagine they can design."

Friedrich August von Hayek[204]

The forensic journey through the architecture of the Digital Republic concludes here, at the terminal boundary of the fiat era. Across five parts and nearly twenty chapters, we have documented the transition from the hollow man economy—a system predicated on the strategic friction of debt and the stealth confiscation of the producer's life-energy—to the crystalline reality of digital realism. We have moved from the jurisdictional fog of centralized clearinghouses and the American Bankers Cartel into a verifiable economy anchored in the physics of the asset and the rule of math. The post-fiat horizon is no longer a speculative theory; it is the hardened logistics of a society where value is earned through production, not manufactured through the printing press.

The Post-Fiat Horizon: The Era of Earned Value

A society that operates beyond the fiat horizon is one that has successfully exorcised the ghost of the

---

[204] Staff (2026). "Economics Quotes." Brainy Quote at https://www.brainyquote.com/search_results?x=0&y=0&q=Economics+.

gimmie culture. In this new reality, the velocity of value is not a tool for the administrative state to fund its entangling alliances, but a reflection of the actual productive energy of the active citizen. When money can no longer be printed, the expert fallacy of the "controlled economy" collapses. Without the ability to manipulate the measuring stick of value, the money changers lose their ability to manufacture the pricing fog that has for centuries masked institutional cannibalization. Value in the Digital Republic is a 1:1 mirror of real-world assets, from the 75-acre forest in the Florida Greenbelt to the lunar economy of KStar and KGalaxy.

In the post-fiat horizon, the relationship between the individual and the state undergoes a structural hard reset. The bureaucratic hammer is neutralized by the smart contract constitution, ensuring that public funds are publicly verifiable and that fiscal policy is governed by algorithmic certainty rather than political will. This is the death of the slush fund and the end of the secret bailout. When the standard of value is crystalline and immutable, the social contract is finally honored through the physics of the ledger. A society where value is earned is a society that respects time, rewards innovation, and preserves the sovereignty of the producer against the predatory reach of the wastrel class.

A Call for Economic Sovereignty: Reclaiming the Standard of Truth

The call for economic sovereignty is the final forensic demand of this work. For too long, the individual has been trapped in a jurisdictional cage where their right to a stable unit of account was sacrificed for the survival of debt-ridden institutions. To reclaim this right is to reclaim the very essence of human liberty. Economic sovereignty is the realization that your life-energy should not be subject to the strategic ambiguity of a central bank or the geopolitical whims of a sanctioned rail. It is the implementation of the sovereign vault and the global mesh, providing every active citizen with the hardened rails required to bypass the cartels and engage in the honest friendship of peer-to-peer trade.

Reclaiming a stable unit of account is the ultimate efficiency multiplier for civilization. It removes the information moat that allows the money changers to shave value from the producer, and it installs the rule of math as the final arbiter of truth. We have provided the bypass protocols, the KIROS architecture, and the Cerberus methodology to ensure that this sovereignty is a technical reality, not just a legal theory. The Digital Republic is built on the bedrock of mathematical commerce, where the standard of value is as immutable as the laws of gravity. This is our call to action: to exit the sovereign debt trap, to dismantle the legacy settlement machines, and to stand as the architects of a verifiable economy.

Ultimately, the transition to the Digital Republic is the forensic reclamation of our future. We have moved beyond the "Hollow Man" and the "American Bankers Cartel," entering a state of digital realism where the right to contract is an atomic certainty. The rails are live, the vault is secure, and the standard of truth is now firmly in your hands. The era of the permission slip is dead. The era of the sovereign producer has begun.[205]

---

[205] Coopers Final Logic Check → The experts and the "Wastrels" tell you that this "Post-Fiat Horizon" is a "Dangerous Fantasy" and that without a "Central Authority," the world will fall into "Barbarism." Logic check: If you are at a Farmers Market, and you trade a Basket of Apples for a Gallon of Honey, did you need a Bureaucrat to stand there and tell you if the deal was "Fair," or did the Apples and the Honey speak for themselves? They want to be the "Authority" because they are the only ones in the market who don't have a Basket of Anything to trade—they only have a Printer. In digital realism, the "Standard of Truth" is the Asset. If the apples are real and the honey is sweet, the market is "Civilized." It is time to stop listening to the "Empty-Handed Authority" and start trusting the Weight of your own Basket.

Appendix A: Breakdown and Takedown of the Clarity Act

(This is just letting the AI analyze it)

The **Digital Asset Market Clarity (CLARITY) Act**, which was formally introduced in May 2025 (H.R. 3633) and passed the House in July 2025, represents a significant milestone in U.S. digital asset regulation. As of April 2026, the bill is currently advancing through the Senate, though it remains a subject of intense debate—particularly regarding its interaction with the **GENIUS Act** (passed in July 2025), which focuses specifically on stablecoin issuance.

Below are the major points of the CLARITY Act and their projected effects on the market.

Major Points of the CLARITY Act

1. Jurisdictional Boundaries (The SEC vs. CFTC Split)

The Act establishes a definitive "Mature Blockchain Test" to determine when a digital asset transitions from being a security to a commodity.

- **SEC Jurisdiction:** Oversees "Investment Contract Assets" and tokenized traditional securities.

- **CFTC Jurisdiction:** Oversees "Digital Commodities" and the exchanges, brokers, and dealers that trade them.
- **The 20-Day Rule:** Requires the CFTC to make a certification decision on a digital commodity within 20 days; if no decision is made, it is automatically approved.

2. Stablecoin Classification

It distinguishes **Payment Stablecoins** (designed for payments and redeemable 1:1 for fiat) from other digital assets.

- **Exemption:** Explicitly states that "Permitted Payment Stablecoins" are **not securities**.
- **Anti-Fraud Oversight:** Grants both the SEC and CFTC anti-fraud and anti-manipulation authority over stablecoin transactions occurring on registered platforms.

3. Market Participant Registration & Disclosures

Requires anyone acting as a digital commodity exchange, broker, or dealer to register with the CFTC.

- **Transparency:** Mandates disclosures regarding ownership, financial condition, and affiliate entities.
- **Segregation:** Strictly prohibits the commingling of customer funds with corporate assets.

4. Custody Standards

Rescinds restrictive guidance (like the former SAB 121) and allows state-chartered trust companies to act as qualified custodians.

- **Operational Requirements:** Custodians must provide clear disclosures about material risks and ensure assets are segregated and not lent out without explicit consent.

Positive and Negative Market Effects

Feature	Positive Effects (Producers/Innovation)	Negative Effects (Legacy/Institutional)
Regulatory Certainty	Removes the "Fear of Imminent Enforcement" (Democratization of Assets).	Reduces the "Information Moat" that allowed large institutions to dominate through legal complexity.
Commodity Test	Provides a clear "Exit Ramp" for projects to transition away from SEC oversight as they decentralize.	May allow for faster listings of assets that have not undergone the rigorous vetting traditional securities require.

Feature	Positive Effects (Producers/Innovation)	Negative Effects (Legacy/Institutional)
Stablecoin Rewards	Bipartisan compromise (Tillis-Alsobrooks) allows rewards tied to *activity* (payments/transfers).	**The Deposit Flight Argument:** Banks fear yield-bearing stablecoins will drain their $18 trillion deposit base.
No Commingling	Increases consumer trust; prevents "FTX-style" collapses by mandating segregation.	Increases operational costs for exchanges that previously relied on "Hollow" liquidity.

The "Cooper" Logic Check

The "experts" and banking lobbyists tell you that these new rules are "Risky" because they move power away from the established "Safety" of the SEC and toward "Unproven" CFTC frameworks. Logic check: If you're at a Fruit Stand, do you want the Building Inspector to decide if your Orange is a "Security," or do you want the Market Master to just make sure the orange is not Rotten? They want the "Inspector" because his rules are so complicated only the biggest orchards can afford to follow them. In digital realism, the CLARITY Act is the Market Master. It stops the guessing game and lets the producers get back to work. It is time to stop letting the "Inspectors" suffocate the "Market."

Status Note: While the House passed the bill with a bipartisan 294-134 vote, the Senate Banking Committee is currently the "chokepoint" as of April 2026. The primary dispute remains the "Yield Prohibition"—whether stablecoin issuers can pay rewards, a move the American Bankers Association is fighting tooth and nail to prevent "deposit flight."

Appendix 2: More Clarity in 7 Pages or Less: The Crypto Legislation and Markets Act (CLAM

Preamble: The Crypto Legislation and Markets (CLAM) Act

Whereas, the current jurisdictional fog surrounding digital assets has created a state of terminal repugnance to economic logic, stifling the sovereignty of the producer and favoring the information moat of the American Bankers Cartel;

Whereas, the legacy administrative state has utilized strategic friction and the expert fallacy to enforce a gimmie culture of selective enforcement, leaving the active citizen in a jurisdictional trap that prevents the true realization of a verifiable economy;

Whereas, it is the forensic duty of the Republic to provide hardened logistics and neutral rails that protect the individual's right to a stable unit of account and the atomic settlement of their life-energy;

Whereas, the distinction between an investment contract and a digital commodity must be determined by the rule of math and the physics of the ledger rather than the subjective whim of a bureaucratic hammer; and

Whereas, the implementation of crystalline transparency and real-time auditing is the only hard reset capable of ending the era of the hollow man and the stealth confiscation of the producer's wealth;

Whereas, the United States is falling behind the rest of the world in digital asset security;

Be it enacted by the Senate and House of Representatives of the United States of America in Congress assembled:

Section 1. Short Title

This Act may be cited as the **"Crypto Legislation and Markets Act"** or the **"CLAM Act."**

Section 2. Purpose and Findings

The purpose of this Act is to provide an efficiency multiplier for the Digital Republic by:

1. **Dismantling the Clearinghouse Cartel:** Replacing legacy settlement machines with autonomous, peer-to-peer protocols that ensure real-time finality.
2. **Establishing the Standard of Truth:** Providing a clear, non-state medium of exchange through the recognition of payment stablecoins as RWA mirrors of tangible underlays.
3. **Defunding the Gatekeepers:** Eliminating extractionary clearing fees and institutional

cannibalization by allowing for the direct custody of digital assets by the producer.

4. **Protecting the Sovereign Ledger:** Ensuring that the right to contract remains an immutable reality, immune to the geopolitical kill-switches and the strategic ambiguity of the administrative state.

5. **Providing Regulatory Certainty:** Ensuring that the Office of the Comptroller of Currencies has the ability and authority to regulate Cryptocurrencies and Exchanges under this Act.

6. **Currency Test, Commodity Test and Security Test:** To provide a clear understanding of which agency works with the Office of the Comptroller of Currencies when Digital Assets fall within a special case.

7. **Stablecoin Reward System:** To protect the ability of the Defi Community and the Traditional banking Community to offer yields on stablecoins.

8. **Increase Consumer Trust by Prohibiting "Commingling":** To prevent FTX style problems by requiring classification as RWA or Stablecoins to have some form of auditable reserve held by a third party or in conjunction with a third party for all liquidity and payment tokens.

9. **Ban on Non-Cryptocurrency Digital Assets Claiming to Be Cryptocurrency**: to prevent scams, misinformation, and corruption in the developing space.
10. **Protecting Exchanges and Wallet Systems**: to ensure that wallets and exchanges are following best practices and the United Nations DCBAS Model Law.

Section 3: Dismantling the Clearinghouse Cartels

May it be enacted that the Office of the Comptroller of Currencies shall, by the year 2030 prohibit through regulation any clearinghouse activity which does not have an auditable record stored to the blockchain with access to Federal and State agencies to which they will be able to comply with treaty obligations for Anti-Money Laundering and Know Your Customer efforts in prevention of Terrorism, Drug Transshipment, Sex Trafficking or any other domestic or international crimes.

Section 4: Establishing A Fair Playing Field

May it be enacted that the Office of the Comptroller of Currencies, with the full force of the federal government, enact a requirement that any liquidity or payment provider, either digital or fiat (including the Federal Reserve), require and maintain a reserve of AT LEAST 7% by the end of 2027. Further, the Office of the Comptroller of Currencies will require that all institutions and issuers which fall under this requirement shall elevate this by 2% per year, until 2036 where they have a minimum of 25% reserves for their product. These reserves may be either digital, physical, security, or commodity and must maintain the 25% reserves, with a six month cure period should the reserve drop below this. The State shall also issue a “reserve grading system” by 2036 where S rating is 50% or more, “A” rating is 40% or more, “B” Rating is 30% or More, C Rating is 25% or more and “F” rating is less than 25% and in risk of losing their status and being reduced to “non-holdable” in traditional banking or credit union systems, as either a custodian or account manager. The 25% reserve requirement exempts local institutions (credit unions and local banks) with a deposit record of less than $1 Billion.

Section 5: Providing Regulatory Certainty

May it be enacted, that in all cases where a cryptocurrency does not fall into a special category, as under §6 of this Act, that it shall be managed by the Office of the Comptroller of Currencies. In special cases, as noted under § 6 of this Act, there may be co-jurisdictional issues under the Commodities and Futures Trading Commission or the Securities and Exchange Commission.

Section 6: Currency Test, Commodity Test, and Currency Test

Be it enacted, that in any case regarding a digital asset, the following tests are used to determine the categorical oversight of the federal government. This supersedes any tests established in any other jurisdiction by judicial fiat or state law.

§1. Security Test-

In any case that an underlying asset within the token is ruled to be a security, or the token contains both of the elements of value (tradable or market value) and governance rights (even within a DAO), then the token shall be deemed as a security. No token shall be deemed a security if there are not governance rights in the token or in the underlying asset. When a question of joint enterprise or expectation of profit is present, the following rules shall be followed

§§A. In the event that there is no management ability of the token holder to oversee the operation of the company managing the asset or the asset itself, then it shall be deemed not a join enterprise for the purposes of this law. If the token holder has any voting rights as to the operation of the token or the company issuing and/or managing the token then it shall be a joint enterprise.

§§B. In the event that there is a question of whether the buyer expects a profit, the standard of review is whether the issuing company issued that the primary purpose of the token was to generate profit. If the token is issued with a stable growth vector, a stable price, or with the concept of being a "meme" or "casino" token, the buyer is assumed to know the risk that is associated with the token. I this event, it cannot be declared an "expectation of profit."

§§ C. In the event that a token is deemed a security then it shall be overseen jointly by the Securities and Exchange Commission and the Office of the Comptroller of Currencies, with the SEC deferring to the OCC.

§2. Commodity Test-

In any case where the underlying asset backing a token is deemed to be a commodity, or the token itself meets the definition of a commodity being used to represent an unfinished fungible product, the token itself shall be deemed a commodity token. In this case, the jurisdiction under which the token is governed shall be the jurisdiction of the Commodities and Futures Trading Commission overseen by the Office of the Comptroller of Currencies.

§3. Currency Test-

If a token is a stablecoin, a token designed to be used for retail or institutional purchases or a liquidity token, then it shall be assigned to the office of the Comptroller of Currencies for jurisdiction. Utility tokens shall also be assigned to the OCC.

§4. Meme, NFT, or Collectable Test-

Any token which falls under the Meme, NFT, or collectable category shall be government by State and Federal Contract law. Tokens attempting to use this subcategorization to avoid regulation under category §1-3, shall be prohibited from trading in the United States. All meme projects must be labeled "meme" or "casino" tokens, they may not be sold on regulated or general cryptocurrency exchanges unless they have a "meme" or "casino" section. Tokens attempting to use this subcategorization to avoid regulation under category §1-3, shall be prohibited from trading in the United States and all holdings shall be seized, national and international, if the company purposefully avails itself upon the United States and the executives shall be subject to criminal penalties under Section 8.

§5. Non-Cryptocurrency Digital Assets-

If a digital asset is not stored on a blockchain or block matrix and/or is not a digital representation of fiat currency through electronic transactions via a bank, it may not be traded or listed on exchanges in the United States and United States citizens, residents or those holding visas may not own, possess, sell or trade such assets. This does not include reward programs or gift cards.

Section 7: Stablecoin Reward Systems

The prohibition on stablecoin issuers or defi institutions holding stablecoins allowing for yield generation created by the GENIUS ACT is hereby repealed. Any token with real world assets backing it at 10% or greater of the in circulation supply may offer yield. Companies offering yield must carry insurance from the FDIC for losses related to errors and omissions, business losses, or theft. Losses due to fluctuations in prices shall not be covered.

In order to be insured, companies must have fractional, auditable reserve accounts with a third party or third parties. These defi institutions would also be required to meet FDIC standards for being a depository and insurance would be limited to $500,000. The DeFi insurance of the FDIC would be a separate insurance fund and not funded by traditional banks, and the funds from the digital insurance fund would also not be used to fund traditional FDIC insurance, they are completely separate policies.

Section 8: Prevention on Commingling

Within three years of the first sale of tokens, companies must have an auditable reserve of 10% of the value (either in token or in other assets) to claim that the token is a “Real World Asset”. This reserve must be held by a third party company or multiple third party companies to ensure that the issuer cannot “rug pull”.

§1. Rug Pull Legislation- A rug pull is committed when:

- A company liquidates a portion of their token (more than 10%) to profit off of the sales prior to the market being able to sell.
- Those with insider information selling the token prior to a known price drop.
- The company intentionally drains liquidity for any price other than price maintenance.
- Team members leaving the company without theft right before a known price drop or rug pull action.
- Influencers or team members, paid or not, known to the company making false claims to increase FOMO (such as promising $10,000 a token) in a concerted effort to drive up the price.
- Developers dumping their tokes at a rate of more than 5% per quarter.
- Code hidden in the project that prevents investors from selling their tokens by limiting sell orders.
- Anonymous teams- all team members at an executive or director level, or persons holding more than 5% of the company must be disclosed.
- Removing websites, social media, community chat after tokens have been dumped.

§2. Non-Rug Pull Elements- The following elements are not signs of a rug pool.

- Shutting down liquidity for routine maintenance
- Shutting down liquidity to change liquidity providers
- Shutting down liquidity for price adjustment in milestone based coins
- Using a declared Executive Entity as a minority member of the company.
- Termination of employees for cause.
- Legitimate marketing with realistic expectations.
- Managed and published team token unlocking schedules.
- Code based price controls on milestone based token systems (non-market tokens or NMT liquidity tokens).
- Removing websites after a company has entered into receivership or has be shut down by due process in a jurisdiction.

§3. Penalties for Rug-Pulling

- Disgorgement of up to ten times the amount lost by those affected by the rug pull
- Jail time of no less than five years and no more than twenty years.
- Permanent Ban from every holding public office
- Permanent ban from voting in any election

- Permanent ban from working in the financial sector
- Permanent ban from working in digital assets, lobbying, consulting, or any profession which is a position of trust.
- Lifetime ban on receiving any income from financial or technology sectors.
- Seizure of any an all funds stored in foreign bank accounts or wallets, unless funds from these accounts are turned over to the government, the felon shall be considered in contempt of court and the measurement of the time in prison shall not start being counted until the money is turned over.

Section 9: Prohibition on Fake Cryptocurrencies

Any token which is not on a blockchain or blockmatrix, and advertises itself as a cryptocurrency, shall be in violation of this law and the purveyors shall be subject to the same penalties as the Rug Pull felons from Section 8.

A blockchain must be immutable (lost blocks immediately disqualify a digital ledger from being a blockchain), transparent (the United States does not recognize privacy chains), and cryptographically secured.

This section does not prohibit traditional “zero knowledge” systems, rather it requires the blockchain to record the wallet from whence the transaction originated and the wallet to which the transaction was transferred to. Chains are not required to publicly make the amount available; however, the chain must be able to show the amount should a warrant be issued for one of the wallets.

Section 10: Protecting Wallet and Exchanges

The United States adopts the United Nations Model law (IFG/DCBAS) on Digital Assets and Exchanges, and assigns the Office of The Comptroller of Currencies as the registration agencies. The United States also accepts the taxation regime expressed in the Model Law and notes that RWAs shall be taxed at an effective rate of 0% the same as stablecoins because of the definitional difference created by the Genius ACT.

Section 11: Economic Protections

§ 1. Federal Prohibitions

No member of the federal government, nor their immediate families, shall hold, trade, buy, or sell stocks, commodities, or cryptocurrencies except through a blind trust during their term in office. This prohibition extends to all federal employees. The blind trust must be managed by a third party of which the federal employee shall not a have relationship with other than being a client. In the case of federal employees in the financial sector, the blind trust shall record them as a number with the OCC having the list of numbered accounts.

§2. State Prohibitions

Any state receiving any grant money from the federal government shall implement a state level law in accordance with Section 1 for state employees to prevent corruption at the state level within two years of the passing of this law, or the state will lose all federal grants until such a time as the law is passed and in effect.

§3. No Collusion

Any collusion, circumvention, or attempts to avoid this law for personal enrichment shall be immediate cause for termination upon the finding of judge, special council, or the non-partisan committee created by congress to enforce this section. For the President or members of Congress (House or Senate), finding of collusion, circumvention, or attempts to avoid the law shall by the committee shall be seen as a mandatory impeachment referral to the house where any implicated members must stand mute from the time the referral is announced and, upon impeachment, will refer the matter to the Senate for an adjudication within 60 days. For all other federal employees, including judges, the termination from their position shall be immediate with all vesting, retirement, and other benefits immediately struck.

§4. Confidentiality

§§ A. Any termination under this clause shall be public record, for the amount and type of violation. The Congressional shield against "in office activities" shall not protect the impeached member from lawsuits from person affected by the trading.

§§B. No matter in the United States shall be classified unless it pertains to defense plans, intelligence sources, national cryptography of messages, and communications with foreign governments related to the above categories. Information which is embarrassing or may implicate government officials in a crime which is suppressed or classified shall result in ALL officials involved with the classification of the information (except whistleblowers) being terminated under Subsection 3 of this section.

Section 12: Definitions

Section 12: Definitions

For the purposes of this Act, the following definitions shall apply:

1. **Atomic Settlement:** The instantaneous and programmatic exchange of assets where the transfer of one asset is cryptographically linked to the transfer of another, ensuring that both occur simultaneously or not at all, without the use of intermediary clearinghouses or T+ settlement delays.

2. **Autonomous Peer-to-Peer Protocol:** A set of self-executing code (smart contracts) deployed on a blockchain that facilitates transactions directly between users without the requirement of a centralized matching engine, escrow agent, or administrative intermediary.

3. **Blind Trust:** A financial arrangement meeting the standards of 5 U.S.C. app. § 102, wherein the official has no knowledge of the specific holdings and no power to direct trades, managed by an independent fiduciary with no prior relationship to the beneficiary.

4. **Blockchain:** A cryptographically secured, distributed ledger that is immutable (historical data cannot be altered), transparent (all transaction history is auditable), and decentralized (governed by a consensus mechanism rather than a single authority). The loss or "pruning" of blocks to hide transaction history immediately disqualifies a ledger from this definition.

5. **Block Matrix:** A non-linear distributed ledger technology (such as Directed Acyclic Graphs or DAGs) that records transactions in a multi-dimensional structure rather than a single sequential chain, provided it maintains the standards of immutability and transparency required of a blockchain.

6. **Digital Commodity:** A digital asset that represents a fungible, unfinished product or resource, governed by the rule of math and protocol-level scarcity, and which lacks governance rights or a centralized management team that creates an "expectation of profit" through entrepreneurial efforts.
7. **Governance Rights:** The encoded power within a digital asset to vote on protocol upgrades, the allocation of treasury funds, the hiring/firing of executive entities, or any decision that alters the fundamental economic or operational nature of the issuing entity or DAO.
8. **Life-Energy:** The finite time, labor, and cognitive effort expended by a human being to produce economic value, the fruits of which are represented by a stable unit of account and protected as a fundamental right of the producer under this Act.
9. **Payment Stablecoin:** A digital asset designed to maintain a stable value relative to a reference asset (typically the U.S. Dollar) and backed by a 1:1 or greater auditable reserve of Real World Assets (RWAs) as defined in Section 8.
10. **Non-Cryptocurrency Digital Asset:** Any digital representation of value that fails the

definition of a Blockchain or Block Matrix (Section 12, Subsections 4 & 5).

11. **Producer:** The individual or entity that originates value through creation, extraction, or service, and who retains the sovereign right to the atomic settlement of their wealth without extractionary gatekeeping.
12. **Real World Asset (RWA):** A digital token that serves as a verifiable, programmable mirror of a tangible, off-chain underlay (including but not limited to real estate, physical gold, or legal securities) held in a transparent, third-party custody arrangement.
13. **Utility Token:** A digital asset that provides the holder with a specific right of access to a digital service, product, or protocol, and which does not function primarily as a medium of exchange or a security.

Section 13: Severability

If any provision of this Act is held to be invalid, the remainder of the Act shall not be affected.

Section 14: Rule Construction

This act preempts any state or territory act which is contrary to the nature or increases taxes on actions within the act. This includes any money transmitter laws or laws similar to and including New York's Bitlicense.

Section 15: Effective Date

The effective date is the beginning of the next congress after the passing.

Made in the USA
Monee, IL
05 November 2026

67845304R00285